THE MANHATTAN PROJECT

THE MANHATTAN PROJECT

A THEORY OF A CITY

DAVID KISHIK

STANFORD UNIVERSITY PRESS
STANFORD, CALIFORNIA

Stanford University Press
Stanford, California

Library of Congress Cataloging-in-Publication Data

Kishik, David, author.
  The Manhattan project : a theory of a city / David Kishik.
    pages cm. — (To imagine a form of life, III)
  An imaginary sequel to Walter Benjamin's Arcades project.
  Includes bibliographical references and index.
  ISBN 978-0-8047-8603-4 (cloth)
  ISBN 978-1-5036-0277-9 (pbk.
  1. New York (N.Y.)—Social life and customs—20th century. 2. New York (N.Y.)—
Civilization—20th century. 3. Cities and towns—Philosophy. 4. Civilization,
Modern—Philosophy. I. Title. II. Series: Kishik, David. To imagine a form of life , 3.
  F128.52.K54 2015
  974.7'10904—dc23
                                                        2014033655
  ISBN 978-0-8047-9436-7 (electronic)

Designed by Bruce Lundquist

Typeset at Stanford University Press in 10/14 Adobe Garamond

CONTENTS

FOURTH PART

FIFTH PART

SIXTH PART

I CAN'T AFFORD TO ♥ NY

WALTER BENJAMIN, whose spirit hovers over the surface of every page in this book, had a special knack for subverting literary conventions. He did, however, admit that he is a faithful observer of at least one established rule: "Never use the word 'I' except in letters."

This was more than just a matter of style. Like every good philosopher, or like every good criminal, Benjamin employs this device in an attempt to leave minimal evidence that could implicate him in the writing of his own work. By scrubbing his identity off the text, he wishes to give the impression that his arguments could be made by anyone and be as true; that the *I* in *I think* is no one in particular.

Friedrich Nietzsche, whose spirit will never rest in peace, came to realize that a great philosophy is always "a confession of faith on the part of its author, and a type of involuntary and unselfconscious memoir." Nevertheless, this book is no ordinary philosophy, let alone a great one. So I would like to begin by speaking frankly, rather than obliquely, about the personal circumstances that led to its composition.

I FLEW TO NEW YORK with my two best friends a few days before our high school graduation ceremony. It was my first time on a plane, or abroad, and the farthest away I had ever gotten from my family's home in Jerusalem.

It may sound corny but the honest truth is that during our tour of the city I did not fall in love only with this place but also with one of my friends. This was a tricky situation, because the other friend had already been half-secretly in love with her for months.

After we got back, my feelings only intensified, and she felt the same. So after a few months we had to tell our mutual friend about what was going on behind his back. Unfortunately, understandably, it drove a wedge between him and us for a very long time.

But then she left to study dance in New York of all places, while I stayed in Israel until I was released from the army. We had a long-distance relationship for three years. I guess that the mental image of our future selves living together in the Big Apple made this romantic limbo slightly less painful.

SHE WAS SUPPOSED TO BE WAITING FOR ME in the fifth-floor walk-up apartment she had just rented for us in the East Village. But when I arrived from the airport, a neighbor told me that she had been taken to the hospital three hours earlier. I dropped my suitcase in the half-furnished bedroom. A few unnerving minutes passed until the phone rang. She said she was fine. Probably just something bad she ate the day before.

Since the beginning, my two objects of desire got all mixed up in my then-young mind, just as Eden and Eve likely did in Adam's. The fact that the initials of her name were the same as the initials of our city surely didn't help. The I ♥ NY cheap white T-shirts carried for me an entirely different, personal meaning, of which the tourists were cheerfully oblivious.

Back then, in the late 1990s, there was a large mural on the corner of Broadway and Houston with the letters *DKNY* forming a black-and-white aerial view of the cityscape. It was beside the point that it was a commercial logo of a clothing label in a particularly hectic spot downtown. As Victor Hugo "read an *H* in the towers of Notre Dame," I was narcissistically convinced that the brick wall spelled the initials of my name and her name, or my name and the name of my adopted city, advertising these bonds, writ large, at the epicenter of the world, at least as I perceived it.

For the next twelve years we lived together in the same small apartment. After six we got married in her parents' backyard. Our mutual high school friend (we eventually reconciled) presided over the ceremony. This is her at the top of the World Trade Center when she was seven.

F. SCOTT FITZGERALD admits that he much prefers large parties: "They're so intimate. At small parties there isn't any privacy." I guess that this is another way of explaining what attracted me to New York in the first place and what made me stay that long.

I always had this strange urge to disappear in a crowd, to disconnect from my surroundings, to be absent while present. The city fulfilled my perverse desire, and then some. This meant that I never got invited to the right parties, either large or small. Instead, I spent most of my days in New York by myself, either reading or writing, usually in coffee shops and libraries.

This fortress of urban solitude probably contributed to my mental development, which was the exact opposite of a child's. Almost all my memories of New York formed during my first year of living there. Everything that followed was more or less a blur. But this observation has its exceptions.

First, it ignores that morning when we stood on our roof, still in our pajamas (maybe we were also holding hands), watching the Twin Towers collapse in the near distance. I also still remember the muffled voices of the protesters against the subsequent war in Iraq. They were chanting on Forty-Second Street while I was sitting inside the public library, reading Hegel's *Phenomenology of Spirit*.

BY THE TIME I FINISHED the initial research for this book, the actual city receded to the background. Real New York was no longer necessary. It even became a hindrance. Besides, there was no way to deny that, both personally and professionally, I was heading in the same, wrong direction. So I moved, by myself, to Berlin. When I was half through the first draft, I realized that I got priced out of Manhattan and loved out of my marriage. Or maybe it was the other way around.

Either way, I now know that what began with juvenile infatuation evolved into full-grown bitterness. But I want to make it clear that this is only *my* unsuccess story, not the city's. As deep and as common as this sense of disenchantment may be, it is not meant to be understood as a general claim about the meaning of New York.

WHAT THEODOR ADORNO and Edward Said had in common was more than their shared fate as exiled intellectuals living in twentieth-century Manhattan. This Jew and this Palestinian also shared the conviction that "the only home truly available now, though fragile and vulnerable, is in writing."

If anything, working on this project has further estranged me from the city to which it is dedicated. It has also made me more familiar with the failings of my own thought. Although the first lines were written by a man with a delusion of epic grandeur, the last lines were written by a man who has come to realize that dwelling in one's own literary production may sound romantic on paper but is fairly hollow in reality.

It is one thing to be an expatriate; it is another to be an ex-libris.

THE MANHATTAN PROJECT

INTRODUCTION THE ROSEMAN HYPOTHESIS

THIS IS A STUDY of a manuscript that was never written. The author of the imaginary text is real. His name is Walter Benjamin. Here are a few well-known facts about his life:

1892   Born in Berlin to a wealthy family of assimilated Jews.

1912   Begins his university studies, concentrating on philosophy and literature.

1918   Dora Pollak, whom he married a year earlier, gives birth to Stefan, their only son. The marriage will not last long.

1921   In disguise, next to Alice Croner, who passed away in the late 1980s.

1925   The University of Frankfurt flatly rejects his postdoctoral dissertation, without which it is impossible to get a decent teaching job in Germany. Academically, he will remain a complete failure for the rest of his life.

1927   Begins independent research for *The Arcades Project*, also known as *Paris, Capital of the Nineteenth Century*. He will work on this book off and on for the next thirteen years. It is a unique fusion of philosophy, history, and literary criticism into an unprecedented theory about our modern condition. Written for the most part in the French National Library, this work, though never completed, will become his magnum opus.

1932   During a stay in Ibiza, where the cost of living is still within his dwindling means.

1937   Benjamin's income from his work as a freelance writer fails to improve his poor economic condition, and his life in Paris during the Third Reich fails to secure his precarious political situation. One of his last rays of hope comes from the Institute for Social Research in New York, which gives him a monthly stipend and will later secure him a US visa, as well as an apartment on Central Park West.

1940   Fleeing the advancing German army, he reaches Portbou, a Spanish town on the French border. Because he lacks the required exit visa for his trip to America, the local authorities are determined to send him back to occupied France. The precise circumstances of his death remain unclear to this day, but it is believed that in an act of desperation he swallows a lethal dose of morphine.

1947   *The Arcades Project*, hidden away by Georges Bataille in the archives of the French National Library during the war, is retrieved and then delivered to New York.

1982   The belated publication of the book in its fragmentary form solidifies Benjamin's position as one of the great intellectuals of the twentieth century and cultivates his almost mythical status among future generations of scholars and writers.

Whereas this chronology is factual, the following one is counterfactual, fictional, or hypothetical:

1940   Faced with the desperate situation in Portbou, there was only one way for Benjamin to save his life. With the help of a Spanish doctor he fakes his suicide and produces an unclaimed body as his own. He arrives in Lisbon with forged identification papers and boards the next ship to New York. The man who had already published his essays under quite a few pseudonyms becomes Carl Roseman, in tribute to Karl Rossmann, the protagonist of Franz Kafka's *Amerika* (originally titled *The Man Who Disappeared*). Notice, however, that he eliminates the fateful *K* from his anglicized name.

1941   A man he met on the ship from Europe secures a job for him in the mailroom of the Daily News Building on Forty-Second Street and Second Avenue. Benjamin decides against contacting his many expatriate friends living in the United States (such as Ernst Bloch, Theodor Adorno, Max Horkheimer, Siegfried Kracauer, Bertolt Brecht, and Hannah Arendt), or anyone else for that matter. Guarding his complete anonymity under his borrowed identity, he assumes the position of a kind of specter living an afterlife—haunting and haunted by his new city. Rather than contest the reports about his death, he embraces this new solitary life, this posthumous existence, as if it were his personal resurrection.

1957   After retiring from his job with a modest pension, he begins frequenting the main branch of the Public Library on Fifth Avenue, up the street from his old workplace. His daily research leads to the composition of a sequel to *The Arcades Project*, which he calls either *The Manhattan Project* or *New York, Capital of the Twentieth Century*. This manuscript will remain his sole occupation for the rest of his long life. It is "the theater of all his struggles and all his ideas."

1977   A photo taken at the library's main reading room may or may not be of Benjamin at work.

1987   Leaving the library building one rainy day in early November, he slips and falls down the grand staircase. His ninety-five-year-old body cannot sustain the injuries, and he is declared dead (for the second time) before reaching the hospital. After the ambulance departs, Beatrice Wald, a librarian who was his only known acquaintance, takes possession of the briefcase he left behind. It contains all of his surviving papers.

1996   Before her death Wald bequeaths the manuscript of *The Manhattan Project* to the New York Public Library, where it is filed away as the Carl Roseman Papers, without attracting any scholarly attention whatsoever.

2008   Inadvertently, I come upon the manuscript while browsing the library's catalog. It is preceded by Wald's letter that recounts the above biographical details (she is, though, unaware of Roseman's true identity or importance). A thorough investigation proves beyond reasonable doubt the true authorship of the text.

THE TWO QUESTIONS that guide this book are as tricky as they are absurd: What if this is all true and *The Manhattan Project* does exist? What will we read in this book that was never written? Benjamin really (and cryptically) wrote shortly before his death: "The historical method is a philological method based on the book of life. 'Read what was never written,' runs a line in Hofmannsthal. The reader one should think of here is the true historian." If we take Benjamin's advice literally, we can also take the previous questions seriously, rather than as some postmodern legerdemain. To follow the Roseman Hypothesis means that the proverbial lines dividing reality from fantasy, the text from its commentary, the author from his interpreter, are from this point on suspended. This will definitely raise a question about the text's voice: Is it him or is it me, or one of the many sources quoted by either of us? To which someone once replied, "What does it matter who is speaking."

What follows is my attempt to make sense of the hundreds of loose pages, written in miniature script and somewhat broken English, which the unearthed manuscript comprises. Since further biographical details will be kept to a minimum, and since quotations from the text itself will be restricted to Benjamin's own citations from his numerous sources, my book is designed as a work of pure textual interpretation. In other words, this is not a reproduction of his *Manhattan Project* but only its analysis. It may therefore be understood as a work of secondary literature, insofar as we bear two things in mind: first, that Benjamin treats the urban setting as a book that must be constantly read and interpreted; second, that his actual writings are also structured like a metropolis. These are his "city-as-text" and "text-as-city."

The subject of my book is equal parts an author named Walter Benjamin and a city called New York. Yet its success or failure should be measured by its fidelity to a place more than to a thinker. Like virtually anyone who has ever written anything of value about New York, Benjamin must be relegated to the position of the city's "ghostwriter." Following Rem Koolhaas, we could say that, like many public figures, the city has neither the time nor will nor ability to contemplate its own life and recount it in orderly chapters. Instead, it hires a host of spectral scribes who are more than happy to do this job for it. Benjamin's *Manhattan Project*—this epic montage of quotations from, and reflections on, a seemingly endless array of texts revolving around New York—should certainly earn its ghostly compiler a seat of honor among his shadowy peers. But if this is indeed the case, then I am no more than the ghostwriter of a ghostwriter of a ghostwriter.

❧

IN GREEK, *hypothesis* means "that which is placed under." Like *The Arcades Project*, *The Manhattan Project* takes an actual place and places it under. These texts can perform this neat trick by not pretending to make a statement about the reality in which we live (a thesis). Instead, they are allowing us to observe what happens to our duly accepted reality once their ideas are placed underneath it. What is placed under can function either as a pillar or as a bomb. Though a hypothesis as such does not make a direct claim for truth, the truth depends on the hypothesis that lies, or lurks, under. Sometimes using a lie is the best way to tell the truth.

But there is another important thing that a hypothesis can do. In ancient theater, the term *hypothesis* denotes something like the program that, nowadays, is handed out by the ushers before a play begins. A classical hypothesis supplies a compact plot summary, describes the setting, identifies the actors, and gives various notes about the production and the playwright. *The Manhattan Project* can be understood as a hypothesis in this sense as well, for it is meant to elucidate in a condensed form the elaborate drama that unfolds in front of our eyes—not only in this specific city but also, by synecdoche, in other parts of this world.

"One can read the real like a text," Benjamin writes. "We open the book of what happened." But a philosophical book dedicated to a city is different from the scientific Book of Nature. Besides, in the same way that philology is commentary on a text, it is theology that Benjamin treats as "commentary on a reality." It is uncertain whether God is still watching us up there, but even if he is, it is possible that he no longer bothers to record our names in the Book of Life and the Book of the Dead. Instead, he probably just peeks at Benjamin's manuscript from time to time, as theatergoers peek at their playbill whenever the show becomes too confusing or too overbearing.

FIRST PART

Benjamin merges his life into a setting.

—SUSAN SONTAG

FIRST CHAPTER

BENJAMIN IN NEW YORK

"THERE IS NOT ENOUGH TIME remaining for me to write all the letters I would like to write." What we believe to be Benjamin's last recorded words from 1940 could not have been further from the truth. His tragedy verges on comedy. So before we begin, let me quickly deflate your possible enthusiasm. Reading *The Manhattan Project* and *The Arcades Project* side by side might give the impression that these are the brainchildren of two different authors. It is not unlikely that those who are familiar with Benjamin's early European writings will be taken somewhat aback by the turn his later work took. For the devoted followers of Saint Walter, this is probably going to be sacrilege. Yet it is the spirit, not the letter, of his work on Paris to which his American writings can still be compared.

Consider, in this respect, the circumstantial factors that must have caused his change of heart: the trauma of the war; his new identity, city, language, and culture; the sixteen years of silence while enduring his menial job; the shifting intellectual and political postwar climate; his monastic existence and advancing old age. This is not to suggest that *The Manhattan Project* can be dismissed as the inconsequential, senescent afterthought of a displaced or disoriented mind. Assuming that the composition of the manuscript under consideration indeed consumed the final three decades of his life, one can only imagine how scrupulous and deliberate his work on his last word was.

"Speech conquers thought," runs Benjamin's personal motto, "but writing commands it." Even though his ascetic lifestyle excluded him from the conversation of his contemporaries and exposed him to only the thinnest sliver of what New York had to offer, his immersion in the endless accounts of the city, readily available and continuously accumulating in the stacks of the Public Library, was apparently enough to satiate his voracious intellect.

"Action can, of course, be as subtle as thought. But a thought must be crude to find its way into action." Benjamin learned this lesson from Brecht in the 1930s. Yet two decades had to pass before he finally found a way to put it into literary practice. In comparison with many of the knotty texts predating his staged suicide, the plain and pragmatic language of his postcontinental work seems to be influenced by some of what American literature has to offer. The prose of *The Manhattan Project* is like an open fist. Its crude theory can be described as *minima philosophia*. It deliberately defies our academic expectations.

On the first page of the manuscript is an epigraph from W. H. Auden: "Sad is Eros, builder of cities." In Benjamin's case "builder" should be replaced with "philosopher." Notice also that, despite his sadness, it is still Eros, the Greek god of love and Freudian symbol of the life instinct, who presides over this urban experiment, or experience. The melancholic angel who hovered over Benjamin's European texts still visits the New York manuscript occasionally, but Benjamin's last book project is the product of much more than spleen.

In an essay Arendt wrote about Benjamin in 1968, she recalls that he was not looking forward to his planned trip to America, "where, he used to say, people would probably find nothing to do with him except cart him up and down the country exhibiting him as 'the last European.'" But as I was reading *The Manhattan Project*, I began to realize that his fear was unjustified. Although calling Benjamin an American writer would be off the mark, and though not once throughout the manuscript does he explicitly refer to himself as a New Yorker, I couldn't help imagining him as "the last New Yorker," writing his book in between saturnine strolls through the remnants of his beloved city after its entire population has been wiped out by some apocalyptic event, like a flood.

IN THE SKY OF POSTWAR NEW YORK Benjamin lived his life like a "star devoid of atmosphere." The fact that this invisible man avoided as much human contact as possible, despite dwelling in the most populous spot on earth, could have easily led him to imagine that he was living on a deserted island. For this reason it is not impossible that the initials of Carl Roseman are a reversal of Robinson Crusoe's. Since a city is often compared to a language, it makes sense that Benjamin was at home neither in New York nor in English. But precisely because he was keeping his distance from his subject matter—while inhabiting its very heart—he managed to see this undeserted island as no one else did.

Think, for example, of how the encounter with the same place during the same period triggered in Adorno his strong critique of "mass" culture, his warning to readers of an array of ostensible modern ills ranging from jazz to laughter. Benjamin appreciated Adorno's ability to reveal many of the insidious traps of twentieth-century life. But unlike those thinkers "who so thoroughly studied every shade of avarice," and without losing sight of their insights, Benjamin sensed that his own contribution must be different. Following Carl Andre's distinction between art and culture, he declares at one point: "Philosophy is about what we do. Critique is about what is done to us." Adorno's warning, in a letter from 1935, against Benjamin's "abandonment of the category of Hell" is therefore not entirely unjustified.

In New York, Benjamin was trying to write a report on what he once called an "eddy in the stream of becoming." He says as much in a long passage copied from *The Arcades Project* verbatim, save for his substitution of "Manhattan" for "Paris":

> Few things in the history of humanity are as well known to us as the history of Manhattan. Tens of thousands of volumes are dedicated solely to the investigation of this tiny spot on the earth's surface. . . . Many of the main thoroughfares have their own special literature, and we possess written accounts of thousands of the most inconspicuous houses. . . . At work in the attraction New York exercises on people is the kind of beauty that is proper to great landscapes—more precisely, to volcanic landscapes. Manhattan is a counterpart in the social order to what Vesuvius is in the geographic order: a menacing, hazardous massif, an ever-active hotbed of revolution. But just as the slopes of Vesuvius, thanks to the layers of lava that cover them, have been transformed into paradisal orchards, so the lava of revolutions provides uniquely fertile ground for the blossoming of art, festivity, fashion.

Another interesting similarity between Benjamin's analyses of Paris and New York is that both are the fruits of a careful literary montage, intentionally left in fragmentary form. The difference is that the European Benjamin still held on, even if only halfheartedly, to some holistic view of an original, "organic totality." He therefore had to understand the fragment within the context of a tragic reflection or an experience of disaster. The American Benjamin, however, upholds the fragment without reverting as he did in the past to notions of ruin and loss, mourning and catastrophe. Like Walt Whitman's poetic reflection on the city's ensemble of specimens, Benjamin's theoretic diffraction results in a mosaic of forms of life that may still constitute the apparent homogeneous whole that we call New York, but only as a conscious abstraction, only as long as any suggestion of a grand urban narrative is understood as mere fiction. Like Edgar Allan Poe's portrayal of the metropolitan crowd, this philosophy of New York (or is it a *paraphilosophy*?) demonstrates that "the description of confusion is not the same as a confused description."

SECOND CHAPTER   NOT TO LOOK UPON

THE EVENTS OF *ULYSSES* take place on June 16, 1904. Today this date is celebrated as Bloomsday, a tribute to Leopold Bloom, the novel's protagonist. But at the time James Joyce was working on his modernistic masterpiece, it had completely different connotations, similar to those that September 12, 2001, might bring to mind today. Joyce knew that he was setting his narrative on the day after, when newspapers around the world reported on their front page about that most "terrible affair" in which "all those women and children excursion beanfeast burned and drowned in New York. Holocaust." On June 15, the *General Slocum*, a steamboat carrying members of St. Mark's German Lutheran Church from the Lower East Side, caught fire and sank in the shallow waters just off the Bronx shore. More than a thousand of the thirteen hundred passengers were killed. Most were women and children. Until the end of the twentieth century this event was the worst tragedy in the history of New York. Unlike the Triangle Shirtwaist Factory fire and the *Titanic* disaster a few years later, *General Slocum* nearly vanished from the city's memory. Yet nothing is more telling than an event that should be commemorated but is not. I found this photo of the victims, their faces shrouded in white fabric, at the bottom of the box containing the manuscript of *The Manhattan Project*. It is the direct gaze of the standing men that I find almost unbearable.

ALTHOUGH BENJAMIN'S THOUGHT is devoted to a city he regarded as the capital of the twentieth century, the dates January 1, 1900, and December 31, 1999, can be only the arbitrary beginning and end points of his investigation. A more convenient and convincing beginning for the New York Century might be the 1898 consolidation of the adjacent municipalities into the five boroughs of the present megacity. But for Benjamin the New York Century really begins only on the day of the *General Slocum* disaster. The magnitude of the tragedy, he reasons, delivered such a powerful shock to the city's psyche that, for the first time, New York became conscious of its own significance and was able to contemplate its own worth. Mourning the dead led the living, as it often does, to come to terms with their own existence. Following Joyce, Benjamin sensed that this quintessentially modern trauma (the steam engine, that machine of progress, can also be a machine of mass destruction) presaged what the new century held in store. The odyssey is shipwrecked. But he also noticed that this event became instrumental in focusing the attention of all nations on New York City, which emerged during the same years as the de facto world's capital.

It is generally accepted that New York reached its apogee in the years following the end of the Second World War, with 1950 often cited as a convenient turning point from the city's meteoric rise to its almost inevitable decline. If we must locate a certain event that could symbolize this turn, then the "Shot Heard Round the World"—when Bobby Thomson hit a home run to win the National League pennant for the New York Giants in the final game against the Brooklyn Dodgers—will do just fine. "Isn't it possible," Don DeLillo asks in *Underworld*, "that this midcentury moment enters the skin more lastingly than the vast shaping strategies of eminent leaders, generals steely in their sunglasses—the mapped visions that pierce our dreams?" DeLillo writes that this baseball game at the uptown Polo Grounds on October 3, 1951, "doesn't change the way you sleep or wash your face or chew your food. It changes nothing but your life." Or the city's life, if we were to ask Benjamin, who was not present at the game and did not particularly care about baseball.

As for the symbolic moment the New York Century ended, it must be the other great tragedy in its history, after which the curtain had to fall (though many people remain seated, awaiting a rumored encore). Again, the sense of loss acts as the most effective catalyst for making people appreciate what they no longer have. Disaster works like divine revelation in a society driven by risk. In the aftermath of September 11, 2001, the public resolved that life would go on and business continue as usual. Still, there is a growing sense today that living in New York somehow resembles an afterlife, just as before the morning of June 15, 1904, the city was, in retrospect, still in its embryonic state.

One could claim that this has been the closure of only one project, that of Manhattan, and that the twenty-first century ushered in a new formation—let's call it the Brooklyn Project—which operates according to a different constellation of ideas and an alternative set of values. But even though New York was a powerful place before the definitive ninety-seven years in its history and will continue to play a central role for many years to come, its two great catastrophes still serve as the perfect prologue and epilogue for an urban biography so extraordinary that its comparison to another historical city becomes rather obvious. "In one respect," an English visitor observed already in 1776, "this town is like Athens: Though it has little or none of its Refinement or its Literature, 'it is always seeking to hear or see some new thing.'"

IT IS ONE THING to imagine the day airplanes will crash into skyscrapers, as E. B. White did in "Here Is New York," his classic essay from 1949. It is another to analyze in precise terms the city's future demise through a close reading of White's text, as Benjamin did in the early 1970s, as the Twin Towers were being built. "It used to be," White writes, "that the Statue of Liberty was the signpost that proclaimed New York and translated it for all the world. Today Liberty shares the role with Death." Being-toward-death becomes the modern city's decisive existential condition, whereas the Enlightenment's being-toward-freedom (an ideal that belonged to Paris more than to New York) is somehow pushed to the side.

As in Kafka's *Amerika*, the Statue of Liberty, that displaced Parisian immigrant, holds not a torch but a sword. Benjamin therefore talks about this "gloomy awareness that along with the great cities has evolved the means to raze them to the ground." The nineteenth-century aristocracy's fear of the amorphous mob, which turned into the fascination of twentieth-century media with the obscure mobster, is mutating today into the government's watchful eye over the elusive terrorist. But of course, the true enemies of twenty-first-century New York are less the specters of terrorism—those who turn the city into a "lofty target scraping the skies"—than those who pretend to exorcize them. The city's demise may coincide with the most conspicuous attack on its buildings and people. But the cause of this decline lies elsewhere. The real disaster movie in the history of New York, the one that actually brought it to its knees during Benjamin's years of living there, features no aliens, no ghosts, no natural forces, and no diabolical villains.

An entire cloud of cynicism can condense into a drop of mortality. In the last lines of his essay, White seems to insinuate that, like the biblical Garden of Eden, modern New York guards within its boundaries nothing less than the Tree of Life, which he describes as an old, battered, barely standing willow in an interior courtyard of a Midtown apartment building. This tree, he insists, must be saved, because "if it were to go, all would go—this city, this mischievous and marvelous monument which not to look upon would be like death."

Henry James articulates a similar sentiment when he writes, "What makes the general relation of your adventure with New York is that, at bottom, you are all the while wondering, in presence of the aspects of its genius and its shame, what elements or parts, if any, would be worth its saving, worth carrying off for the fresh embodiment and the better life." The spirit of this advice evidently informed Benjamin's thought as early as 1939, when he made an attempt to distill his years of intellectual labor on *The Arcades Project* into a single, short, essential text. It was meant to function as a clearing in the middle of his seemingly boundless forest of quotations and reflections. Inspired by the letters he received from his friends in New York, he titled this piece "Central Park."

THE PERSISTENT DIFFICULTY is to put one's finger on a plausible explanation for the attraction New York has had on so many. "The right reason," the journalist Joseph Mitchell confesses, "is something obscure and way off and I probably don't even know it myself. It's like the old farmer who wouldn't tell the drummer the time of day." The shortest version of this story goes something like this:

An old farmer, carrying a jug of applejack, boarded a train heading back to his home in South Jersey. As the train pulled out of the station, he took his watch from his vest pocket, looked at it, and put it right back. Across the aisle sat a young drummer who leaned over and said, "Friend, what time is it?" The farmer took a look at him and said, "Won't tell you." The drummer was confused by the harsh reply, so he asked again, only louder, but the farmer didn't budge. "Well, look here, for the Lord's sake," said the drummer, "why won't you tell me the time of day?" "If I was to tell you," the farmer replied, "we'd get into a conversation, and I got a jug of fine applejack next to me, and in a minute I'm going to take a drink, and if we were talking I'd offer you to drink with me, and you would, and eventually we would drink some more, so by the time the train would pull up to my stop I'd invite you to get off as well and spend the afternoon with me, and you would, and we'd get to my front porch and drink and sing until evening, and then my wife would come out and ask you to take supper with the family, and you would, and after we're done we'd drink some more, and I'd offer you to spend the night in the spare room, and you would, and along about two o'clock in the morning I'd get up to go to the pump, and I'd pass by my daughter's room, and there you'd be, in there with her, and I'd have to get out my pistol, and my wife would have to get dressed and go down the road and get the preacher, and I don't want no God-damned son-in-law who don't own a watch."

THIRD CHAPTER BACK TO THE FUTURE

"IN A DREAM," Benjamin wrote in the mid-1920s, "I took my life with a gun. When it went off, I did not wake up but saw myself lying for a while as a corpse. Only then did I wake." Awakening is the ultimate task of Benjamin's two monumental book projects. What changes is what is identified as the fantasy and what is identified as the reality. The awakening in his early project assumes that the Paris of the nineteenth century is essentially a dream, even a nightmare, which his twentieth-century reader must snap out of. His theoretical work is presented as a dreamwork of the past. It is meant to help his contemporaries to wake up and smell the bourgeois miasma, to enable them to confront the present situation with eyes wide open.

Born at the end of one century, Benjamin can be read as the voice of a generation that came to its senses at the beginning of another. Writing in uncertain times, he found the European dreams of his parents neither attainable nor desirable. This may explain why his work resonates so powerfully with our confused experience of the twenty-first century, as well as with our skeptical attitude toward the American dreams that suffused the twentieth. Despite its uneasy relationship with the current zeitgeist, the New York manuscript can still be approached with the following advice in mind: "Before we have learned to deal with things in a given position, they have already changed several times. Thus, we always perceive events too late, and philosophy always needs to foresee, so to speak, the past."

Billed as a history of the present, *The Manhattan Project* is meant to set an alarm clock for its future dozing readers. It is *our* current state of dogmatic slumber to which Benjamin responds. Every epoch, certainly our own, dreams of the preceding one. Just as retro fashion cites specific decades, it is very likely that before long the entire twentieth century will consolidate in our minds into a distinct point of reference. This temporal comportment can also be conveyed through the title of a movie that was released shortly before Benjamin's death, *Back to the Future*—not in the sense of return but of refusal.

The gesture of turning around to gaze at the city from which one flees is so irresistible that, in the biblical story of Sodom and Gomorrah, it is stronger than God's word. It therefore feels as if *The Manhattan Project* is written in a new, odd tense, the *past future*, as in, "Tomorrow was the party." This, however, is not an attempt to "repeat the past," Gatsby-style, but to make it replete with revolutionary potential.

IN BENJAMIN'S MIND almost everything is treated as an allegory for something else. We will see how many elements of his earlier work on Paris are prefigurations that arise in a different guise in his later study of New York. As to what his investigation of the capital of the twentieth century could possibly be an allegory for, we will see that the most reasonable though unpredictable reply would be that it is essentially a profane retelling of Saint Augustine's *City of God*. It is undeniable that "the gaze of the allegorist, as it falls on the city, is the gaze of the alienated man." In Benjamin's detached brand of urban studies, no city, not Paris or New York, not even Berlin, is approached as a native ground or a homeland. Nothing is experienced in an immediate or unmediated way.

It is, however, necessary to add that the city is also never conceived in Benjamin's work as a utopia—a word that literally means "no place." The whole point about his *Manhattan Project* is that it is a philosophical work grounded in an actual topos, not an imaginary one. For all that the historically informed New Yorker knows, Utopia is the name of a neighborhood in northern Queens, originally designed in the early twentieth century to house the impoverished Lower East Side Jews. But it is also true that in the collective imagination of the twentieth century New York did not lose its fading position as a eutopia (a homophone that means "a good place"). Justifiably or not, *The Manhattan Project* remains Benjamin's most sustained attempt to give an account of a profane order that is still "erected on the idea of happiness."

Aristotle supposedly said that hope is a waking dream. This could be what Benjamin had in mind when he remarked that although there is infinite hope in New York, none of it is for him. It is Ernst Bloch's *Principle of Hope*, written during the Second World War while its author was living in the United States, that left a faded imprint of this disposition on the theoretical scheme of *The Manhattan Project*. "Philosophy," Bloch asserts, "will have conscience of tomorrow, commitment to the future, knowledge of hope, or it will have no more knowledge." But this is certainly not the type of wide-eyed, self-centered hope of those who arrive in the city for the first time or the sort of benevolent, charitable hope of those who have already made it here. Those hopeful creatures only fill Benjamin with despair.

It is actually his growing awareness of the desperate situation of the city in which he lived from 1940 to 1987 (arguably its most challenging hour), his attention to this place where destitution and dereliction and danger were lying around every street corner, that triggered Benjamin's search for a new saving power—not in some unknown future but in his known present. He seems to assume that such fraught living conditions are less conducive to the sort of comfortable sleep that degrades concrete hope into fluffy dreams. He was, after all, fully aware, long before Frank O'Hara, that true meditations are always "meditations in an emergency." Like O'Hara, he often sees the city as a cluster of signs that, by and large, signify "that people do not totally *regret* life."

REM KOOLHAAS CALLS MANHATTAN the "20th century's Rosetta Stone." Deciphering the city is supposed to unlock the mysteries of the epoch. Benjamin is similarly hyperbolic when he predicts that the same island will become the philosopher's stone of the twenty-first century. This means that in both the literary and alchemical sense *The Manhattan Project* can be regarded as his true magnum opus. But to this I should immediately add one crucial caveat: in this case he is obviously referring only to his *idea* of New York rather than to an actual, physical reality. He still approaches his city as a subject of philosophical speculation, mainly because he suspects that by the time you read this, it will have to come to terms with its new position among the other great cities in the nursing home of the past. Anyway, Wallace Stevens suggests that "we live in the description of a place and not in the place itself."

Benjamin sees himself not only as the angel of history (whose back is indeed facing the future) but also as the owl of Minerva (the Roman goddess of wisdom). It is an allusion to these famous lines from G. W. F. Hegel: "A further word on the subject of *issuing instructions* on how the world ought to be: philosophy, at any rate, always comes on the scene too late to perform this function. As the *thought* of the world, it appears only at a time when actuality has gone through its formative process and attained its completed state. . . . When philosophy paints its grey on grey, a form of life has grown old. . . . The owl of Minerva begins its flight only with the onset of dusk."

Nietzsche illustrates this Hegelian sentiment by showing how the great Greek philosophers began to thrive only after the urban culture around them dwindled, only after the powerful way of life in the Athenian *polis* was experiencing an inevitable process of decay. To write a philosophy of (or even just in) New York is thus a clear indication of the imminent death of the place. It is a sign that the chaotic Dionysian forces of the city can surrender to the rational Apollonian forces of the philosopher. Yet the urban philosopher is still moved by a strange kind of love. It is strange because it is not love at first sight but rather what Benjamin calls "love at last sight." He explains: "It is one and the same historical night at the onset of which the owl of Minerva (with Hegel) begins its flight and Eros (with Baudelaire) lingers before the empty pallet, torch extinguished, dreaming of bygone embraces."

Unlike nostalgia, philosophy was alien to the dominant spirit at the height of New York's power. During this vital peak, the journalist A. J. Liebling pointed out, "It is very vulgar not to be dead, and this is what many writers hold against New York." Philosophers, however, differ from other writers in that they usually feel most comfortable not with the dead but with the dying. Whereas most writers know how to phrase beautiful eulogies and formulate succinct epitaphs, philosophers are at their best when they supply palliatives and support the infirm.

Like Hegel, Benjamin knows that philosophy is meant not so much to rejuvenate a shriveling life as to comprehend its incoherent mumble. Unlike Karl Marx, his primary concern is less to change the city and more to interpret it, like the philosophers of yore. This may explain why he copied a couple of sentences from *The Arcades Project* as a sort of disclaimer at the beginning of his final work: "Nothing at all of what we are saying here actually existed. None of it has ever lived—as surely as a skeleton has never lived, but only a man."

FOURTH CHAPTER   **THINK LOCALLY**

THE SLOGAN "think globally, act locally," which began to circulate toward the end of Benjamin's life, can be traced back to Immanuel Kant, not because he ever uttered it but because he embodied this sentiment quite perfectly in his very life and work. Though he never, not even once, set foot outside Königsberg, his Prussian hometown, Kant remains the great champion of the universality of reason, which could transcend, or so he believed, such differentiating factors as place, time, and culture. As scattered across the globe and unalike as we might be, the basic principles behind the way humans think are supposedly pretty much identical.

It should also be noted that although Königsberg was a respectably sized preindustrial European city with a slightly cosmopolitan air, and though Kant was a very congenial resident and a must-have addition to every dinner party, what encouraged the esteemed philosopher to "think globally" was less his involvement in local activities than his role as an armchair traveler, voraciously reading about a vast world that he would never see in person.

Within the philosophical tradition, Benjamin offers one of the best alternatives to Kant's position, which brings the former closer to one New Yorker with

Königsbergian blood and distances him slightly from another. On the one hand, Hannah Arendt, who grew up in Kant's city, is a typical global thinker who solved international problems in her writings the way most people solve crossword puzzles in the daily paper. On the other hand, Allan Stewart Konigsberg, better known as Woody Allen, is a distinctly local thinker whose best work remains, before all else, a contemplation of the life and times of his own city.

This does not mean that Allen and Benjamin's literary or cinematic works make sense only within the boundaries of New York. In fact, their worldwide appeal seems to only increase as their sense of place intensifies. Although there is no reason to assume that their work and their life simply mirror each other, these two sides of the same coin (what we call a lifework) still converge in a specific location, which happens to be called Manhattan. "Can we actually 'know' the universe?" Allen reproaches Kant in "Critique of Pure Dread." "My God, it's hard enough to find your way around in Chinatown." All knowledge is situated knowledge.

For Kant and Arendt, acting and thinking, even mind and body, fail to coincide in the same spot. Whereas it is possible to pin down the physical whereabouts of these two philosophers on a map, their writings can be said to be all over it. Unlike Kant, Arendt was an intellectual globe-trotter. Yet she wholeheartedly believed the answer to the question "Where are we when we think?" to be "Nowhere." As an intellectual who emphasized so enthusiastically the importance of acting in the public sphere, she nevertheless personally preferred to withdraw as much as she could from its harsh light. On one occasion, she asked a young friend who was living out of town to come over to help her with what she only described as a pressing matter. When he arrived, she made him attend a board meeting of her co-op building while she waited for him in her apartment. She explained, "You have to understand that there is an enormous difference between knowing what should be done and actually doing it."

Whereas Arendt's personal motto had always been *"amor mundi"* (the love of the world), and her fellow New York intellectuals were constantly "arguing the world" among themselves, Benjamin's vision was decidedly nearsighted. One of the things that this condition allowed him to see as he was examining the writings of some of his farsighted, contemporary, local (and, so it happened, usually Jewish) intellectuals, whom he never met in person, was that the path from *amor mundi* to *odium urbis* (the hatred of the city) is the path of least resistance. It is perhaps only after Marshall Berman, one of the last survivors of this venerable group, resolved to put New York at the empathic center of his thought that the familiar discussions about world politics and world literature reoriented themselves around the local, urban situation.

This may explain why Benjamin begins the section of his *Manhattan Project* dedicated to this set of questions with Allen's joke from *Annie Hall* about the merger of the New York intellectuals' two major magazines, *Dissent* and *Commentary*, into a new publication called *Dysentery*. Then Benjamin goes on to observe that there is no need to spend time and money on sending New Yorkers to psychoanalysis in order to know how they really feel about themselves. Instead, it is better to casually ask them what they think about their own city and then, while they go on and on about how horrible or spectacular or irreplaceable or impossible it is, to simply substitute the words *New York* with *my life*.

THE DESIRE TO THINK LOCALLY must be placed at the very core of Benjamin's work. This is the reason that he refers on more than one occasion to his writings on New York, Berlin, Paris, and a few other cities he happened to visit as works in *local philosophy*. This sounds like an oxymoron, given that universal application and validity seem to be the high aspiration of every philosopher. It is very likely that Kant is responsible, at least in part, for deepening the roots of this far-from-obvious assumption in our modern minds. There is, however, no philosophy that manages to go against this grain so effectively, that arises from such a direct involvement with a specific place, and that remains a resolute contemplation of this place than Benjamin's lifelong dedication to the cities in which he was living. In the mind of this local thinker, the worst thing that one can say about another's ideas is not that they are false but that they are provincial.

A philosophy of *a* place, however, is not the same as the philosophy *of* place. In the latter case, place is treated as an abstract, nonlocalizable notion. Specific places are meant to serve only as examples of a general understanding concerning the significance of place. But where, Benjamin wonders, does the thought about place take place, or what is the place of place, understood as a philosophical concept? When one reads theoretical musings about the subject, one usually gets the impression that they could have been written anywhere and be about anywhere. Benjamin therefore shows very little interest in ideas *about* place. Instead, he draws his attention to the ideas arising from *this* place. His is one of the rare philosophical works that begins with the question *where* rather than the usual *what* or *how* or *why*. Call it, for the time being, a *topology*, or a theory in situ. Benjamin calls it "presence of mind."

It would be unfortunate to exclude this approach from the discipline of philosophy on the grounds of its failure to tap into the universal rather than allow it to expand our understanding of what philosophy can do or be. It would also be unfortunate to stigmatize local philosophy as a brand of relativism. First, any representation of New York's condensed amalgam of cultures (not in the United Nations but in its actual neighborhoods) is a simple and concrete refutation of the relativist belief in the unbridgeable chasm that separates different forms of life. More to the point but perhaps also more problematically, Benjamin nowhere claims that every place can have its own philosophy.

True thinking means for Benjamin, above all, the "arrest" of thought's movement from place to place, from idea to idea. Only in New York did he finally come to a full stop in front of an urban constellation saturated with tensions. Paris, he came to realize, was only a station. Manhattan was his intellectual terminus. This standstill enabled him to crystalize his thinking about his new city into what he called a "monad." A monad, he learned from Leibniz, has no windows that open into the world. It is self-contained. So we cannot think about it globally. Nevertheless, Manhattan-as-monad remains, in Leibniz's own formulation, a "perpetual living mirror of the universe." It is still a paradigm for something larger than itself. It can entail consequences that go far beyond its temporal and geographic limits. As Archimedes of Syracuse puts it, "Give me a place to stand, and I will move the world." Or as Sinatra of Hoboken puts it, "If I can make it there, I'll make it anywhere."

⸎

AS AN ACTOR, Benjamin was pretty much helpless wherever he went. His *vita activa* was rather elusive. He acted neither globally nor locally. One might say that his actions were otherworldly, but the truth is that he was, simply and sadly, unworldly. Following Arendt, he knew that his destiny as a thinker was to live a life in hiding, to be unnoticed, unmarked, to see but not be seen. This, after all, is probably the best part about being declared dead, and he made sure to take full advantage of this unusual situation.

But his motivation was not escapist. He did not wish for his mind to be unshackled from his body or transported to heaven. He was not trying to become an Aristotelian thought that thinks only of itself, nor was he aspiring to become an Augustinian saint who transcends the city of man. Instead, his project was based on the decision to commit his thinking to the concrete place in which his body was to be found. In this sense, he is an embodiment (or ensoulment) of what

Antonio Gramsci called an organic intellectual, who is rooted in his own environment and articulates its form of life rather than imagine himself as an autonomous agent operating independently of his local fabric.

Long before Kant's attempt to think globally, René Descartes was already busy trying to divorce thought from extension. He insisted that only extended things (bodies that have geometrical shapes) had a place within his famous system of x and y coordinates, whereas thinking things (or minds) lacked a definable location in space. Though he came to trust *that* he thought, *where* it was that he thought remained a matter of the greatest uncertainty. Benjamin's main criticism is consequently not directed at Descartes's problematic dualism of mind and body but at the usually less noticed (though closely related) detachment of thought from the place in which it finds itself. "In this large town where I live," Descartes wrote about Amsterdam circa 1631, "everyone but myself is engaged in trade, and hence is so attentive to his own profit that I could live here all my life without ever being noticed by a soul."

Benjamin argues that the fact that your surroundings fail to notice you does not give you the license to fail to notice your surroundings. In a way, he reverses the famous Cartesian position: The only certainty and knowledge comes from the world (or the city) around the philosopher, whereas the self (or the thinker) becomes the main source of doubt and error. This, by the way, is precisely the position of Walter Benjamin within *The Manhattan Project*.

FIFTH CHAPTER   IMPLOSION

ONE OF MARX'S ASTUTE OBSERVATIONS is that the ruling class controls not only the economic sphere but also the realm of ideas. The ideology and spirit of those who are materially in power are gradually abstracted from the concrete, local circumstances from which they are derived and considered instead to be universally applicable. After Gramsci, we call this phenomenon cultural hegemony. The interests of the rich are henceforth treated as the interests of all of humankind, as the only rationally valid option. Marx's example is that when the aristocracy is dominant, "honor, loyalty, etc.," are the dominating values, and when the bourgeoisie rules, freedom and equality are esteemed above all.

In order to steer clear of this trap, Benjamin, the purveyor of local philosophy, while investigating what was arguably the most powerful place in the world at the time, never abstracts his findings from their context; he never presents them as objective, universal truths. He makes it very clear that the philosophical potency of the ideas investigated in his *Manhattan Project* are inseparable from the material conditions, the subjugations, and exploitations that enabled New York to become the capital of the twentieth century. It is a point worth remembering while reading the book in your hand just in the event that its writer did not.

It is not the spreading of thoughts across lands and peoples but rather their concentration into a small island that truly fascinates Benjamin. He therefore describes New York as a perfect manifestation of what Lewis Mumford calls an "urban implosion." This gives an ironic twist to the title of Benjamin's manuscript, because the process that generates a metropolitan center like Manhattan is the opposite of the way an atomic bomb detonates. Rather than send out an explosive spray of particles from a single core to a large area, a city forces more and more disparate elements—ideas, commodities, skills, persons, interests, fortunes, beliefs, desires, practices, aspirations, sensibilities, ideologies, stupidities—to come closer and closer together, to congest into a single limited space. The more a city draws different elements into a dense mass, the more it attracts exceedingly distant elements, the more powerful it becomes. From this perspective we could say that *The Manhattan Project* is an interdisciplinary work simply because the city is.

During the first half of the twentieth century the consensus among urbanists, with Mumford at the helm, was that this process of implosion had reached its demographic and architectonic limit. They believed that once a city achieves a certain level of congestion, it becomes self-destructive and begins to disintegrate into its peripheries. The majority of planners treated this reversal of the urban process, this scattering of elements away from the center, as a desirable development. "During the last fifteen years," Mumford wrote three months before the Second World War began, "a few hundred thousand Manhattanites have permanently left the island. As a result, the rest of us have a little *Lebensraum*."

The paradigm shift occurred only after Jane Jacobs published in 1961 *The Death and Life of Great American Cities*—a book that Benjamin (whose own life after death should not be dismissed offhand) considered the New Testament of urban thought. The attempt to thin down the inner-city population through slum clearance and suburban sprawl is revealed in this book for what it really was: an insidious *urbicide*. The motive, Jacobs shows, was an ideological commitment of urban thinkers who were actually deeply antagonistic to metropolitan life. She thus contests their claim that urban flight is a natural development and a scientific necessity.

In a chapter titled "The Need for Concentration," Jacobs dismantles this argument by countering the emotionally charged assumption that "human beings are charming in small numbers and noxious in large numbers." She argues instead that people who gather in city centers can be considered a positive good "because they are the source of immense vitality, and because they do represent, in small geographic compass, a great and exuberant richness of differences and possibilities, many of these differences unique and unpredictable and all the more valuable because they are."

THE REASON GOD DECIDED to foil the people's plan to build the Tower of Babel had little to do, despite what is often assumed, with the skyscraper's height. God was clearly threatened, above all, by the prospect of so many people concentrated in the same place, building together a single powerful city: "If as one people with a shared language they have achieved this," we hear him musing while surveying the imposing metropolis, "then they could achieve any project they conceive of." Instead of rejoicing in this human potentiality, God decides to scatter people across the land and confuse their shared means of communication, all in an attempt to stop the construction of Babel and thus to secure his superiority.

The Babel story enables Benjamin to connect the phenomenon of urban implosion to a mystical theory about the creation of the world that he first encountered in Gershom Scholem's notes for the lectures he delivered in 1938 at the Jewish Institute of Religion in New York. When the book based on these lectures was published three years later as *Major Trends in Jewish Mysticism*, Scholem dedicated it to the memory of Benjamin, his presumably dead friend.

In Kabbalistic cosmogony, Scholem explains, "*tsimtsum*" is the name of a process that preceded the creation of the world as we know it from the first chapter of Genesis. In the beginning before the beginning, God's infinite light contracted or withdrew from the entire universe in such a way that it imploded into itself. The world as we know it could then be created in this empty dark space that is essentially devoid of the divine light, besides a few sparks. This is one way to explain why two of God's most important names in Judaism are *HaMakom* (the place) and *Shekhinah* (dwelling). In opposition to common belief, God is neither everywhere nor nowhere, because he *is* somewhere: "God is the place of the world," writes the author of *Genesis Rabbah*, "but the world is not His place."

The city represents for Benjamin a modern process of *tsimtsum*, as the light/life of vast areas around the globe are constricted into a small place, leaving behind only remnants of glimmers in an otherwise dark land. Baruch Spinoza equates God with nature, the entire universe with the divine. Benjamin claims that today we are witnessing how this absolute immanence goes through a gradual process of contraction, imploding into a few points across the globe, each becoming what we call a *cosmopolis* or world-city.

Though Benjamin never treats the *cosmos* as a *polis*, the world as city, he views the *polis* as the true *cosmos*. Contrary to current practice, this is a better way to approach cosmopolitanism. Rather than view the world as a gigantic, single city, it is more helpful to treat the city as a complete miniature world. For example, try to match each borough in New York with one of the five continents. Cosmopolitanism could be understood in this sense as an argument for localism rather than as the usual argument for the erasure of all locales. Seeing the world as a global village is also a way of treating all its inhabitants as provincial or marginalized villagers. Rather than everyone being included in the same fictional village, everyone is now excluded from the same imaginary city.

For the "citizen of the world" (a term that goes hand in hand with the term "refugee"), cities are mere nodes in an accelerating network or launching pads for international operations. When financiers and artists, merchants and academics, shuttle over this seemingly homogeneous global landscape by hopping from one indistinguishable airport to the next, they also reach a point at which their different occupations seem to lose their distinctions. The philosopher Agnes Heller once asked a businesswoman who sat next to her on a transatlantic flight which place she considered home. Her answer was, "My home is where my cat lives."

This is not to deny that, as Benjamin knew firsthand, New York is a little like Paris and a little like Berlin and probably like a few other big cities. If you have managed one, you can probably manage the others. But he also knew that living in different cities is a bit like sleeping with different members of the same family. You'd better not mix them up. Modernity has changed a lot of things about the way we live, but neither cheap air travel nor high-speed Internet has managed to refute these simple clichés: where you live is who you are; location, location, location.

Even though cities existed, exist, and will exist in various configurations and degrees of congestion, New York, capital of the twentieth century, remains Benjamin's paradigmatic example of an imploded world-city. So instead of talking about New York, we often find him speaking of *the city* in general. But New York is not just a placeholder. This becomes clear when one notices its nearly mystical position in Benjamin's thought. New York, he claims in an otherwise empty page of the manuscript, is the real *Aleph*, by which he refers to Jorge Luis Borges's name for "the place where, without admixture or confusion, all the places of the world, seen from every angle, coexist."

SIXTH CHAPTER   SHEER LIFE

IF I WERE TO SUMMARIZE the intricate theoretical argument of *The Manhattan Project* in a single sentence, it would be its claim that the city is a "landscape built of sheer life." It is easy to miss this phrase (borrowed from Hugo von Hofmannsthal) when it first appears in Benjamin's *Arcades Project*, buried among thousands of other quotations. But when he applies this proposition to New York instead of Paris, it suddenly becomes definitive; it crystallizes his vision of the city in such a way that the expression "sheer life" transforms into the manuscript's decisive term of art, into a hinge on which his entire argument turns.

Benjamin does not usually revert to his native German in the New York manuscript, but here he finds it necessary to clarify that sheer life is a translation of *lauter Leben*. He distinguishes it from *bloßes Leben*, or "bare life," a term he used in a few of his early essays. Bare life is a life that is separated from its form or its way, from its qualities or its attributes, from its meaning or its possibilities, from its human rights or its political status. It is just life, stripped to its mere biological necessities.

For the young Benjamin, bare life served mainly as a theoretical and polemical notion. He did not imagine how close he would personally get to this inhuman condition during the Second World War and how real it would become for the estimated fourteen million civilians who were exterminated by Nazi Germany and the Soviet Union between 1933 and 1945. So when the stories about the death camps began to trickle into the back pages of the *New York Times*, it was with precisely this early concept that he chose to describe these almost indescribable places. Auschwitz—he writes in one of the most decisive pages in the whole manuscript—is a terrain of bare lives. New York, he then continues without pause, is a landscape built of sheer life.

This stark comparison between the camp and the city, Auschwitz and New York, bare life and sheer life, receives no further elaboration. But it certainly remains one of Benjamin's elementary axioms. It contrasts two ideal conditions— the inhuman and the human—which may or may not coincide with the complex historical facts associated with these two actual geographic locations. Benjamin seems to posit an abstraction of this particular camp and this particular city in order to treat them as theoretical paradigms, as the symbolic, extreme limit cases between which his thought, but also our reality, oscillates. Though the word *Auschwitz* appears but once in the entire manuscript, it still functions as the polar opposite of New York, thus charging his text with a particular tension that renders his political commitment unequivocal. As Italo Calvino points out, "each city receives its form from the desert it opposes."

Since the days of Aristotle, the *telos* or ultimate aim of the city is not considered to be the protection of our mere bodily existence. Although the city originated in "the bare needs of life," it exists, above all, "for the sake of a good life." One of the problems, however, is that once this singular, limited, focused space that the ancient Greeks called the *polis* expands into vast states and intercontinental empires, the good does not necessarily follow suit. Instead, the basic idea that the end of politics is to facilitate a life according to the good in this world tends to dissipate; more often than not, it is not even acknowledged. Seasoned politicians and regular citizens alike habitually forget that the original political goal is to find ways to have a "share in happiness," while the philosophers who are still bothering to figure out what exactly the good or happy life amounts to interest almost no one.

All things considered, Benjamin still seems to imagine that the lives that pass by him in the streets of New York contain the same kernel of the good that Aristotle first glimpsed more than two millennia ago in the streets of Athens. Whereas he considers bare life the most minimal and meaningless human existence imaginable, in which different forms of life are eliminated, it follows that sheer life is understood in his work as the most intricate and significant human existence possible, where different forms of life are constantly being produced. This is what Benjamin wished to bring to the fore, not merely through casual people watching but by means of his scrupulous scholarly legwork.

TO BETTER SEE what Benjamin means by sheer life, we need to take a short detour to his theory of photography, a subject very dear to his heart both before and after his alleged suicide. It is well known that because of the long exposure time required by early photographic techniques, only static objects were able to impress their image on the final result. Whatever moved, even slightly, disappeared. One might therefore expect that the first photograph of a human being would be one of those early studio portraits in which the privileged subject was instructed to sit absolutely still for a painfully long period of time before his image registered on the photographic plate.

The real story behind this monumental event is quite different. In 1838, Louis Daguerre decided to turn his camera's lens from still objects in his Parisian studio to an open window facing the Boulevard du Temple. As he predicted, when the silver plate was developed, the lively midday bustle was completely wiped out. The picture showed only buildings and an empty tree-lined street. The multitude of people, carriages, and pushcarts were all gone. But then, at the boulevard's curve, Daguerre detected a clear silhouette of a single man lifting his leg, apparently to get his shoe shined. Because he happened to linger in this position while the camera's shutter stayed open, this anonymous man was the first to ever be photographed.

More than a century after the medium took its first baby steps, eventually allowing the amateur photographer to snap a picture in a millisecond, the old method of long exposure was resurrected to produce, in the name of art, some of the strangest images of New York City. Benjamin first discovered these photographs in the Public Library's Art and Architecture Collection. He was immediately drawn to their deception. There is something eerie about the ability of long-exposure photos to transform the busiest spot on earth into a lifeless wasteland. In the age of the bomb, this depiction of a deserted Fifth Avenue may even resonate as apocalyptic.

BENJAMIN, however, for whom the Manhattan Project meant the opposite of what it meant for a New Yorker by the name of Robert Oppenheimer, interprets these pictures very differently. From his point of view, these hyper-daguerreotypes that manage to erase every single living being down to the last one who stopped to get his shoe shined are so wrong that they are almost right. As representations of New York, they are precisely the opposite of what he took to be the city's deepest truth. Because their deceit is so perfect, all that is needed to discover what he took to be the proper representation of the city is to find a way to negate them completely.

Inspired by his discovery that in many ancient cultures variations of the cross were the symbol of life and variations of a circle enclosing a cross (or crossroad) were the symbol of the city, Benjamin wonders what would we see if it were technically possible to take a picture that erases everything that is static but registers everything mobile in a particular instant? Imagine a photo of a busy street corner in New York with no buildings, no stores, no parked cars, no sidewalks, no signs, no fire hydrants: just a blank image dotted with pedestrians and dogs, bikers and drivers, pigeons and rats, all seeming to float in a void. This, he claims, would be the true image of the city; it would be a landscape built of sheer life.

SEVENTH CHAPTER   A SECRET ABOUT A SECRET

SOMEWHERE IN THE MIDDLE of *The Manhattan Project* one can find a sentence attributed to Marx that echoes Benjamin's basic intuition: "Men can see nothing around them that is not their own image; everything speaks to them of themselves. Their very landscape is alive." He also discovered one particular photographic image that beautifully illustrates this observation. It is a contact sheet developed in 1957 by Diane Arbus, showing two consecutive snapshots she took in Times Square. The upper image is a study of a blonde woman in an elegant black coat as she walks down the street with a cigarette in her right hand. The one below is dominated by the buildings and neon signs of the nightly square, though at the bottom of the shot one can detect a man in a suit next to an American flag, waving his fist in the air, pontificating fervently to indifferent passersby. In what was most likely only a happy darkroom accident, Arbus used the technique of double exposure to impress her self-portrait in between the two images, superimposing her own face over these city scenes.

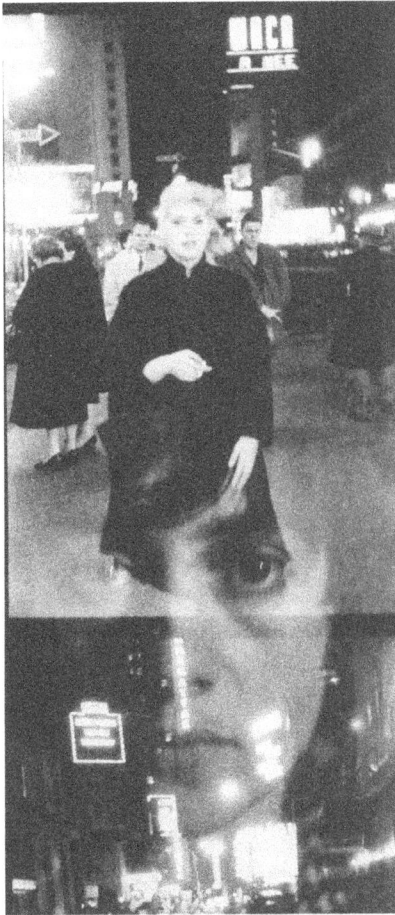

IN A WAY, Arbus's entire body of work is an elaborate, piecemeal self-portrait. It is the modern, fragmentary, urban version of Narcissus's pond. She could see nothing around her that was not her own image. Everything spoke to her of herself. When one looks at many of her portraits, the presence of the photographer can be sensed almost as strongly as the presence of the person being photographed (something that seldom happens in cinema). For this reason all the strange (some might say freakish) characters who populate her photographs rarely provoke in their viewers some sort of detached fascination with the exotic or less fortunate Other. Consider "Seated Man in Bra and Stockings, N. Y. C. 1967." The ease of the subject in front of her camera (held at waist level, thus allowing him to look her in the eye) does not convey the impression that he is being either praised or ridiculed, either documented or cataloged. This and all her other photos appear to be remembered in her mind's eye, like mental images.

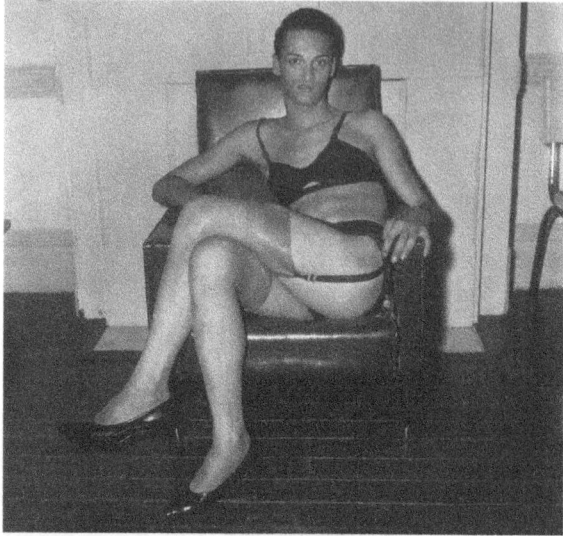

AUGUST SANDER'S candid portraits of German people in the 1920s were a prime inspiration for Arbus's own photographic style. When the Nazis began to question the anti-Arian ethos of Sander's work, he simply switched from portraits to landscapes. The closest thing to a landscape in Arbus's oeuvre is that of cheap wallpaper in a building's lobby that depicts a romantic lake, with the corner of the drab room cutting through the center of the wallpaper and an electric socket protruding at the bottom of it. The Arbusian landscape is almost always alive, though not as a natural landscape teeming with animals and plants, away from civilization's reach. It is dominated by the different individuals she discovered in the city and its environs, who cannot be reduced to social types, which is what Sander's work tends to do.

If Benjamin had to place in a sealed time capsule the only items by which future generations would remember the New York of his time, he would select no books, not even the montage of texts that is his *Manhattan Project*. Instead, he would choose some of his favorite Arbus portraits of outcasts, along with some of Helen Levitt's slum scenes, some of Weegee's crime scenes, and other works by a handful of New York photographers. The focus of these photos is not the city's imposing buildings but the multiplicity of its people, especially its more marginalized and less visible dwellers—those who rarely show up in the official pages of its history.

Instead of trying to say what this place was all about, Benjamin would try to show something by means of a visual Noah's ark. "A photograph," Arbus writes, "is a secret about a secret. The more it tells you the less you know." But Benjamin's selection would be enough to make his intention very clear. Through the medium of photography, by means of this "mirror that remembers," he wants to transform our usual conception of the city as a *built form* into a vision of this place as a *lived form*. It is not the solidity of walls but the precariousness of lives that stands as the ultimate horizon of his thought.

PHOTOGRAPHY IS NOT HISTORY. A photograph does not pretend to have a past or a future, a before or an after. As such, it offers neither judgment nor explanation. By itself, it gives no clues as to how the person in the picture arrived at his condition, where he is headed afterward, or what can be done to alter his inferred situation. For a critic with liberal inclinations like Susan Sontag, the tendency of the medium not to take sides in the usual social and political discourse about our place in history—how did we get to where we are, how can we move forward, how should we intervene—leads to her deep dissatisfaction with the way photography can often leave the viewer morally crippled. As Marx reproaches philosophy in general and Hegel in particular for only trying to understand the world rather than change it, Sontag reproaches photography in general and Arbus in particular for abandoning even the attempt to understand the world. Instead, she argues, most photographers simply "propose that we collect it."

Benjamin came to appreciate photography's ability to crystallize the homogeneous, linear flow of history into heterogeneous, still images pregnant with tension. He actually cherished the ability of the medium to prove that any human being in this mass society of ours can be transformed into a singular (but also solitary) living monad, into a world, undistracted by the illusion of progress, unvictimized by the context. A photographic document is not necessarily a document of barbarism, as Sontag would have it.

Some of us cringe when we see our own pictures, but for others, even those who have never met us, this medium is a surprisingly effective window into the soul of the photographed subject. But this soul is not eternal, simply because the exposure of every photo correlates with a well-defined segment of time (painting, Benjamin notes, lacks this "chronological specifiability"). In other words, without photography the fleeting living landscape that Benjamin glimpsed at first in Paris and then, even more vividly, in the streets of Manhattan, would have gone unnoticed. This explains why twentieth-century New York "was as important to photography as photography to New York." The medium and the place somehow brought each other to their senses; they enabled each other to see in sheer life their shared raison d'être.

NOT EVERYTHING THAT WE SEE when our eyes are open can be called an image. Because our visual field changes as we move about, we barely notice it as such. We do not see that we see, so to speak. We might have noticed the old man who just crossed the street on our way to the subway, but we don't necessarily think of what we just saw as an image proper. Only on special occasions do we sense that what we observe in front of us crystallizes into a true image. So what, exactly, is an image? Benjamin's definition is as simple as it gets: "When one knows that something will soon be removed from one's gaze, that thing becomes an image." A section in his *Manhattan Project*, curiously titled "New York Elderhood around 1980," is essentially a long literary montage of such thought-images, of little prosaic snapshots of his daily city life.

Taking a photo is an act of preemptive mourning, an attempt to hold on to a present life that is certain to pass. Arbus describes her own pictures as "the proof that something was there and no longer is. Like a stain." Even though, or precisely because, we know that everything that is solid will eventually melt into air, we cannot help trying to freeze being in time, to make life stand still. Notice that the faster life changes, the more pictures we take. But Arbus had no intention of holding on to the passing life toward which her camera was directed. By attending to the stillness, not the movement, of her subjects, she was, in all earnestness, trying to redeem them. Benjamin's *Manhattan Project*, which could easily be compared to a photo album made entirely of words, is driven by a parallel attempt to redeem the passing life of a city that, similarly to his own life, was vanishing like a match's flame.

But we are still here, at least for now, looking at the stained tablecloth after the feast is over, gazing at the pictures of those frozen, calcified, past lives whose "stillness," Arbus observes, "is boggling. You can turn away but when you come back they'll still be there looking at you." In Benjamin's manuscript, however, the word *looking* is crossed out, above which he wrote *leaping*.

FIRST THRESHOLD INTERPENETRATION

ONE OF THE NOTICEABLE SHIFTS in Benjamin's thought as he moved from Paris to New York can be explained with the help of three pairs of simple (some might say simplistic) categories: reality/fantasy, politics/economics, heaven/hell. These function like three dimensions within which any element that is a part of any big city can be found. Nevertheless, there is no need to treat these conceptual axes as necessary truths but only as pragmatic ones. They hold only because and as long as they work, only because they enable us to make some sense of the chaotic and fragmentary urban happening.

Another reason to familiarize ourselves with the logic behind these opposing categories is that it will help us orient ourselves within the theoretical maze of Benjamin's *Manhattan Project*. You may have noticed that I have divided this book into six parts. These are meant to reflect the trinity of elemental polarities Benjamin employs in his attempt to grasp how New York works. The first part revolves around the city as a fantasy, and the second deals with its reality. The third part is about the political power of the city, and the fourth is about its economic power. Finally, the fifth and sixth parts are dedicated to New York's hellish and heavenly aspects, respectively.

This schematic division leads to another surprising discovery. It appears that Benjamin's three polar opposites also fit rather neatly into Kant's three fundamental philosophical questions when applied to the city. Seen in this way, in the first and second parts of this book Benjamin focuses on the question, "What can I know?" In the third and fourth parts, he wonders, "What ought I to do?" Then the fifth and sixth parts can be read as his attempt to ask, "What may I hope?"

Our three dualisms may also be handy for anyone trying to get a better grasp of *The Arcades Project*. There, however, they clearly tend toward what might be called their negative side. First, hell trumps heaven. Benjamin describes his book on Paris as a "theology of hell," as his attempt to awaken us from a nightmare. Second, fantasy trumps reality. Nineteenth-century Paris is repeatedly treated as a "dream city" or a phantasmagoria. Third, private or economic considerations trump public or political ones. The entire city is seen as an interior, or an inside with "no outside."

The arcades of Paris, the main metaphoric vehicle of Benjamin's early work, are also the symbolic point at which the three negative elements converge into a "world in miniature." When those covered passageways that cut through an entire city block became the center of public fascination in the first half of the nineteenth century, they immediately evoked the modernist chimeras of vitality and novelty. The most opulent shops of the arcades catered to the cream of society by offering what was meant to be an all-embracing shopping experience. But Benjamin shows that it was not long before the daydream turned sour, before the spectacular structures became derelict, before the coveted commodities were covered with layers of dust, and before the elegant shops were visited by an assortment of unsavory characters.

One can read *The Arcades Project* as a cautionary tale about the chain reaction that goes into effect once the open street morphs into a kind of interior room, which then turns into a dreamscape, which then becomes a wasteland. Privacy, phantasy, and purgatory go hand in hand. The later Benjamin could not help detecting the same process in the shopping malls that plagued suburban America during his afterlifetime. He saw how yesterday's sparkling-new mall that sucked the life out of Main Street became tomorrow's outdated piece of undesirable real estate. Yet he also notes that these malls, these suburban nightmares, never manage to gain a substantial foothold in New York City. By rejecting the model of the mall, which is the arcade's next of kin, twentieth-century Manhattan proved its ability to resist the dark magic exercised by one side of Benjamin's trinity of polar opposites, which had ruled so effectively over nineteenth-century Paris.

NO ONE in his or her right mind would claim that in New York heaven wins over hell, reality overcomes fantasy, or the public has a priority over the private. Instead, the argument advanced in *The Manhattan Project* is that each aspect of these three conceptual dichotomies operates like a magnet with more or less equal force of attraction as its opposite. It is as if the city hovers somewhere in the middle of this field of tensions, at the zero point of this x, y, z graph. So even though New York can be described as the "capital of perpetual crisis," it may also be a "jealous custodian of its own inner tensions." Rather than lead to a colossal collapse, those opposing forces create and maintain a very delicate urban equilibrium.

In the same way that standing a wrong idea on its head does not make it right, standing a right idea on its head does not make it wrong. The factual or the notional, the celestial or the infernal, the personal or the communal can claim for themselves only momentary and localized triumphs in a place like New York. The result is that any theoretical separation or distinction that one can think of becomes inoperative, because the multitude of concrete, opposing elements that populate the city constantly *interpenetrate* one another. Or, to use Marx's formulation, everything in New York "seems pregnant with its contrary." Or, as Marshall Berman puts it, New York is a "forest of symbols" that are "endlessly fighting each other for sun and light, working to kill each other off, melting each other along with themselves into air." But whereas Berman perceives constant movement and change, Benjamin claims that the overall dialectical ebb and flow of the city results in a curious standstill—not because nothing happens but because so much happens.

Benjamin quotes Brecht: "Do not insist on the wave that breaks on your foot. As long as it stands in the water, new waves will break on it." In the grand scheme of urban things, the three pairs of polar opposites reach a point where their oscillation is so rapid that they appear to be at rest. The more hectic New York appears to be, the more serene it turns out to be. The more six-sided dice are cast in the city's casino, the more time stands still.

A. J. Liebling gives us one of the nicest illustrations of this strange urban condition: "The finest thing about New York City, I think, is that it is like one of those complicated Renaissance clocks where on one level an allegorical marionette pops out to mark the day of the week, on another a skeleton death bangs the quarter hour with his scythe, and on the third the Twelve Apostles do a cakewalk. The variety of the sideshows distracts one's attention from the advance of the hour hand." In other words, the history of New York, unlike that of Paris, is not a "dialectical fairyland." It is a dialectical Sabbath, where all dualistic structures melt into immanent events.

ABOVE ALL, it is Henry Miller who helped Benjamin better understand this urban dialectics at a standstill. In *Tropic of Capricorn* Miller explains that on every map of Williamsburg, his childhood neighborhood, Grand Street functions as the boundary separating the North streets from the South streets. Yet to his young mind Grand had no significance whatsoever. Another street, North Second (later renamed Metropolitan Avenue), was for him the indisputable boundary between two incommensurable worlds.

The curious implication is that Miller lived between two frontiers, the first real or public and the second imaginary or private. According to the first boundary, his home was located in the north. According to the second, he lived in the south. It is this zone of indistinction between two frontiers that he perceives as paradigmatic. Between Grand and North Second there is a short block called Fillmore Place. This, Miller argues, is the *ideal* street "for a boy, a lover, a maniac, a drunkard, a crook, a lecher, a thug, an astronomer, a musician, a poet, a tailor, a shoemaker, a politician . . . each one a world unto himself and all living together harmoniously and inharmoniously, *but together*, a solid corporation, a close knit human spore which could not disintegrate unless the street itself disintegrated."

Any conceivable dialectical distinction between thesis and antithesis (north and south, heaven and hell, rich and poor, good and evil, nature and culture, private and public, fantasy and reality) must assume a line that divides everything into two more or less distinct sides. By following Miller, it becomes possible to divide this line itself down the middle—not crosswise but lengthwise—thus opening a new space between two established boundaries. In geography, we know of two such lines: the Tropic of Cancer and the Tropic of Capricorn, not incidentally the titles of Miller's two masterpieces (one set in Paris and the other in New York).

Benjamin speculates that New York City as a whole operates within this in-between conceptual space. This simple (topo)logical device, which he borrows from Miller in an attempt to undermine our inveterately dualistic thought, is what allows the city's chaotic multiplicity of polarizing elements—each seemingly independent of (and agonistic to) the other—to nevertheless interpenetrate, to form a single spore.

SECOND PART

Things are real before there is an image of them.

—JANE JACOBS

EIGHTH CHAPTER **LIVINGRY**

AS MUCH AS HE BECAME INFATUATED with photography, Benjamin grew quite impatient with architecture. His claim that physical structures have become mere distractions from city life is not easy to digest, though he does make the intriguing point that seasoned New Yorkers rarely stop to look at the buildings around them, and during the fleeting moments that they do, they tend to feel a bit like tourists. That this observation entails his conclusion—that modern buildings are meant to lead us astray by turning the gaze away from the life in the street—is hardly obvious. In any event, Benjamin never speaks, metaphorically, about the architecture of his book, and only rarely does he treat the built city as an aesthetic object. "Some people," Andy Warhol concurs, "say Paris is more aesthetic than New York. Well, in New York you don't have time to have an aesthetic because it takes half the day to go uptown and half the day to go downtown."

Augustine distinguishes between *urbs* (the brick-and-mortar physical city) and *civitas* (the communal city made of people), which logically precedes his celebrated split of the *civitas* into its heavenly and earthly manifestations. Benjamin continues this line of thought by claiming that a focus on New York's architecture implies that the Shakespearean question, "What is the city but the people?" is not a rhetorical one. If skyscrapers could speak, they would probably try to convince us that New York is more than just a landscape built of sheer life. In order to prove them wrong, to demonstrate that the true measure of a city is not a beautiful building but a beautiful life, some of the most animated pages in *The Manhattan Project* are dedicated to a methodical dismantling of architectural discourse. If we assume that society is a spectacle and New York is a stage, then Benjamin has a point in comparing architecture to the curtain, or to the wings, or to the person in the seat next to you who intermittently coughs throughout the show. Buildings are veils drawn over life's face.

Because Benjamin treats the city's built form as an apparatus of concealment, it makes sense that photography is his favorite device of *un*concealment, that he approaches this medium as an aperture of truth. Prior to his turn away from architecture and toward photography, he sought in vain for a type of New York building that could assume the role of the Parisian arcade. He needed an architectural metaphor to encapsulate the essence of his new city. Then, instead of dwelling on the decay of a certain kind of architectonic structure, he became interested in the decay of architecture as a discipline. He realized that his inability to find a satisfactory solution *was* the solution. This happy failure led him to treat *The Manhattan Project* like a long-exposure photograph turned "inside-out." All buildings dissolved into indistinct shadows, while all lives became absolutely crisp.

🕊

THE PROBLEM IS that the built form remains the single most powerful apparatus opposing the lived form. No one in the city dares do anything that might anger the almighty god of real estate. Whatever other deities the New Yorker chooses to worship, the lord of the land must receive the first and most substantial sacrifice. The primordial, though usually unacknowledged, fear of the typical city inhabitant is not to be excommunicated in this world or suffer the everlasting fire of hell in the next but to be homeless. As long as they have a roof, New Yorkers will sacrifice whatever they hold dear to keep it over their urban heads. Even their closet space.

The built form reveals its reactionary face when it hinders the inhabitants' ability to change the form of their life. Consider the flight of the bourgeoisie from New York to the suburbs after the Second World War, which led to the cataclysmic devastation of many neighborhoods throughout the city and the devaluation of properties. A less expected consequence of this so-called white flight, which occurred in tandem with an industrial flight, is that the low rent facilitated one of the most creative and revolutionary periods in the cultural and social history of this place. Think of the hip-hop scene in the Bronx, the art scene in SoHo, or the punk scene in the East Village. When the construction cranes are silent, the muses are loud and clear.

But those days are pretty much gone. Today it is tacitly understood that life can be different or radical only insofar as it (or its parents) can also pay the rent. Seen from the perspective of the real estate agent, the use value that may arise from living in the city is outweighed by the staggering exchange value of its properties. Like Paris, New York runs the risk of being reduced to merchandise and its inhabitants to customers: "The great goal so long sought," writes a nineteenth-century observer, "had finally been achieved: that of making Paris an object of luxury and curiosity, rather than of use . . . a display city placed under glass . . . an object of admiration and envy to foreigners, unbearable for its inhabitants."

Architects may be driven by the best of intentions. But in the definitive urban tension between people and buildings, lives and walls, they not only serve the wrong side; they also blur this basic struggle by disguising the oppressive force behind a charming facade and a show of consideration for the human scale. For example, Benjamin was not the first to notice that some of the most socially conscious housing projects of the twentieth century turned out to be the most obvious machines of urban oppression. Architects have a hard time hiding the fact that they are the priests of Moloch "whose eyes," as Allen Ginsberg writes, "are a thousand blind windows . . . whose skyscrapers stand in the long streets like endless Jehovas."

THIS IS THE CONTROVERSIAL CONTEXT in which Benjamin takes special aim at the inventor Buckminster Fuller and his notion of "livingry"—a neologism for whatever enhances life that contrasts with weaponry, which annihilates it. "The architectural profession," Fuller asserts, "has always been the place where the most competent thinking is conducted regarding livingry, as opposed to weaponry." Probably the best example of this naive attitude at work is Fuller's own design of a spherical dome meant to cover the entire Midtown section of Manhattan from river to river in a perfect two-mile diameter, reaching its highest point around the Public Library's main branch on Fifth Avenue and Forty-Second Street.

A first impression might speak to the spectacular benevolence such a structure seems to exude on behalf of the public. A less enthusiastic or more paranoid reading would be to claim that the Manhattan dome (from *domus*, Latin for "home") is secretly meant to domesticate and maybe even dominate anyone and anything within its scope. If city air indeed makes us free, then wouldn't such a "city indoors" make us prisoners? If, as Fuller's plan implies, home is anywhere, then isn't it also nowhere? Would the Manhattan dome be a convenient haven for the homeless, protecting them from the harsh weather, or would such a mega-shelter inevitably lead to their systematic banishment from this circumscribed sphere, along with all other natural elements?

Just as every umbrella eventually breaks and is left mutilated on a street corner, the dome's promise of "one umbrella over all heads" might be less durable and more questionable than it appears. By en-doming the Midtown area, Fuller's project resonates with the messianic vision of Isaiah, who prophesied that in the end of days Jerusalem will be covered by a "glorious canopy," as well as with the practical vision of a nineteenth-century science-fiction writer, who speculated that by 1987 Paris will sport a retractable "crystal canopy" for rainy days. Even more to the point, it seems that the Manhattan dome is an attempt to realize on a grand scale what the Parisian arcades were supposed to achieve on a smaller one, which is the reason that it also falls into the very same traps that Benjamin analyzed in his *Arcades Project*.

By documenting how those covered Parisian streets faded into obscurity, by showing how these structures that were meant to enrich nineteenth-century city life (thus functioning, according to Fuller's logic, as a kind of livingry) turned out to slowly embalm it (and thus serving as nothing less than urban weaponry), Benjamin was ideally positioned to shatter Fuller's own utopian vision of an ultimate arcade (which, to be honest, no one in New York ever took seriously). There was little doubt in Benjamin's mind that the Manhattan dome, which in Fuller's rendering looks very much like an explosion of a hydrogen bomb over the center of the island, was the exact opposite of a protective shield. It was, again, a transparent act of *urbicide*.

BENJAMIN'S POLEMIC against architecture is admittedly a militant one. It often sacrifices theoretical subtlety and attention to detail for the sake of a strategic decision not only with respect to the background and foreground of his image of New York but also his urban friends and foes. Whereas architectonic discourse wants to convince us that buildings and people can harmoniously complement one another, the task of *The Manhattan Project* is to point out their basic conflict of interest. Besides, it is not the physical buildings as such but rather the proliferation of meanings we readily attach to them that stand at the center of Benjamin's constructive criticism. The city's architecture, he argues, determines its destiny much less than imagined. Like the weather, it is something the inhabitants sometimes relish but usually just learn to cope with and endure. And like their conversations about the weather, their conversations about buildings are usually not much more than small talk.

In a place where the fetishism of the architectonic commodity had reached fantastic levels, at a time when buildings were elevated to high art and architects were revered as deep geniuses, Benjamin took upon himself the improbable task of devaluing their field, dimming its aura, and thus reducing its detrimental effect on the urban landscape of sheer life. Turning again to the photographic model made by Fuller to promote his own Manhattan project, we can also interpret this transparent dome as a sacred or divine halo radiating from the world's densest concentration of buildings and capital. Benjamin's project is an attempt to dispel or to profane this speculative halo.

That buildings are needed and useful is a given. But what makes us certain that the financial, theoretical, moral, and aesthetic values we readily attach to them are solid and permanent? How can we be so sure that such value is not inflated or even invented, that it will not burst like a stock market bubble? Benjamin, who saw the repression at work behind this false confidence, describes his *Manhattan Project* as the work of a specter haunting a city. But he no longer saw himself as the specter of communism. He had become the specter of sheer life.

NINTH CHAPTER # THINGIFICATION

THE WIDESPREAD VIEW of the city as a built form rather than as a lived form stems from a strange logical fallacy with a fittingly strange name. *Reification* comes from *res*, Latin for "thing," which has led some to suggest instead the silly-sounding *thingification*. Even though Manhattan is almost entirely human-made, it can be easily reified as a given, as a fact, as an objective thing, independent of the human context, the form of life, or the social relations that brought it into being and continually perpetuate its existence. Coming to terms with the forces, interests, ideas, and a myriad of other factors that stand behind the production and reproduction of this urban space is the best way to resist the reification of the city. And what this attention is meant to bring to light is nothing but the lived form behind every built one.

Though Jane Jacobs never talks about reification in any of her books, she does offer a devastating criticism of what she calls "thing theory." This is the widespread (though often unacknowledged) assumption among urban planners that what a city in trouble needs in order to prosper is this or that physical structure: a power plant, factory, housing project, highway, bridge, airport, theater, school, what have you. Cities, Jacobs demonstrates, are not clusters of independent things. Development is an intricate and interdependent organic process, not the result of an object that can be artificially manufactured and physically added to the urban landscape. Accordingly, when Benjamin speaks of New York, he speaks of much more than its physical makeup. Rather than reify or thingify his subject matter as a simple object in space, he approaches it as a continuous project, as a complex field of interrelated forces.

"For all reification," Adorno writes in a 1940 letter to Benjamin, "is a forgetting." Benjamin was aware of this curious logical slippage that occurs once the attention to the life of the city wanes. Graffiti is a case in point. When one forgets the social situation and human condition from which it emerges, one tends to reify this phenomenon and treat it as such, as a thing divorced from the life that produced it. It is thus usually perceived as a nuisance (like rain or pests) that should somehow be mitigated. But reification is only the first misstep.

The next comes once people begin to fetishize graffiti, to attribute to it special values, or even the sort of aura that surrounds canonical works of art. In the fetish stage the emotional reaction may be positive; the wish to get rid of graffiti may transform into the desire to own it. The fetishization stage is not, however, the antithesis of the reification stage but rather its intensification: we are now twice removed from the origin, from the form of life of the graffiti writer (who, as a person, can also be reified and then fetishized, which is one way to explain what happened to Jean-Michel Basquiat).

This leads to a third misstep, in which the life that turned into a thing that turned into the aura of the thing is further transformed into a pure spectacle, a mere simulacrum, or a phantasmagoria. Once that occurs, graffiti can function as decoration in a new supermarket, a backdrop for a fashion shoot, or a welcome addition to an otherwise gentrified neighborhood, one that makes it feel more authentic or gritty.

The slippery slope leading from reification to fetishism to spectacle is a process that Benjamin also detects in the general way New York as a whole gradually came to be treated in the documents that he discovered in the Public Library's archives. His *Manhattan Project* is an attempt to resist this slippage and correct this skewed perspective. When he first noticed this problematic process during his work on *The Arcades Project*, his proposed remedy was to de-reify Paris by his studious animation of its seemingly dead structures. For a man of letters like Benjamin, "the most poignant realities . . . are not spectacles but studies." Hence his intense engagement with the arcades, panoramas, catacombs, mirrors, lights, iron and glass constructions, commodities, articles of clothes, street advertisements, and so on.

This early attempt to invert the reification of Paris became one of his main targets of self-criticism once he moved to New York. It became difficult for him to imagine how a densely written manuscript filled with lofty theoretical formulations could serve as a reality check for a city that was turning into its own phantasmagoria. He came to the sad realization that his work on Paris only enhanced the fascination of his reader with the physical city and helped to fetishize it even further. It is yet to be seen whether *The Manhattan Project* can counter the tendency of today's New York to turn into a mere copy of itself.

The day will come, Benjamin predicts with a strange mixture of self-aggrandizement and self-loathing, when the Parisian arcades will be resurrected and once again become fashionable, in great part because of the influence of his *Arcades Project*. Maybe one of these retro arcades will be renamed Passage Benjamin in his honor and will house a little souvenir shop that sells an eponymous line of merchandise, tailored to the rising market of literary tourism. As his pseudo-posthumous fame spread during the last decades of his secret life, it dawned on Benjamin that not only the work of art but also the work of theory must be reassessed in view of its mindless reproduction by the insatiable culture industry.

WHEN A CITY BECOMES A MERE SPECTACLE, a different brand of reification may come in handy to remedy or at least alleviate this predicament. Benjamin first came to rethink the process of reification while reading Hannah Arendt's *The Human Condition*, where she cleverly upends the negative connotations that many Marxists traditionally attached to this term. Reification, for Arendt, means the transformation of an abstract idea into an actual thing. For example, a carpenter who builds a table is reifying his mental image of the design, turning a blueprint into a physical, three-dimensional object by means of his handiwork.

Benjamin therefore approaches the city—by far the most complex and most impressive human artifact ever created—as the sum of all its reified thoughts. In a typical Marxist reification we are led to forget the subjectivity of our human agency, to treat the city around us as an objective given. In Arendtian reification, however, we realize subjective ideas in the objective city and thus change it, even in the most minuscule way. Of course, Arendtian reification precedes the Marxist one. Humans must create something before they can forget that they are responsible for it.

Although Arendt restricts reification to *homo faber*, the human being who fabricates artifacts like tables and houses, Benjamin claims that whatever people have a hand in, even the political sphere that Arendt considered the highest level of human existence, could be treated as a thing, a *res*, as the word *republic* suggests (*res publica*, the public thing). Politics—like philosophy and religion, or whatever else some Marxists call the superstructure—could still be seen as some*thing* that, despite its immaterial nature, is the outcome of Arendtian reification, by persons who act and speak with one another. Maybe even what Arendt considers the low-est level of human existence, the labor that aims not at the fabrication of new things but only at life's sustenance, is still the result of a process of reification that produces something, as impermanent and insubstantial as it may be—a meal, a salary, a place to sleep—that was not there beforehand.

Also notice that for those who believe God to be the creator of this world, even natural things—such as mountains and hurricanes and stars and flowers—are the direct result of divine reification, again in Arendt's sense of the term. The perspective of those who fail to see this point is impaired, according to the believer, by Marxist reification: by the secular inability to recognize the existence of a divine thought or spiritual design behind this material, natural order and occasional disorder. Yet for the unbeliever, the error lies in the religious reification of a human-made God.

Clad in this conceptual armor, Benjamin is ready to confront the architectonic dragon in a slightly more sophisticated manner.

TENTH CHAPTER   REALITY OVERDOSE

ALTHOUGH BENJAMIN APPROACHES nineteenth-century Paris as a phantasmagoria, he comes to see twentieth-century New York as a place where all ideas, ideals, and ideologies, every program, philosophy, and utopia pass through a powerful reifica-tion machine. As ephemeral thoughts materialize into concrete things, whatever fails to undergo this ruthless process loses its reason for existence; in fact, it sooner or later simply stops existing. But even if something does get reified and solidified, it is only a question of time before it also melts into air. Despite all the potentiali-ties and dreams and promises that glaze the eyes of new New Yorkers, Benjamin is not interested in what the city could or should or would be but in what it actually is. His New York is ultimately not a city of "wishful frivolity," as Jacobs calls it, but one of hard-won and often arbitrary reality.

These considerations help position *The Manhattan Project* vis-à-vis *Delirious New York*, Rem Koolhaas's influential theory of the city's architectonic legacy, which also doubles as one of the more appealing attempts to write a philosophy of the place. That book begins with a clear nod to the question of reification. Its first epi-graph is borrowed from Giambattista Vico, who argues that "since the world of na-tions is made by men, it is inside their minds that its principles should be sought." The second is from Fyodor Dostoevsky, who wonders, "Why do we have a mind if not to get our way?"

Koolhaas's reading of these propositions does not lead him (as it does Arendt) to consider the ways ideas turn into things and fantasies become realities. Instead, he decides to bracket off the actual, concrete city in order to study a *"theoretical* Manhattan, a *Manhattan as conjecture*, of which the present city is the compromised and imperfect realization." In theory, he argues, the aim of the city is to "exist in a world totally fabricated by man, i.e., to live *inside* fantasy."

By describing New York as a "factory of man-made experience, where the real and the natural ceases to exist," Koolhaas is not implying that the city is the result of some well-ordered, rational, or enlightened design. Even the 1811 Commissioners' Plan for the city's gridiron of numbered streets and avenues—this "two-dimensional discipline" of Manhattan's urban expansion—is meant to facilitate its "three-dimensional anarchy." Since the city's covert strategy is one of "indefinitely postponed consciousness," it is not to be understood as the outcome of the reification of a certain prethought theory or ideology or philosophy, all of which can be gathered only after the fact. What Koolhaas tries to do in his book, which he bills as a "retroactive manifesto for Manhattan," is thus at odds with Benjamin's basic approach. For Koolhaas, the true essence of New York is not its sheer life but its buildings' sheer delirium, as the book's cover illustration makes clear: the city's two iconic skyscrapers are curled up in bed (their sex undecided) next to a lamp made from the Statue of Liberty's torch and a rug that doubles as a map of Manhattan, while other buildings enjoy the peepshow through the open window.

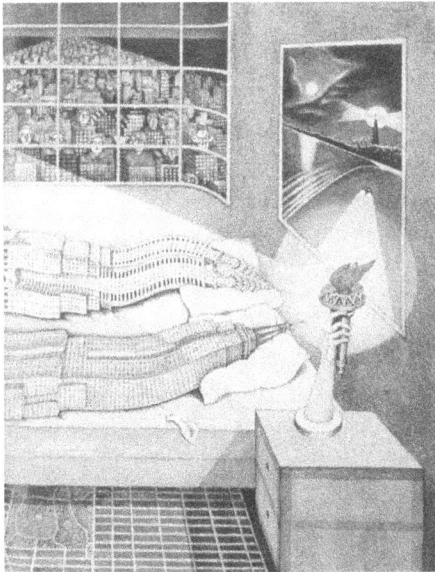

BENJAMIN CONSIDERS Koolhaas's thesis more befitting of nineteenth-century Paris, at least the way it is presented in *The Arcades Project*, than of the twentieth-century New York of which his *Manhattan Project* struggles to make sense. A turning point in his assessment of *Delirious New York* can be found in his gloss on the concept of "Reality Shortage," which Koolhaas explains thus: "As the big toe of a saint's statue gradually disappears under the onslaught of his devotees' kisses, so the Big Toe of reality dissolves slowly but inexorably under perpetual exposure to the continuous Kiss of mankind. The higher the density of a civilization—the more metropolitan it is—the higher the frequency of the Kiss, the faster the process of consumption of the reality of nature and artifacts. They are worn out so rapidly that the supply is depleted."

What triggers Benjamin's gloss on this passage is Koolhaas's curious choice of metaphor. The statue of the saint is, after all, the most elementary example of religious fetishism, of that mysterious aura that a mere physical object (such as an icon or a relic) acquires when the believers attribute to it special values and magical powers. This usually happens only after they have successfully forgotten that the object is human-made. Marx shows that a very similar thing happens in capitalism (which may or may not be distinguished from religion) whenever the use value of an object gives way to its exchange value. By turning something into an intense object of desire, we crave its possession more than we probably should. We are enchanted by the electronic gadget or the fashion accessory in a slightly irrational way. It is surrounded by a halo that draws us to it like moth to flame.

To return to the statue of the saint, is it possible that what gets worn out by the repeated kissing of the saint's toe is not reality but fetish? Recall again Benjamin's story of how the sense of euphoric intoxication brought on by the Parisian arcades quickly gave way to an irritating hangover. It is, then, the fuzzy aura of an object, not its concrete reality, that slightly fades every time it is used. What keeps a thing sacred is first of all the ban on its everyday use. Once we have easy access to it, once we can readily touch it, the fetish tends to go away.

The poet Edwin Denby claims that the endless parade of eyes and hands that come in contact with everything in New York is like a camera's shutter that never closes: "So many a day makes anything like forever: So a hydrant is. . . . In a split second a girl is forever pretty." In this sense, Manhattan's density makes it less delirious or fantastic, more concrete or grounded. Even the fake or artificial elements in this city are treated after a while as natural, as integral parts of the real. Central Park—which was landscaped with the help of rock blasting that consumed more gunpowder than the entire Battle of Gettysburg—is a case in point.

Maybe New York is suffering from an overdose, not a shortage, of reality. Koolhaas wants us to consider Coney Island and especially Dreamland, its most extravagant amusement park in the early twentieth century, as a "fetal Manhattan." Benjamin only states the obvious when he replies that Manhattan is not the actualization but the exact antithesis of Coney Island, which was created so that New Yorkers could escape every now and then from their daily reality overdose to a conveniently located and reasonably priced mirage. "Luna parks," he observed already in 1928, are only a "prefiguration of sanatoria."

Nothing dissipates faster than a dream. The moment you wake up and describe it to your partner (if you have one), the initial excitement begins to lose its potency. By the time you eat your breakfast and leave home for the day, the dream has more or less been forgotten. To use a more historically pertinent example, think of Freedomland; the world's largest amusement park in the early 1960s, it has left the faintest of traces in New York's collective memory. Designed in the shape of a map of the United States, it was built in the Bronx as the East Coast's answer to Disneyland. Four years after it began operating, it was razed to the ground and quickly replaced by a mammoth residential project called Co-op City.

If Koolhaas is correct in his diagnosis that Manhattan, like Luna Park (the original Coney Island predecessor to Dreamland), is an "experiment in moral weightlessness," then the actual city would have long ago disappeared into the stratosphere, like a helium balloon lost by an inattentive child. A hundred years after its heyday, rickety Coney Island is but a dim memory of its dazzling past, while Manhattan is almost as real and vital as it ever was. I say almost because the gradual transformation of the twenty-first-century city into a giant theme park certainly jeopardizes its chances of survival.

When Dreamland burned to the ground in 1911, the Manhattan newspapers neglected to report the event for twenty-four hours because they assumed it was a publicity stunt. This had something to do with the fact that the best attraction in Dreamland was a show simulating fire in a tenement building. The spectacle obfuscates the actual. When the World Trade Center collapsed ninety years later, the postmodern patter about the confusion between reality and its simulacrum mysteriously came to a halt. Even the conspiracy theorists agree. It happened. Amending his thesis from the 1970s, Koolhaas published a short article two years after the terrorist attack, titled "Delirious No More." Benjamin, however, is not convinced that New York was ever delirious in the first place.

ANOTHER OF KOOLHAAS'S EXAMPLES that backfires is an anecdote involving Salvador Dalí. When the artist first arrived in New York in 1935, he planned to disembark from his ship carrying a fifty-foot-long baguette. (Un)fortunately, the oven on board his ocean liner was capable of accommodating only an eight-foot loaf, which Dalí held while facing the eager New York press in an attempt to shock them with this surrealist stunt. The reporters asked him a variety of polite questions, but none of them mentioned the bread that rested so conspicuously on his shoulder. For Koolhaas, this story shows that "surrealism is invisible" in New York, because something like an oversized baguette is "just another false fact among the multitudes." Surrealism demands contrast. Otherwise—if it is only a drop of delirium within a phantasmagoric ocean—it loses its shock value.

Benjamin knew a thing or two about surrealism, and his understanding of this episode is very different. The surrealist work, he points out, is *supposed* to be directed at a society in a state of deep sleep. Like *The Arcades Project* itself, surrealism has an explicit political task. It is meant to bring about an awakening, specifically from the bourgeois dream of nineteenth-century Paris. This explains why Benjamin claims that "surrealism was born in an arcade" and why his early project was born from his encounter with surrealism. He goes so far as to claim that "no face is surrealistic to the same degree as the true face of a city."

Just as the explicit aim of *The Arcades Project* is not to perpetuate a certain urban mythology but to bust it up, the surrealists' employment of dream images and unhinged thoughts is not meant to enhance the delirium of urban society but, like an Indian dreamcatcher, to purge it. By turning the subjective interiority of a dream into a public, collective experience, the surrealist work of art challenges the dogmatic slumber that people *presume* to be the objective reality, proving to them that their reality is itself just another elaborate fantasy. Understood in this way, it seems that Dalí's stunt fell on deaf ears when performed in New York not because it was a dream within a dream but because it was an attempt to awaken a place that was already fully awake, to sound an alarm in a city where, as Benjamin used to say, the clock "in each minute rings for sixty seconds."

A last anecdote clarifies this decisive issue: "During the war," Edwin Denby recalls, "Bill [Willem de Kooning] told me he had been walking uptown one afternoon and at the corner of 53rd and Seventh he had noticed a man across the street who was making peculiar gestures in front of his face. It was Breton and he was fighting off a butterfly. A butterfly had attacked the Parisian poet [and father of surrealism] in the middle of New York."

André Breton was not delirious, and this was not a surrealist performance.

The butterfly was not imaginary. It was (a conspicuous symbol of the) real, teasing the professional dreamer rather than the other way around. Reality, in short, bites. Or is it just another fantasy? Here is how a different Parisian visitor by the name of Simone de Beauvoir puts it: "There's something in the New York air that makes sleep useless."

ELEVENTH CHAPTER   # THE DISENCHANTED ISLAND

IN 1809 WASHINGTON IRVING published his satirical *History of New York*, though he claimed it was really written by a man named Dietrich Knickerbocker. Two years earlier, Irving nicknamed the city "Gotham," after a village on the outskirts of Nottingham. English lore has it that Gotham was a village of fools, though of a very special kind. The Gothamists' legendary foolishness was actually a cunning strategy for subverting sovereign power. One day, the story goes, the king's emissary arrived at the village with the intent of delineating a path for a new royal highway. The inhabitants, who much preferred to be left alone, all pretended to be mad. They were found "pouring water into a bottomless tub" and "painting green apples red." This sight was all it took to scare the land surveyor into having the road bypass the village.

"More fools pass through Gotham than remain in it," according to an English saying. The American city of Gotham can also trick the outsider into thinking that it is a rather delirious place. But like that of the English village, New York's delirium is, to a great extent, a front that allows the city to escape unwanted attention from gullible external forces. New York certainly does its best to fend off repeated attempts to subordinate its way of life to the state apparatus. In 1790 it lost its position as the capital of the United States to Washington, D.C. Though at the time many local inhabitants saw it as a disastrous move, in retrospect it came to be seen as one of the most fortuitous events in the city's history.

When the first skyscraper was under construction in lower Manhattan, skeptical onlookers referred to it as "the Idiotic Building." But if the city's architecture stands for anything, then Benjamin argues that it is the exact opposite of a foolish ignorance of reality. At the beginning of the twentieth century, when the Flatiron Building was the most conspicuous skyscraper in New York, *Life* magazine ran on the cover of its Christmas issue an illustration of Santa Claus's sleigh crashing into the top of this iconic building during his nightly gift run. This seems like the right pictorial articulation of the essence of the city's built form, which the architectural historian Manfredo Tafuri sums up with a word he borrows from Max Weber: *disenchantment*. The true function of a New York building is not to produce dreams (as Koolhaas would have it) but to crush (or crash) every single one of them.

PREDATING KOOLHAAS'S ANALYSIS by a few years, Tafuri's competing account of New York's architecture takes its cue from a simple observation. In classical antiquity, a building was meant to reflect particular, discernible values. With the advent of capitalism, though, a rift is created between *eidos* and *ethos*, between the way buildings are built and the way life is lived. The consequence is that the architectonic form begins to send conflicting messages. For example, a wall made of glass may be an expression of fascism, socialism, or capitalism.

On this point, Tafuri sees almost eye to eye with Koolhaas, who will call this condition the "Great Lobotomy." The life that takes place inside a modern skyscraper, Koolhaas observes, has very little to do with the building's external facade. The lived form on the inside fails to reflect the built form on the outside. This process leads to a decisive crisis because, Tafuri writes, "architectural ideology no longer has any purpose." Buildings are no longer informed by either theory or utopia; they convey neither a philosophy nor an ideal.

Whereas New York provides an excellent example of architecture's ideological crisis, Washington, D.C., plays a diametrically opposite role. "It is not by mere chance," Tafuri claims, "that the least economically necessary city in America is also the most 'configured.' . . . In Washington, the nostalgic evocation of European values was concentrated in the capital of a society whose drive to economic and industrial development was leading to the concrete and intentional destruction of those values." Pierre L'Enfant's plan for the new US capital is meant to be a seamless dialogue between value and form, the ideal and the real, emanating from the mind of a single, rational, European individual. His monumental design for the city is seldom driven by pragmatic considerations, which necessarily change over time. The plan for the city reflects to this day the same spirit of the Enlightenment that the people of the eighteenth century held dear.

In New York, on the contrary, form is subordinate to function, which is always multiple and shifting. The hand directing the city's built form is not invisible but nonexistent, or at least feeble. In contrast to Washington's, the Manhattan cityscape cannot be considered a theater in which the buildings, like well-trained actors, express a coherent thought and present a consistent character that reflects a written script or the artistic choice of a director. Nevertheless, to say that there is some reason to New York's madness is no less true than to say that there is certainly some madness to Washington's reason.

Adorno and Horkheimer show that the Enlightenment's attempt to disenchant the world, to place rationality where belief once stood, "to dispel myths, to overthrow fantasy with knowledge" led to the creation of new mythological forces that might very well be even more deceptive and violent than the previous ones. Reason can easily beget madness rather than defeat it. *The Manhattan Project* is Benjamin's own attempt to shake off the mythical nightmare, though some detractors will claim that he is falling back into a new phantasmic order. His working hypothesis is that although the "elevation of urban life to the level of myth" is one of modernity's most basic gestures, this spell is most effectively cast on outsiders. Urban insiders are measured not by the number of years they have lived in the city but by their growing sense of disenchantment with it. For this reason E. B. White describes New York as the only city "that takes itself with a grain of salt."

THE PROTAGONIST in Tafuri's account of New York is a man named Raymond Hood, an architect at odds with the mythological stereotype of his profession during the first half of the twentieth century, best exemplified by the individualistic and charismatic visionary Frank Lloyd Wright, or by Ayn Rand's Howard Roark. In Hood, the architect is inseparable from the businessman. A building site is understood not as the concentration of ideas but of capital. Whatever the style of the facade turns out to be (there is little consistency in the design of his different buildings), Hood regards it as an "added value."

Hood assumes that buildings are built because of exigent demands and not as a result of a burst of creative inspiration, an overarching rational plan, or an explicit ideological commitment. The fact that Hood's name remains virtually unknown only proves his point: an architect is not an auteur. That the designer and his ideas are forgotten while his building continues to be profitable to its owner, functional to its user, as well as inoffensive to its onlooker is one straightforward way to demonstrate the designer's success. From this perspective, Hood's four Manhattan projects seem to prove, almost a century later, their solid worth. Whatever *eidos* his buildings may have, their ethos remains the same: to achieve complete and utter reification.

Tafuri and Koolhaas agree that Rockefeller Center, Hood's most important design, is the slightly surprising apogee of New York's architectonic legacy. But their interpretations of the man and his work diverge. At this point, Benjamin's text follows almost squarely in Tafuri's footsteps, as I will do in the remainder of this chapter.

Whatever ideas were incorporated into the construction of Rockefeller Center, Tafuri argues that they "were stripped of any utopian character." Even the conventional position of the architect as the building's sole creator was supplanted by a committee of designers (though Hood is still considered to have been their driving force). The cluster of buildings has no aspiration to contest the established institutions around it. The three Midtown blocks are like an island that does not interrupt the city's flow. This leads Tafuri to claim that Hood's design "represented the final result of the general debate on the structure of the American city. In response to attempts at comprehensive control of the urban organism [as in Washington, D.C.], it demonstrated that the only type of undertaking with any real possibility of influencing urban dynamics was one limited in scale and wholly in keeping with the existing, traditional laws of urban growth."

Rockefeller Center is an object lesson in what Tafuri calls "the disenchanted mountain." This is a single building, or a cluster of buildings, designed according to a variety of private and public interests, a multiplicity of capitalist and collectivist forces, which fight and play with one another until a certain equilibrium is literally set in stone. The instrumental success of Hood's design was thus the final nail in the coffin of visionary city planning: "The realism that characterized the creation of Rockefeller Center—to the point of cynicism—marked the end of any utopian ideal of comprehensive public control over the urban structure."

From that point on any attempt to restore the lost enchantment of an urban adventure (as Koolhaas and the other starchitects of the twenty-first century still try to do, though usually in cities other than New York) can be anachronistic at best and opportunistic at worst. What dominates the metropolitan landscape after the magic of its architectonic form has been revealed as sleight of hand are, according to Tafuri, only isolated disenchanted mountains, pure structures pitted of meaning, "intent on communicating nothing besides their own surreal presence."

It is no coincidence, Tafuri therefore speculates, that in 1933, as Rockefeller Center was in its final design stage, King Kong was killed on top of the recently completed Empire State Building, thus symbolizing how "technological civilization conquers the irrational sentimentality of the 'noble savage.'" In this sense, the skyscraper that used to be the symbol of humankind's skyward aspirations and indomitable will becomes an agent of ruthless demystification. In New York, anything that looks enchanting eventually solidifies into concrete.

For the remainder of the century, more and more corporations built their insular urban headquarters in the form of such super-skyscrapers, each of which constituted "a city under a single roof." But a city within a city is really an anti-city. The corporate tenants were only able to escape or retreat from, rather than understand or affect, the apparent chaos and irrationality of the urban landscape that surrounded their steel-and-glass structures. The typical post–Rockefeller Center skyscraper rarely tries to dazzle or shock the observer. In this sense its delirious effect is reduced to near zero. Its only tangible appeal to the public is through the obligatory designation of small plazas predominantly used by office workers on their lunch break, like high school cafeterias for adults.

Nevertheless, as the New York built form went through this process of disenchanting reification, as the aura of the skyscraper began to disintegrate, it was also possible to achieve a subtle shift in the way we perceive the city. When the fetishism of architecture diminishes, when one abandons all hope of treating physical buildings as if they were living, thinking things, it becomes a bit easier to see the real life lived in their shadows. *Forma mentis* turn into *forma vitae*.

AS A WORKER in the mailroom of the Daily News Building, Benjamin was intimately familiar with one of Hood's groundbreaking designs. Passing every morning through the grand entrance on his way to the skyscraper's basement, he must have noticed that above the main door's lintel there is a *mise en abyme*: an engraving depicting workers entering the Daily News Building. In other words, the ethos or ideal exalted by Hood's building was nothing other than the building itself.

Once inside the lobby, Benjamin passed by a giant globe, half sunk into the floor, rotating slowly around its tilted axis under a black, shiny dome. In Grand Central Terminal, two blocks to the west, the high turquoise ceiling depicts the nightly constellations. Curiously, it was painted not from our perspective on earth but from God's perspective in heaven. In the News Building the workers are also made to feel as if they are observing the earth while hovering in outer space. This feeling appears to inform Hugh Ferris's drawing of the lobby, which was presented along with Hood's plans before construction began. Rather than walk united as one humanity under a shared heaven, Benjamin and his coworkers were being tacitly isolated from each other, lonely satellites orbiting the earth in a dark void.

Like Clark Kent, who worked as a journalist for the *Daily Planet* (modeled after the *Daily News*), Benjamin was essentially an alien. With his double identity, he did his best not to draw attention to his philosophical alter ego. Going up the stairs from his subterranean office, exiting the building every day at dusk, he could have seen in the eyes of his fellow New Yorkers what Nietzsche saw in Venice: that eight million deep solitudes together form the city and that this, not its buildings, is the true source of its enchantment.

TWELFTH CHAPTER DEMOCRACITY

MODERN ARCHITECTS, like modern artists, can be divided, according to Tafuri, into "those who search into the very bowels of reality in order to know and assimilate its values and wretchedness; and those who desire to go beyond reality, who want to construct *ex novo* new realities, new values, and new public symbols." As the art world's center of gravity moved to Manhattan during the second half of the twentieth century, Benjamin began to reflect on the underlying dissimilarities between surrealism (the last definitive artistic movement, some would claim, to emerge from Paris) and the new artistic movements that were indigenous to New York. His first impression was that much of the New York art scene, particularly during the 1960s and 1970s, revolved around a continuous, dogged attempt to be receptive to, and expressive of, the real. "Delirium is elsewhere," he writes, in clear reference to Breton's "existence is elsewhere."

Benjamin also treats Manhattan's two main train stations, Grand Central and Penn, as "factories of dreams," as portals into the deep sleep of suburban America. He was able to marvel at Penn Station's old beaux arts structure before it was demolished in the 1960s and replaced with today's dismal underground hub. The architectural critic Vincent Scully said that through the old Penn Station "one entered the city like a god," whereas "one scuttles in now like a rat." Benjamin adds that no matter what the architecture looks like, whether the commuter enters the city like a god or like a rat, he hopes to leave it at the end of the long workday like a mensch. W. H. Auden explains: "From the conservative dark into the ethical life the dense commuters come, repeating their morning vow: 'I *will* be true to the wife, I'll concentrate more on my work.'"

THE ARCADES PROJECT documents Benjamin's fascination with a variety of popular nineteenth-century techniques that created an illusion of reality, such as panoramas and dioramas. These primitive fantasy machines had all but disappeared after the invention of cinema. Yet no technological innovation (be it television, video games, or the Internet) had changed the basic modern fact that people will go to extraordinary lengths to be entertained by apparitions they know perfectly well to be unreal. After Guy Debord, we know that our society is coextensive with the spectacle it continuously produces and reproduces.

Phantasmagoria, another of cinema's ancestors, was a very popular nineteenth-century horror show, created by the projection of shadows, usually in the shape of ghosts and skeletons. It relied on the use of a hidden magic lantern called a phantascope, which changed its position so that the silhouettes looked alive. Following Marx, Benjamin uses the word *phantasmagoria* to denote the imaginary aspect of modern capitalism. His favorite example of a phantasmagoria is the World's Fair, with which the Parisians were so enamored that they hosted six of them between 1855 and 1937. These universal exhibitions were the ideal occasions for nations and industries to display the latest innovations and most coveted commodities to the gawking masses. The objects, however, were not to be touched, used, bought, or sold but only seen.

In *The Arcades Project* Benjamin tries to convince us that the capitalist machine turned nineteenth-century Paris into a nightmarish phantasmagoria from which we ought to wake up. But calling the city a phantasmagoria is not as straightforward as it seems. It turns out that it is less a standard Marxist critique of urban space and more a covert urban critique of a dated Marxist dogma. Benjamin eventually came to realize that the real problem is the phantascope, the magic lantern that transforms a real thing into an illusory horror show. It is an ideological phantascope that turns the actual city into a parade of imaginary, shadowy specters. It is a device that leads us to fear a place that would otherwise be desired. The true nightmare, then, is often the very perception and representation of the city as a nightmare. These considerations put Benjamin in the position not of a ghost or a ghostwriter but a ghostbuster.

🐦

IT IS USUALLY IMPOSSIBLE to pinpoint the exact moment a new idea dawned on a thinker. We are fortunate enough to be able to identify almost to the day the event that triggered this turn in Benjamin's thought. It appears that shortly after he arrived in New York, in October 1940, he took advantage of the opportunity to go to Queens to visit the World's Fair, which was going to shut down at the end of the same month. His account of the fair in *The Manhattan Project* leaves little doubt that it is based on firsthand experience, even though the foci of his recollections are two of the fair's most famous attractions: a film called *The City*, narrated by Lewis Mumford; and a diorama called *Democracity*, which was housed at the center of the fairgrounds, inside a gigantic white sphere.

The diorama and the film offer a comprehensive vision of the "city of tomorrow." Thanks to the advancements in rail, air, and especially automobile travel, the future city will be rid of pedestrians. Residents will either live in isolated skyscrapers surrounded by endless greenery or in meticulously planned suburban tract housing, also surrounded by natural expanse. They will commute to discrete work zones through tunnels and overpasses, enjoying the clean and wholesome life that they are deprived of in the present urban conditions. In this vision, the city as we know it is condemned to die not of old age but as punishment for its inexcusable crimes. To this end, fairgoers are shown footage of dirty factories polluting the lungs of men, corporate offices polluting the souls of women, and even poor children playing in the gutter while their friend is run over by a passing car.

In his script for *The City* Mumford predicted that the new towns and highways would put an end to the miserable life in city centers, which would have to be demolished and then rebuilt according to a new master plan. Urban chaos, lawlessness, and congestion would give way to a well-ordered, efficiently controlled, and evenly dispersed society. The city of tomorrow is consequently not really a city. Curiously, the model metropolis in the diorama featured no human beings. Images of people, or their Platonic representations, were projected on the round ceiling, where they could observe the fake urban spectacle from their detached firmament.

Benjamin immediately realized that this was a perfect representation of the true fantasy of the twentieth century. He sensed that the new dream that enchants the citizens of modernity no longer involves the city but the suburb. For his contemporaries, the irresistible illusion was that of the pastoral-yet-convenient outdoors, not that of the opulent-yet-stuffy indoors, as was the case in nineteenth-century Paris. The nightmare from which the New Yorker had to awaken is that seemingly benevolent and progressive spectacle projected on the curved walls of the white sphere from which Benjamin emerged into the northeastern October chill.

For nearly the rest of his life Benjamin would closely observe how the American suburbs and exurbs flourished while the dense urban clusters crumbled.

For him it was a clear triumph of fantasy over reality. He was not alone in sensing that the moment of awakening is inevitable, that it is just a matter of time before people will realize that this bucolic dream is unsustainable. He was, however, probably one of the first to compare the Mumford-orchestrated requiem for the city from the early parts of the century with the requiem for the suburb that will mark its end. Phantasmagorias never die; they just relocate to a new zip code.

It is, after all, a similar redemptive promise that midcentury, middle-class Americans associated with their escape from the city that filled the hearts of their end-of-the-century, bourgeois children who were reclaiming the urban frontier. Benjamin was in no way elated to see this process taking place. He predicted that the city itself was about to be suburbanized, that its own reality was going to be compromised, and that it would slowly but surely turn into another fantasy that, like all fantasies, would eventually clear the way to painful disillusionment.

The American dream does not become more reachable, or its inherent optimism any less cruel, its escapism less of a trap, once monotonous Levittown turns into gentrified Nolita, or when the stereotypical man in the gray flannel suit turns into the yuppie with the expense account and the soccer mom in her van turns into the millennial on her bike. A walk-up apartment cannot save the souls of the young, just as a sub-urban, single-family house with a little backyard was incapable of saving the souls of their parents. Real estate has very little to do with real life.

"I COULD MAKE PROMISES to myself and to other people and there would be all the time in the world to keep them. I could stay up all night and make mistakes, and none of it would count." The writer Joan Didion portrays her first years in the city as a continuous dream. It never occurred to her that she was living a real life. To actually live in New York, she surmised, was "to reduce the miraculous to the mundane." But then, in 1962, something happened and she woke up. "That was the year," she confesses, "my twenty-eighth, when I was discovering that not all of the promises would be kept, that some things are in fact irrevocable and that it had counted after all, every evasion and every procrastination, every mistake, every word, all of it."

THIRTEENTH CHAPTER **(AD)DRESS**

ON JANUARY 23, 1931, three thousand guests arrived at the Astor Hotel in Times Square. They were invited to an extravagant costume ball, billed by the organizers as a celebration of modernity. The main attraction of the evening was "The Skyline of New York." It was a strange performance piece by seven of the city's most prominent architects, who entered the stage dressed as the buildings that they were most known for. As a photo that both Koolhaas and Tafuri reproduce in their studies shows, William Van Alen stood out among his boxy colleagues with a streamlined costume representing his Chrysler Building. Only a year earlier his skyscraper had surpassed the Eiffel Tower as the tallest structure in the world, though in the year of the costume ball it had already lost its title to the Empire State Building.

"Houses of the best taste," Henry James opines, "are like clothes of the best tailors—it takes their age to show us how good they are." Fashion is one of Benjamin's original fields of research for his book on Paris. In *The Manhattan Project*, though, he makes use of the anecdote about the architects' burlesque, along with this line from James, to introduce his translation of the critique of fashion he developed in *The Arcades Project* into the biting analysis of architecture that dominates his later thought. He treats this photograph as a symbolic turning point in one of his main theoretical targets: from dress to address.

"EVERY FASHION," Benjamin writes during his Paris days, "stands in opposition to the organic. Every fashion couples the living body to the inorganic world. To the living, fashion defends the rights of the corpse." Sexual desire, not to speak of sexual fetish, has something to do with this blurring of the line between an inanimate thing (the clothes) and an animate body (the flesh). Usually we are attracted neither to the mere clothes nor to the mercilessly naked body as such but rather to the interplay between the two, to this dialectics of striptease and dresstease. Even nudity can be seen as a kind of dress, if only because "the beauty of the body is merely skin-deep," under which the strongest of attractions easily gives way to gore.

Our natural, naked, aging life can almost be forgotten behind the layers of the ever new, artificial garments that cover it up. It is no surprise, then, that professional models are rarely instructed to look vivacious. Life is often a marker of irrelevance in the fashion world. Deadpan is de rigueur for the mannequins who mechanically strut up and down the catwalk, that sanitized version of a bustling city street. Following the poet Giacomo Leopardi, Benjamin can thus attach to fashion quite an unflattering nickname. In *The Arcades Project* he calls it "Madam Death" and considers it the antithesis of sheer life.

In New York's version of this urban drama, architecture, not fashion, assumes the role of Madam Death. A building in twentieth-century New York is comparable to a nineteenth-century Parisian garment in that both of them "inhere in the darkness of the lived moment." Even more than our clothes, buildings do an excellent job of hiding the mechanics of our bare, biological life (unless one is homeless, in which case sleeping, eating, and sometimes even more intimate human functions must take place in the public street). In this context we should also ask ourselves which fetish is more irresistible today: a fashionable dress or a fashionable address?

"To dwell means to leave traces," Benjamin already wrote in *The Arcades Project*. These traces, he noticed during his work on *The Manhattan Project*, are all but absent from the homes featured in the interior design magazines he apparently leafed through in the periodical room of the Public Library. Like the fashion model's expressionless gaze, the rooms in those glossy photos never feel lived in, which makes them so appealing. The same is true of hotels. How utterly disconcerting it is to discover an orphaned sock or a crumpled tissue under the bed of a room into which we have just checked in. It hinders our ability to repress the obvious fact that thousands of people have slept here before. In the twentieth century, Benjamin observes, "dwelling is diminished: for the living, through hotel rooms; for the dead, through the crematorium."

The Parisian fashion of the nineteenth century was mostly restricted to the ruling class. "Poor people," Benjamin explains, had "fashions as little as they had a history, and their ideas, their tastes, even their lives barely changed." Fashion was therefore a "camouflage for quite specific interests of the ruling class." It gave the false impression that things were on the move. It deceived the gullible onlooker into the belief in the progress of history. It made people assume that change was on the way, when in fact everything remained the same, which is just what the ruling class wants. With their shifting fashions, well-to-do Parisians appeared to be different every few months, but under their expensive clothes, beneath their urban camouflage, they were always the same privileged class. From this perspective, the common association of fashion with new possibilities, with change, with life, is rather suspect. Benjamin knew that Parisian fashion was a clear indication of the old order, of stasis—indeed, of death.

A symmetrical argument is employed against architecture in *The Manhattan Project*. Consider, for example, the way a different neighborhood in New York becomes hip every few years. This may convey dynamism in the city's social order. But in fact it is always the same sort of people moving in and the same sort of people moving out once an area is designated by the journalists as the new hot spot. It is also important to remember that only the ruling class can afford the latest architectonic style, the most cutting-edge interior and exterior designs. As a result, the city's poor are less promiscuous than the rich about their relationship to the built form. Once again, as the architectonic terrain changes, one might get the impression that the city changes. For Benjamin, this is only the hellish, eternal return of the same; only a slow petrification into the "always new, always identical 'heathscape'" of modernity.

*

AT THE BEGINNING of the twentieth century the New York garment industry helped revolutionize the strict Parisian law according to which one's dress was the ultimate marker of one's social class. As clothes got cheaper, the poor were no longer excluded from the fashion game, and they were quick to embrace it with such ferocity that, by the end of the century, the rich lost their position as the sole dictators of style. In fact, the ruling class less and less acts as the avant-garde in matters of fashion, because at least since the 1960s, trends are more and more being set in the street rather than in the manufactured reality of the exclusive fashion show.

Nineteenth-century fashion is "the barrier—continually raised anew because continually torn down—by which the fashionable world seeks to segregate itself from the middle regions of society." But as the dress lost its function as a reliable symbol of class, one's address quickly became an almost infallible means of achieving the same goal. In infinite detail, Honoré de Balzac describes in *Père Goriot* the great sacrifices that Rastignac must make in order to become the proud owner of a pair of clean white gloves. In the same way, Tom Wolfe depicts in *The Bonfire of the Vanities* what McCoy has to go through to hold on to his Park Avenue duplex.

At the other end of the social/built spectrum, we see that just as the clothes of the poor in nineteenth-century Paris were their inescapable mark of Cain, no twentieth-century New Yorker could avoid being branded by the slum, housing project, or faraway subway stop in which he or she lived. The address is the city's tell-all. In Manhattan you don't wear your heart on your sleeve; you nail it to your doorpost.

While theories of architecture proliferated in the twentieth century, fashion was less susceptible to such a meta-discourse about its deep values and conceptual significance. Whereas architecture had solidified its role as Madam Death, twentieth-century fashion slowly regained contact with the living. New York fashion even managed to slightly undermine the lobotomy of *eidos* and ethos, the separation of how one looks and how one lives, of costume and custom. Using Tafuri's observation about classical architecture, Benjamin argues that fashion in twentieth-century New York even became a sphere in which radical identities and controversial agendas were able to present themselves unequivocally (dress comes from *directus*, "direct path" or "straight line"). This may explain why New Yorkers are "tolerant of your beliefs" but "judgmental of your shoes."

A person's clothes may still serve as a marker of class at first glance. But because people tend to dress up or down, they can also easily give the wrong impression, pointing in either direction of the social ladder. A second look at the garments of most people, and not just dandies, can still convey a variety of subtle sensibilities. "The eternal," Benjamin writes, "is far more the ruffle on a dress than some idea." He even argues that fashion can tell us in advance not only about "new currents in the arts" but also "new legal codes, wars, and revolutions." So despite fashion's inextricable link to economic conditions, we still tend to know how to read people's clothes as a readily available indication of their personal and even political proclivities.

Our clothes do not necessarily reveal the balance in our bank account, but they can still say something rather significant about what we feel, desire, believe, and think of ourselves or of the world around us. In other words, Benjamin would not have become a hipster, if we mean by that someone for whom fashion is an ironic device to hide in public. Maintaining that form of dress and form of life can be close allies, Benjamin tries to diminish fashion's fetishistic aura. A slogan for a clothing retailer in the 1920s sums this up the way only a slogan can: "The New Yorker doesn't follow fashion. Fashion follows the New Yorker."

FOURTEENTH CHAPTER **NONARCHITECTURE**

I HAVE ARGUED THAT no architectonic element in New York inherits the emblematic position Benjamin confers on the arcades of Paris. Now I need to qualify this state-ment. There is in fact one element that he considers absolutely fundamental and deeply symbolic, perhaps even more than the arcade ever was. This unconstructed structure, this anti-building, or nonarchitecture, is invoked by the *New York Times* critic Herbert Muschamp when he writes about "the integrity of that most demo-cratic, social, informational, commercial, accessible, hard-working and efficient piece of infrastructure yet devised by humankind—the New York City street."

I can already hear the objection that the street is neither a new invention nor unique to New York, as the arcade presumably was to nineteenth-century Paris. But this is exactly the point. The street is neither a product of modernity, nor is it distinctly pre- or postmodern. The street is like a gorge in history. Don DeLillo calls it "an offense to the truth of the future," but it is as much an offense to the truth of both past and present. Consider the changes to the buildings that line the street on both sides. Consider the traffic that flows through it. Consider the hours of the day and seasons of the year. Might the very emptiness of the street be the closest thing we have in an urban space to a taste of eternity?

Everything in the city but the street eventually dies. It is precisely because it is not another enclosed space, like an arcade, that the street is more or less impervi-ous to time. It may seem to be in a state of flux, as stores open or close, as facades crumble or undergo renovation. Strictly speaking, though, it is the built form that goes through this dynamic process, not those "built canals of air." These in-between spaces are the city's pure potentialities. Vacuums are only fleetingly left empty before new powers take over and fill them in. Not so the street.

THE 1811 COMMISSIONERS' PLAN, which established the city's grid of streets and avenues for generations to come, is neither a conceptual speculation (as Koolhaas claims) nor a capitalist speculation (as Tafuri claims). It is, Benjamin claims, an untimely meditation. The gridiron plan is a delineation of a negative space, to be left untouched. Its sole interest is the *un*built form. It is building-blind. It is concerned with the *un*production of space. It defies, rather than promotes, the spirit of continuous change, the unquenched desire for the new that New York architecture exemplifies so well. (Fun fact: In the entire city there are fewer than thirty buildings predating the American Revolution, only three of which are located in Manhattan, while in Boston and Philadelphia scores of colonial structures are still standing.)

The map produced by the commissioners is meant to delimit the power of speculators, architects, and developers by showing the network of arteries that cannot be appropriated by, or consecrated to, the landlord; it delineates the narrow paths that must remain profane, in the sense that they can be used by anyone. Whereas buildings are strictly prohibited from bleeding into the street, one of the oldest tricks in the architectonic playbook is the street-level setback (exemplified in Mies van der Rohe's Seagram Building), where the space of the built form makes a concession to the space of the unbuilt form. This, however, is only a last-resort attempt on the building's part to regain some of its lost dignity, which was compromised once the ninety-degree grid equalized every location in the city, every block, every structure, democratizing space by eliminating the possibility of centers or squares where more than two streets converge (besides the unavoidable intersection of Broadway with the numbered avenues).

In Paris, the grand boulevards are meant to focus the pedestrian's vista on particular monumental structures that stand at either end. In New York, besides a few exceptions, such as the arch in Washington Square Park, which marks the beginning of Fifth Avenue, all structures must stand to one side, giving precedence to the emptiness between them. This void is the only monumental component within the city proper. The truly commanding physical monument in the vicinity of Manhattan is stranded on an otherwise deserted island in Upper New York Bay. The Statue of Liberty might be seen as sacred only because it has no contact with the profane street. In this context, it is noteworthy that, already in the single mention of New York in the entire *Arcades Project*, Benjamin approaches the city's "absence of monuments" as the distinct mark of its modernity.

The enemy of the street is not the building, without which there can be no street. The danger comes once a few standard blocks of buildings swallow the streets that divide them to form a single imposing superblock. By subjecting the oversized lot to a unified master plan, the existing buildings are usually razed to the ground and replaced with a coherent set of new structures, complete with lush greenery, winding pathways, or expansive plazas in between. In the postwar city numerous housing projects—but also commercial projects like the World Trade Center and cultural projects like Lincoln Center—were allowed to scrap the existing grid and eliminate hundreds of streets across the city's five boroughs. Getting people off the street was considered during those years to be the supreme act of progressive benevolence.

The grid, which can be seen as a totalitarian attempt to impose a rigid plan on the entire city, proves to be a practical way to immunize New York "against any (further) totalitarian intervention" because, Koolhaas points out, the grid posits the single block as a "maximum unit of urbanistic Ego." The superblock is a blatant attempt to undermine this urban system of checks and balances. There are, however, some exceptions. One of the best elements in Hood's design for Rockefeller Center is that it not only keeps intact the two existing streets that run through it but also cuts additional, T-shaped paths in the middle of each to enhance pedestrian circulation and diminish the imposing effect of the single, unified plan. Whereas Rockefeller Center is organically integrated into its surroundings, run-of-the-mill superblocks can often feel like alien bodies dropped into the city from outer space.

The grid was denounced by nineteenth-century romanticists as an artificial infliction of a strict form on the island's varying natural topography. In the twentieth century, however, it became the city's second nature, while the superblock turned into the worst violation of this basic urban law. From this perspective, even large parks are ultimately artificial architectonic structures demarcated by the grid like any other superblock. The basic urban dialectic is not, therefore, between tree and tower but between tree and tower as thesis, and sidewalk and pavement as antithesis.

WE HAVE ALREADY SEEN how Benjamin treats enclosures as sedatives, as incubators of dreams. With enough resources any interior can be faithfully reproduced anywhere in the world. An open street, however, can exist only where it exists. Every attempt to duplicate a particular city block someplace else feels rather fake. This may also explain one of Benjamin's only philosophical engagements with Central Park and his apparent predilection for Sheep Meadow, with its expansive lawn and its view of the skyscrapers that peek from above the surrounding trees. This clearing, Benjamin suggests, allows us to see the true city: the city outdoors. It is there that he first came to the conclusion that what stands inside a "windowless house" can only be false.

Because it is the only urban space that can somehow resist the forces of construction, destruction, and (if you care) deconstruction, the street per se is usually impervious to the processes of reification and fetishization. It is even less susceptible to the forces of the spectacle in which we otherwise live. Like Sirens, billboards and shop windows do their very best to lure the reality of the outer, public street into their fantasy of an inner, private realm. But the street as such is not a thing that can be readily owned or exchanged, simply appropriated or reappropriated, easily reified or fetishized. At least in principle, its value remains that of pure use. Urban legends abound about gullible tourists who were sure they made an excellent deal by buying the Brooklyn Bridge on the cheap, or the Statue of Liberty, or the Metropolitan Museum, or plots in Central Park, from swindlers who claimed to be their lawful owners. No such stories circulate about the selling of certain streets or avenues.

Benjamin is not the kind of thinker to posit a negation as the founding principle of his thought. At the core of *The Manhattan Project* there is no architectonic structure like the Parisian arcade, but there is also no nonarchitectonic structure like the New York street. Instead, the manuscript appears to revolve around a vital structure, a living configuration, or a form of life. This makes his philosophical position much more difficult to understand. But it also makes it more difficult to misunderstand. It is as if with one hand he is searching for the object of his investigation, which he most often calls sheer life, while with the other he assures the "conditions of its inaccessibility."

FIFTEENTH CHAPTER   **TRUTH IS CONCRETE**

"IN THE STREET you learn what human beings really are; otherwise, or afterwards, you invent them. What is not in the open street is false, derived, that is to say, *literature*." Of course, this proposition, taken from Henry Miller's *Black Spring*, is also literature. So my writing here about this piece of writing is just a derivation of a derivation (not to mention my interpolation of Benjamin's interpretation of Miller's quotation). Moreover, the seemingly mystical experience Miller and his childhood friends had in the streets of Williamsburg at the beginning of the twentieth century was efficiently purged by the introduction of the car, then by television, then by deindustrialization, then by crime, and finally by gentrification. In this sense, the real streets of the current neighborhood may also be treated as no more than literature.

It is not important whether Miller's account of the original, prelapsarian street—where one could actually learn, rather than invent, what human beings really are, where one could see the truth rather than mirror it—was ever a historical fact, located in a specific place and time. Even if it was, this seal of historical approval marks the loss of the actual life in that real street; it can only indicate that this exemplary place has ceased to be. Nor should one make the facile claim that this magical street was a mere figment of Miller's imagination, that this special place where one had access to the real was a fake.

For Benjamin, Miller's street is neither fact nor fiction. In his *Manhattan Project*, the street turns into a technical philosophical concept, which is defined as that place, any place, in which we learn what human beings really are, whereas outside this place, we can only invent them. Whatever is false, derived, that is to say, literature, is consequently not in the street: it is indoors. Whatever is true, real, that is to say, sheer life, exists in this narrow opening that he calls "the street."

↟

STREETS, according to Benjamin, are "the dwelling place of the collective. The collective is an eternally unquiet, eternally agitated being that—in the space between the building fronts—experiences, learns, understands, and invents as much as individuals do within the privacy of their own four walls." Since every city consists of different forms of life, the street functions as the natural space of their convergence or clash. But as living beings walk past one another, they only rarely have anything to say to, or do with, one another, for better or worse. They usually share neither words nor deeds, which is what the classical public sphere is supposed to be about. People just pass by. Maybe the pedestrians' consensus (from *con-sensing*, "a shared sensation") manifests itself in a silent agreement rather than in acting and speaking together. They tend to exchange neither opinions nor goods but only quick glances.

Maybe it is precisely this tacit agreement, exponentially multiplied with every momentary chance encounter, that consolidates the sensation of the streets of a city like New York into a surprisingly concrete political consistency. Jane Jacobs writes that the most important thing about city streets, particularly their sidewalks, "is precisely that they are public. They bring together people who do not know each other in an intimate, private social fashion and in most cases do not care to know each other in that fashion." In other words, the Jacobsian human condition stipulates that man is to his fellow man neither a wolf nor a sheep, neither a friend nor an enemy, but a stranger. One neither loves nor hates one's neighbors; more than anything, one is merely indifferent to them.

In big cities the right to association and the right to disassociation carry a similar weight. But because everyone is a stranger to virtually everyone else, the basic distinction between insider and outsider makes much less sense. "By its nature," the theologian Paul Tillich wrote after moving to New York, "the metropolis provides what otherwise could be given only by traveling; namely, the strange. Since the strange leads to questions and undermines familiar tradition, it serves to elevate reason to ultimate significance." Benjamin also noticed that in New York even the natives often feel like strangers, while back in Paris the category of the *étranger*, with all its Camusian connotations, is much better defined and neatly separated from the local scene.

The geographic demarcation of Paris proper and its differentiation from its suburban rings—first by a wall and then by an expressway—creates a very clear sense of inside and outside, inclusion and exclusion. Nevertheless, suggests Arendt in her essay on Benjamin, even in Paris a "stranger feels at home because he can inhabit the city the way he lives inside his own four walls. And, just as one makes an apartment comfortable by living in it, and not merely by using it for sleeping, eating, and working, one becomes comfortable in the city by strolling through it without aim or purpose, stopping off at one or another of the countless cafes that line the streets and past which the life of the city, the flow of pedestrians, moves along."

This strategy, however, does not work as well in New York, where the street, with its curbs and stoops, trash cans and parked cars, tends to function less as a metaphoric duplication of one's claustrophobically cramped apartment and more as a simple escape from it. Benjamin observes that this increasing importance of the streets probably began in Paris, where it can be traced back to Balzac's reaction to the deteriorating urban living conditions: "Soon," the novelist writes in 1855, "it will become necessary to live more outside the house than within it."

In contrast to Paris, where the outdoors can still feel like a cozy indoors, in New York the inside feels more like the exposed outside. "Home," according to one local definition, is "a place to sleep as a last resort." According to another, it is "the place where you dressed to go out." At the same time, one would be hard pressed to treat an avenue or a street in twentieth-century Manhattan as if it were one's personal living room, which is how the nineteenth-century flâneur used to treat the Parisian boulevards and arcades through which he leisurely meandered.

THE PARISIAN ARCADES, like skyscrapers in the first half of the twentieth century, were constructed mainly with iron. This material fascinated the early Benjamin to the extent that he dedicated to it a full section of his *Arcades Project*. Yet the standard New York street, including sidewalk and roadway, is made mainly of concrete, though a thin layer of asphalt coats the latter. In the second half of the past century, reinforced concrete also won out over steel I-beams as the basic ingredient in the construction of new skyscrapers. Since then, concrete has become the number-one building material and "the second most consumed substance on the planet after water." For example, Manhattan adds concrete to its structures at the rate of "approximately one Hoover Dam every 18 months."

In nineteenth-century Paris, cast-iron beams supported glass roofs that let the sun penetrate the structure. In twentieth-century New York, reinforcing iron re-bars (also called carcass) were submerged in concrete to never again see the light of day. Transparency gives way to brutalism. It is therefore not surprising that in *The Manhattan Project*, Benjamin tries to attach some philosophical meaning to this basic material fact. For example, he mentions Koolhaas's observation that by pouring this thick gray liquid into its designated empty mold, the builder manages to "objectify vacuity" or, even better, reify it. To this Benjamin adds that although concrete slightly expands and contracts over time, breaks can usually be avoided by the addition of artificially made cracks. These are the straight lines that divide the continuous New York sidewalk into standard squares, which are the result of a building practice that may be understood as preemptive fragmentation.

These free associations make better sense if we clarify the etymological origin of the word *concrete*, from the Latin *concrescere*, "to grow together," but also "to unite, harden, to take form by cohesion, to become strong by solidification." This becomes a rather straightforward metaphor in Benjamin's work. New York is not a melting pot but a concrete mixer. The plasticity of its human material, before the elements lock themselves into a rigid position—according to the available (social) mold and the reinforcement of (iron) rules—is rather fleeting. Before long, these different lives turn into a solid substance, which is much less amorphous, free-floating, or fragile than might be assumed. This is the message that Hegel passed to Lenin, who passed it to Brecht, who passed it to Benjamin: "The truth is concrete."

AN ARCADE, like a small town, is a space we can easily pass through while traveling from point *a* to point *b*. What distinguishes both from a station is that they do not require a full stop, though they usually make us move at slower speed.

Passage is the word for arcade in French. In English it denotes an "act or process of moving through, under, over, or past something on the way from one place to another." *The Arcades Project*, or *Passagenwerk*, can be distilled into this one word. Benjamin sees modernity as (a) passage. Modern life, not unlike medieval life, is something we pass through. The main difference is that, in modernity, we are not necessarily or not as firmly sure where we are coming from and where we are heading. On the upside, there are some nice stores along the way.

A street is not something we tend to pass through. If we are sitting in a restaurant and looking out the window, the other people who walk by might indeed be said to be passing through. But, oddly, when we are the ones walking, riding, or driving down a street, we usually do not understand this activity as passing through. We also tend to say that we pass through town, even when we are talking of a very big city. This is more than just semantics. *The Manhattan Project* is guided by the observation that streets and cities do not lend themselves to passage as readily and as one-dimensionally as arcades and towns do.

Once the grid of New York streets and avenues renders the Parisian arcades obsolete, an interesting overhaul of Benjamin's definition of modernity becomes necessary. The meaning of modern life, which is absolutely inseparable from the meaning of urban life, is no longer understood as a work of passage. Instead, it negotiates multiple intersections and possible routes; it offers various shortcuts and inevitable dead ends, like a labyrinth with neither entrance nor exit, neither origin nor destiny, whether personal or collective.

SECOND THRESHOLD   INFRASTRUCTURE

BEFORE WE GO ON, it would be helpful to touch on a very important and slightly tricky methodological idea that guides Benjamin's thought throughout *The Manhattan Project*. To do so, let's play a little game. First, find a Marxist, which is not as difficult as it seems. Then, engage the Marxist in a conversation about anything whatsoever. The aim of the game is to defer as long as possible the moment when the Marxist says something like, "Look, you must take into consideration the difference between the structure and the superstructure."

To those who want to know and are afraid to ask what the Marxist means by that, the following may suffice. Poetry and art, philosophy and politics, ideas and culture, laws and institutions do not exist on their own. They are, for the disciplined Marxist, only the effects of the material conditions that, as a whole, are considered to be their causes. The economy is really what determines or underpins even our loftiest human endeavors. The overall *structure* of our social relations and forces of production is the ultimate foundation of the *superstructure* of our intellectual achievements.

When, in 1938, Benjamin sent a preliminary chapter from his *Arcades Project* to the Institute for Social Research in New York, it did not take long for Adorno, the institute's director, to jump the structure-superstructure gun. Given the project's "micrological" method, which assumes a "world of secret affinities" between its fragmentary elements, it was unclear to Adorno whether it could ever cohere into a totality, into an all-embracing, systematic theory about the social whole. Adorno was concerned by this lack of causal inference from the singular miniatures that compose Benjamin's disjointed depiction of the base structure to the general ideas that rule the abstract superstructure. Even in a text published fifteen years after Benjamin's presumed death, Adorno continues to be baffled by this amalgam of reality and philosophy, fact and form, positivism and magic.

Benjamin's unorthodox methodological assumption, which Adorno never managed to fully fathom, is better explicated in *The Manhattan Project*, where it becomes clear that the structure and the superstructure correspond to each other not because one is the cause and the other its effect but because they are both manifestations of one and the same thing, or attributes of one and the same substance, which he calls the *infrastructure*. Though Benjamin is certainly interested in the material structure and immaterial superstructure of New York City, his center of attention is dedicated to this deeper layer of reality that underlies them both. At first it appears that by infrastructure, he means everything that we normally understand by this term: train stations, sidewalks, sewage systems, street signs, and so on. But after a while it becomes clear that the term also has a special, philosophical use.

In *The Manhattan Project*, infrastructure stands for anything that is understood in and of itself, before a thing finds its expression within the fields of structure or superstructure, before, for example, it manifests itself as either an economic phenomenon or a political one. Before Benjamin even considers either the use value of a thing or its exchange value, or its fetishistic aura, or its poetic force, or its theoretical significance, he aims never to lose sight of the thing itself. Early on in his career he even tried to make the seemingly absurd argument that things possess their own language, by which they communicate themselves to human beings. He spoke, for instance, about the "language of this lamp." By invoking the infrastructure of the city, he found a more reasonable way to allow things to have a life of their own, to reveal themselves as such, in their thus-ness, as it were.

A CLASSIC EXAMPLE of an infrastructure is, once again, the arcade. An arcade is not the expression of ideas, whether economic or political, factual or formal, practical or poetic. On the contrary, those ideas can be an expression of this thing that we call an arcade. The place of the arcade within the structure and superstructure of Paris may raise a host of pertinent questions: Is it public or private? Is it some kind of indoor agora or a nascent department store? How does a commodity transform once it enters this space? And what does it do to the person who strolls through it? Yet the meaning we end up attaching to the arcade does not precede its infrastructure but arises from it. Things are expressed through different ideas that may belong to either the structure or the superstructure of a city, "precisely as, with the sleeper, an overfull stomach finds not its reflection but its expression in the contents of the dreams."

The infrastructure thus becomes the secret key with which Benjamin tries to unlock the mysteries of the city. Structure and superstructure are only its secondary manifestations. This point is well understood by those who are trying to undermine the overwhelming power of the metropolis. They know that an attack aimed directly at the structure of the city (the economic establishment) or its superstructure (the political establishment) is almost always doomed to fail. But even slightly tampering with the city's infrastructure can bring it to its knees, just as a tap on the shoulder of a person in deep sleep can change the course of her dream or suddenly wake her up.

Think about infrastructure in rudimentary Freudian terms. Analyzing what is conscious and what is unconscious in Paris or New York, à la Freud's early topographical model of the psychic apparatus, may be of some value. This is very similar to the practice of comparing and contrasting the city's structure and superstructure. Yet Freud's more advanced, structural model—that of the id, ego, and superego—becomes an exceedingly useful tool in Benjamin's dissection of the urban apparatus. Like a good surrealist, Benjamin offers a psychoanalysis not of persons but of things. Infrastructure, in this sense, is the city's id, the origin of both ego and superego, lying or lurking underneath both structure and superstructure.

But what is this id, in Freud, other than *das Es*, literally, the *it*? To come to terms with the city's infrastructure is accordingly to come to terms with the city as an *it* or with the *it* of the city, as in *It is glorious* or *It is hectic*. Also notice that the city's *it* is similar to the weather's *it*, as in *It is freezing* or *It is muggy*. This approach can help us temporarily take our minds off issues like *what* the city is, or *how* it is, or *why* it is and focus instead on the realization *that* it is. Wondering about the very existence of the city is a work reserved for ontology, or first philosophy, which is how *The Manhattan Project* is ultimately meant to be read.

BENJAMIN IS NOT restricting himself here to dead, inert, thoughtless matter. The infrastructure of New York, in his unique sense of this term, also bespeaks its sheer life, which Western philosophy traditionally hid behind a structure-and-superstructure-like division. Long before Marx, the Greeks even had separate words for these two aspects of our human existence. Their first word for life was *zoe*. It stood for the necessary facts of our life—eating, sleeping, procreating, but also earning a living—all of which they relegated to the realm of the household, or *oikos*, from which the word *economy* derives. Their second word for life was *bios*. It stood for the form, the way, or meaning of our life, which they considered the true concern of the city-state, or the *polis*, from which the word *politics* derives.

Even today when we think about city life, we tend to separate the facts of our existence as natural beings from the form of our existence as social beings; or distinguish our biological necessities from our cultural possibilities; or develop a private aspect and a public aspect of our personalities; or even consider ourselves as either bodies or souls. The ontological account of New York as a landscape built of sheer life, as a vital infrastructure, is Benjamin's way of stalling this dialectical machine that overdetermines our existence by simply slicing it down the middle. Thinking beyond this outworn dualistic notion of our lives and cities is not an easy task. However we go about it, it is already clear that calling Benjamin a Marxist is a bit like calling Einstein a Newtonian.

THIRD PART

There are certain sections of New York, Major,
that I wouldn't advise you to try to invade.

—HUMPHREY BOGART

SIXTEENTH CHAPTER **EMPIRE**

ONE SUMMER EVENING IN 1964 Andy Warhol and his crew set up their film camera in a friend's office on one of the top floors of the Time-Life Building on Sixth Avenue. From the window they had a clear view, one mile to the south, of the Empire State Building, the protagonist of the movie they began to shoot as the sun set. They held the iconic building at the center of the frame and filmed it continuously for the next six and a half hours—without moving the camera, without color, and without sound.

The light in their office was turned off, except when the camera reel had to be changed. In one of these few unavoidable moments of illumination, Warhol's profile can be seen reflected in the office window, superimposed over the nightly urban landscape, like a white ghost. Otherwise the changes are minute: the floodlights at the top of the skyscraper are switched on at one point and off at another; a plane goes by; the exposure of the film changes slightly; the lights in various windows are turned on and off but not much more. This did not prevent Warhol from stipulating that the film, simply called *Empire*, be projected in slow motion, extending its duration to more than eight long hours of a barely changing continuous take.

BENJAMIN'S ANALYSIS of this film—which he considers to be Warhol's finest work in any medium—begins with a rather unremarkable examination of some of the artist's well-known, noncinematic pieces, such as his paintings of the Campbell's soup cans and sculptures of the Brillo soap boxes, his serial portraits of Marilyn Monroe, and repetitive wallpaper of a pink cow. This body of work addresses in no uncertain terms a situation that Benjamin was the first to assess: the disintegration of the aura of the unique work of art in the age of its technological reproducibility. Given that his seminal essay on this subject was first translated into English in 1960, and given the influence it had on Siegfried Kracauer and Jay Leyda, two key figures in the New York avant-garde film scene of that time, it is not unthinkable that the link between Benjamin and Warhol is more than accidental. How else are we to understand Benjamin's comment from 1931 about the artistic capacity to "endow any soup can with cosmic significance"?

Warhol devised simple methods to transform the cliché of the inspired, struggling artist into a new figure of an impersonal, productive machine. Though no two Warhols are exactly the same, his silk-screened paintings do away with the masterly brushstrokes and expressionistic paint drips that were previously integral to the authentic work. The result was a streamlined process that was often executed by anonymous assistants. The Factory—as his art studio came to be known during the same years that many manufacturing industries fled the city—was able to churn out multiple, almost identical copies of works that were nevertheless revered as high art, while Warhol, The Factory's owner, was anointed as the greatest artist of his generation.

There is nothing new about this analysis of Warhol's work. What makes it interesting is the way it is mobilized to explain *Empire*'s inapparent significance. A movie, it goes without saying, is only an illusion. What seems to be moving on the screen actually stands still, even though our mind is tricked into believing otherwise. Benjamin therefore decides to approach *Empire* not as a single, continuous motion picture but as a series of approximately half a million individual still pictures, or copies of more or less the same image.

What is the fundamental difference between Warhol's multiple celluloid impressions of the Empire State Building and his numerous silk-screened portraits of, say, Elvis Presley? One could claim that the former are projected one after another and the latter are hung one next to the other. In this sense, the seemingly extravagant running time of *Empire* is actually an attempt to speed up as much as possible the experience of this multitude of singular artworks. *Empire*, to be appreciated, should be screened at an even slower rate than sixteen frames per second, treated like a slideshow rather than a movie. For example, at the speedy pace of one frame per second, it would run for almost five and a half days.

If we take seriously Warhol's approach to his studio as a factory, then *Empire* marks an extremely efficient nightshift in the history of his art plant. In less than seven hours, without breaking a sweat, he produced half a million original works of art, each one ever so slightly different from the others. After examining a reproduction of a few of these consecutive stills, Benjamin mused about the day the film's original reels will be spliced into individual frames and then sold in a massive auction to anyone who has ever wished to own a genuine Warhol but cannot afford his exorbitantly priced paintings.

Wouldn't this be the clearest and truest statement of the philosophy of pop art? In Benjamin's imaginary auction not only the subject matter of the work but the work itself becomes readily available for almost anybody, like collectible baseball cards, or one-dollar bills, or Coca-Cola bottles. "When Queen Elizabeth came here and President Eisenhower bought her a hot dog," we read in *The Philosophy of Andy Warhol*, "I'm sure he felt confident that she couldn't have had delivered to Buckingham Palace a better hot dog than that one he bought her for maybe twenty cents at the ballpark."

REMEMBER THAT when Benjamin first encountered those long-exposure still photographs of the streets of New York, where all movement was effaced and only inanimate objects remained visible, he imagined instead a photograph that would reverse the process, that would focus entirely on what is alive and moving and somehow erase all the motionless buildings. Only after he took the rare opportunity to sit through a screening of *Empire* in its entirety did he realize that this film goes in a diametrically opposite direction from that of his imaginary photo in order to reach the same result: instead of dedicating a still picture to motion, Warhol dedicated a motion picture to stillness.

Warhol's filmography from the 1960s comprises dozens of titles; but as far as Benjamin was aware, *Empire* is the only one featuring an inanimate object as the sole star of the movie, doing away with the image of a human life almost entirely. Nevertheless, movies cannot help being meditations on movement, on life, and *Empire* is no exception. The film's apparent attempt to erase both movement and life is an ingenious experiment set to prove the unavoidable failure of this very attempt. On the face of it, the film is concerned with a built landscape, with still life, not with sheer life. Yet Benjamin believes that even though *Empire* appears to be dedicated to a skyscraper, its true subject is (pun intended) still life.

This point makes better sense once we consider the possibility that War-hol's surprising mid-1960s decision to abandon painting for cinema's sake was spurred by a subtle shift in his artistic interest. It is not easy to reconcile his original obsession with commodities and his subsequent anticommercial, al-most unwatchable films (the most profitable artistic medium in history). It is also difficult to reconcile his early fixation on fame and his later cultivation of a cast of so-called superstars, who were anything but. Something else is going on in these movies.

Following the rise in the status of his art as a coveted commodity and the growth of his personal fame, Warhol's studio gradually metamorphosed from a quiet workplace into an elaborate social scene. As New York became a magnet for the vanguard of the 1960s counterculture, Warhol's Factory was one of its most powerful epicenters, pulling into its orbit some of the most interesting characters in the city during this turbulent decade. At one point he began to wonder if more things were happening because "there was more awake time for them to happen in (since so many people were on amphetamine), or if people started taking amphet-amine because there were so many things to do that they needed to have more awake time to do them in."

With neither cynicism nor resignation, Warhol also noticed that people who went to gallery openings were fascinated not by the art on the walls but by the other people around them. The objects were expendable because life was far more interesting; it was the real art. Instead of fighting this development, Warhol chose to go with it, to embrace it, by dedicating much of his subsequent work to a painstaking documentation of the daily life that was drawn to his aura, as boring and as wacky as this life often turned out to be. And he did so as a passive ob-server, with as little intervention or direction on his part as possible.

Warhol's *Screen Tests* are his most sustained attempt to become the chronicler of the lives that surrounded him. These filmic portraits, documenting hundreds of visitors to his studio, were all produced in a similar manner: The subject was asked to sit in front of a rolling camera that captured him or her from the shoulders up for several minutes. The Factory people used to call these films "stillies" because of the way they wavered between still photography and the moving image. Un-surprisingly, Susan Sontag's stilly is both unsettling and fascinating. It is as if she is mentally struggling, eyes closed, with Warhol's elementary question: "Isn't life a series of images that change as they repeat themselves?"

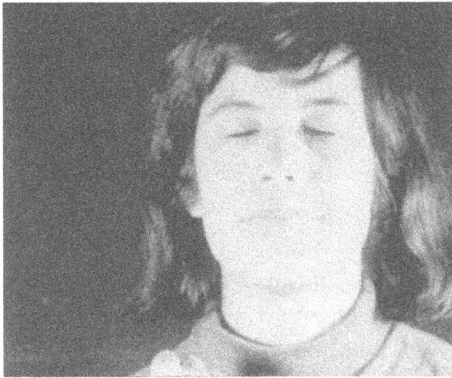

COME TO THINK OF IT, *Empire* is very similar to *Screen Tests*, which date to the same phase in Warhol's career. One difference is that the running time of *Empire* extends to a few hours. Another difference is that the person in the shot is replaced by a building. Other than that, both are silent, black-and-white films, shot in twenty-four frames per second and then slowed down during the screening to sixteen frames per second. They both depict a subject positioned at the center of the frame with minimal movement. If we account for the horizontal orientation of the frame, which was rarely contested in the history of cinema, we could also say that *Screen Tests* are not moving *portraits* but *landscapes* of different lives.

In *Empire*, the absence of life proves to be its roundabout affirmation. To claim that the film is concerned with architecture is like claiming that the Christian cross is concerned with carpentry. Benjamin is far from certain that Warhol, who attended Mass regularly all his life, would have dismissed such a comparison between these profane and sacred symbols. A cross is not merely the wood from which it is made. It is first of all an emblem of a life: that of Jesus and his followers. Benjamin therefore speculates that *Empire* approaches its subject matter not merely as a material building but as another icon of another life: not just Warhol's own life, or the life of his circle of friends, or the life of the people of New York, but an icon of city life as such. It is as if Warhol wanted *Empire* to be the New Cross, symbolizing not the religious form of life but the urban one.

Empire is the only work in Warhol's *catalogue raisonné* that can be said to be dedicated explicitly to New York, the city where he lived and worked his entire adult life. Notice, by the way, that the film is not called *The Empire State Building*, because Warhol is not interested in the landmark building itself, and his film is not about architecture. It is also notable that it is not called *Empire State*. Even though Warhol was quite the patriot, and his film was made when the United States was at the peak of its power, Benjamin does not even entertain the possibility that this artwork is a salute to the American Empire. Many of Warhol's works have American themes, but his only attempt to deal with his country as the explicit subject of his art is in a series of paintings called *Death in America*.

Benjamin therefore concludes that Warhol must have had a very different empire in mind. As often is the case, the philosopher has no qualms about articulating the signified for the artist. The new empire, he argues in *The Manhattan Project*, is anchored in cities, not nations. Instead of the American Century, he talks about the New York Century. Nevertheless, like *Empire*, Benjamin approaches New York only as the icon or emblem or banner of a global urban revolution. This city may die, but others will live. John Locke said that "in the beginning all the world was America." So maybe in the end the entire globe will be Manhattan.

SEVENTEENTH CHAPTER   **THE URBAN REVOLUTION**

DESPITE BENJAMIN'S RAREFIED IDEAS, puzzling literary flourishes, and occasional flights of fancy, his philosophy has a pretty solid empirical basis. The numbers, as they say, speak for themselves. At the beginning of the nineteenth century only 3 percent of the world's population lived in cities. At the turn of that century the percentage rose to 13. By the end of Benjamin's life it was already hovering around 40 percent, with a very clear and consistent trajectory. The scales tipped in 2008. The majority of people are now no longer rural but urban, and their (numerical) domination steadily increases. One conservative estimate is that by 2050 about 75 percent will be city inhabitants, constituting a majority on every continent, including Asia and Africa.

Today we are standing neither in the beginning nor at the end but somewhere in the middle of this most decisive process in human history, which has been transforming the human form of life in the most profound ways imaginable. This is true not only in privileged corners of the Western world but virtually everywhere. If there is a single piece of information that can efficiently sum up the modern world, then this is the one. Other attempts to speak of modernity in terms of secularization or rationalization, capitalism or individualism, the nation-state or technological innovation sooner or later reveal their limited explanatory power.

It is very likely that future historians will not call ours the modern age (from Latin *modo*, "just now") but the urban age. The modern revolution is above all an urban revolution, and it is not even getting close to its post phase. From this perspective, *The Manhattan Project* can be read as a case study of urbanization, treating twentieth-century New York as the paradigm of a phenomenon whose origin and destiny lie elsewhere (London and Paris in the nineteenth century, Shanghai and Mumbai in the twenty-first, and perhaps Lagos and Kinshasa not long after).

When Benjamin talks about the urban revolution, it is safe to say that he is not alluding to the work of the archeologist Gordon Childe, who first coined this term to describe the establishment of ancient cities as the decisive steppingstone in the development of civilization. Instead, Benjamin is most probably inspired here by the work of the philosopher Henri Lefebvre, who applies the same term to our modern condition. In so doing, Lefebvre wants to rewrite the usual narrative of historical materialism, which assumes that the Industrial Revolution should be considered the definitive event of modernity.

Industrial society should not be conflated with urban society. Chances are that you live in or close to a big city and that neither you nor most of the people you know work in a factory. New York, for example, which is still the center of world power, is considered today to be a postindustrial city ruled by a consumer society that wins its bread (and cake) by engaging in immaterial labor. We need to remember that this city underwent this particular metamorphosis at the same time Benjamin was writing his *Manhattan Project*. Following more than a century of feverish industrialization, New York lost within the span of a few decades its status as a predominantly working-class city. But does the fact that we no longer tighten screws in an assembly line, as in Chaplin's *Modern Times*, necessarily mean that we are living in postmodern times? Or should we reassess the equation of modern life with industrial life?

It is misleading to dismiss urbanism as a mere outgrowth of industrialism. Although industrialization usually leads to urbanization, urbanization usually leads to *de*industrialization, to the flight of manufacturers away from city centers. It should also be noted that most major cities, Paris and New York among them, achieved their primacy not because of their industrial prowess but mainly as a result of their prior positions as centers of international trade. Nevertheless, Benjamin is not really interested in this chicken-or-the-egg causal relationship between urbanization and industrialization. As the "painter of modern life," he has no doubt which of these processes serves as a better model for the descriptive work of his prose-picture.

The Industrial Revolution cannot be the essence of modernity but only its precondition. It is apparently a necessary stage in the process of modernization, which at its most basic level inheres in an exodus away from the impoverished conditions of rural society (a preurban society that is easy to romanticize from a comfortable distance). It is hard to come across two thinkers who completely agree on what the modern exactly means, probably because the word is like a "trademark" that, since the days of Charles Baudelaire, has been stamped on almost anything. The urban, however, designates a much more focused and concrete reality, the precise reality that functions as the uncontested source of virtually everything else we associate with modernity.

Modern society has become invariably urban for several well-known reasons. First, whether industrial production is located in the city, the suburb, or a faraway land, the profit is always drawn back into urban centers, whose power only increases as a result. Second, the better the methods of communication and transportation, which enable commodities, information, and people to travel faster and cheaper, the more condensed and powerful cities become (rather than less so, as is often assumed). This happens because cities can now control the rest of the land more efficiently and because their ties to one another become even stronger, leading to what Saskia Sassen calls "global cities."

It is also necessary to add that in developed countries in North America and Western Europe, the very distinction between urban and rural is moot, because the city's range of direct and indirect influence can be felt just about everywhere. A paved road, a general store, a neighbor who once lived in the city, or cell-phone reception is enough to render the most secluded little house on the prairie significantly less so. In a postrural world (a much more accurate descriptive than postindustrial), anything that is not within the limits of the modern city is becoming its colony, in ways that might turn out to be as detrimental as the religious and nationalistic colonial projects of the past.

AMONG BENJAMIN'S NOTES about the urban revolution there is a short list titled "Other Spaces," which indicates the direct influence of Michel Foucault on his later thought. The list comprises a few examples of those modern attempts to secure a controlled other space, ruled by order and discipline, in the midst of a world perceived to be chaotic and irrational. At the top of his list, and underlined, Benjamin places the factory, followed by the corporate office space, the commercial airplane, the public school, the general hospital, the housing project, the army camp, and finally, the concentration camp. The not-dissimilar layout of these superefficient spaces is hardly coincidental, and their comparison to one another is not as outrageous as it seems.

These Foucauldian other spaces are all based on the intentional eradication of otherness within their boundaries, or on the ability to monitor otherness in the most efficient manner, or on the capacity to control different individuals by separating them from each other, or on the ability to impose preordained differences through a meticulous division of labor (the steering wheel assembly line versus the engine assembly line, sales or accounting, chicken or pasta, English or algebra, fever or high blood pressure, middle or low income, yes sir or no sir, life or death). In a second column next to Benjamin's list of these idealized other spaces is only one item: *the urban space/space of otherness.*

Criticizing the inhuman conditions in factories around the world remains as urgent today as it was for Marx. Extending this argument to the inhuman metropolis feels more anachronistic, especially when applied to Paris or New York, whose main problem is not inhumanity but inaccessibility. Following Lefebvre, we could say that whereas the industrial homogenizes and pacifies, the urban can still differentiate and revolutionize. If the industrial is focused on the production of things, then the urban is concerned with the production of space.

Benjamin does not view the urban revolution as an attempt to change history as he does other modern revolutionary movements; it is not a temporal event but a spatial one; it does not insert a break or a brake into the flow of time but alters, block by block, person by person, the human topology that constitutes this living landscape. At the very same time that modern society went out of its way to separate different behaviors, activities, identities, and bodies, by consigning them to different, distinct, well-ordered spaces, the space of a city like New York gave people the opportunity to live a "mongrel" existence, to cite the title Dorothy Parker chose for her unwritten autobiography.

THERE IS SOMETHING even more radical about Benjamin's passages dedicated to the urban revolution than this pluralistic utopia, something that may very well be the most explosive political implication of *The Manhattan Project* as a whole. Remember that, for Marx, the Industrial Revolution of the nineteenth century was a powerful wake-up call. He realized that behind the promising economic boom was endless human gloom. The factory workers who produced a parade of cheap commodities were exploited by their employers, who became obscenely rich while their employees remained wretchedly poor. The workers justifiably felt unjustifiably powerless. They knew that if they asked for more money or better conditions, all they would get in return was the boot. To the naked eye, the workers surely looked like a random heap of suffering individuals. Marx's achievement lay in his creation of a "class consciousness," as it would later be called, a pair of glasses through which the workers could look around and realize that they were actually proud members of a unified class made up of all the workers of the world, wherever they were. This class was so vast and was responsible for the production of so much wealth that it was capable, potentially, of ruling the world.

In a barely disguised similar vein, Benjamin develops an argument that is at once a respectful homage to Marx and a possible criticism. It goes something like this: Although city dwellers are becoming the overwhelming majority in more and more countries around the world, they are still lacking what Benjamin calls *urban consciousness*. Before they identify themselves as members of the lower or the middle or the upper class, before they see themselves as belonging to the Left or the Right, before they play a patriotic role by rooting for this or that nation, it would not hurt the inhabitants of the city to be a little bit more *metriotic*. Without erasing their differences, urban dwellers need to realize that their primary allegiance is to the city, that their true solidarity is to one another, that they all participate in the same project.

To see ourselves as belonging to the city is to realize that we are a part of a global urban phenomenon, not just a local one. If the true revolution is urban, then it is humans struggling in cities, not those toiling in factories, who have played—and will continue to play for years to come—the dominant role in the shaping of modernity. Of course, no one will deny that virtually all the power in the world is already concentrated in big metropolitan areas. The problem is that city dwellers are not considered powerful qua city dwellers. They are usually perceived as influential only because they have a role in the operation of certain corporations or governments. But these private and public sectors remind Benjamin of that joke about the two mice running alongside an elephant, with one mouse saying to the other: "Hey, look at all the dust we are raising."

For more than two centuries, the combined forces of modern economy (predominantly capitalism) and modern politics (predominantly the nation-state) have preferred to ignore the elephant in the room. Once the urban beast forced them to acknowledge its presence, they thought they could tame it. When this strategy proved impossible, the political leviathans and economic behemoths began to claim that the city was their own proudest invention and most precious possession. But what all those sovereigns and CEOs fail to imagine is that the city is not an elephant but a Trojan horse, patiently waiting for night to fall.

EIGHTEENTH CHAPTER **HYPOTHESES ON MODERN CITIES**

LET ME TRY TO ARTICULATE some of Benjamin's basic ideas about the urban revolution with the help of eleven convenient hypotheses.

1. The later Benjamin does not stop at a nuanced, anticapitalist condemnation of the city as the evil epicenter of accumulation and exploitation. Seen as a basic theoretical armature, he finds this approach necessary but not sufficient. Without naming names, his Marxist critique of the city loosely connects the early *Arcades Project* to a range of key urban thinkers. Yet it is Marx himself who perceived the medieval city as the seed of communism (it is, after all, "the first *communio*" or commune) and the modern city as the soil for revolutions of all shapes and forms (not only economic but also political, social, cultural, and intellectual). Nevertheless, there are still those who are willing to throw the baby of revolutionary hope out with the urban bathwater because they are convinced that this water came from the poisonous source of capitalism. Certain anarchists may portray different forces encroaching on the city (the government, the police, the law, the sovereign), yet their dismissal of the urban space as unfit for radical action is quite similar.

2. Consequently, Benjamin feels the need to either bolster or deepen the shaky or uncritical faith in the city, which he understands not just as a revolution of the space in which we live but also as the primary dwelling place of the revolutionary spirit as such. Rather than write the city off and instead imagine some alternative place more congenial to human cohabitation, he deals with the existing urban landscape as the crowded and contested site where all power relations, all forms of life, engage, sometimes without even noticing it, in a daily war to hold their ground. Since Benjamin knows that "cities are battlefields," anywhere else can only be a place for temporary retreat. Whatever revolutionary idea or practice is to be imagined will have to fight for its place within the confines of the agonistic urban space. As pacified as the city can be, it has no *alibi* (Latin for "another

place"). "The revolution in our times," David Harvey recently declared, "has to be urban—or nothing."

3. The urban revolution is not something to wish for, nor is it something we should dread. It is already an accomplished fact. The twentieth century witnessed how good capitalists and good communists became skeptical of this urban reality and even fearful of it for quite similar reasons. They both tried, with dismal results, to quell urban growth and reengineer the topology of modern life to fit their different economic ideologies. They both knew that every city would include pockets of resistance that could easily sabotage their overarching program and undermine their ultimate goals. Benjamin is interested precisely in these anomalies nested within the urban space. His aim is not to caulk the cracks and iron the creases out but to make them even more pronounced. For instance, one of his longtime fascinations is idleness, a phenomenon that neither the communist ideology of labor and equality nor the capitalist ideology of production and consumption can easily stomach. From an orthodox economic perspective, idlers are totally superfluous and thus incomprehensible. Their stubborn presence in every big city destabilizes dogmatic systems of thought. The idler is living proof that the city is more than just a by-product of economic activity, that city life is more than just an extension of factory life. For the Parisian flâneur, the New York homeless, and all the other part-time loiterers sitting on café chairs, bar stools, park benches, brownstone stoops, and sidewalk curbs, the city functions as means without end, as the thing itself, as an object of pure use, or pure enjoyment, but also pure misery.

4. Benjamin is not blind to the fact that the city is the ultimate cradle of capitalist production, consumption, and circulation. He often walked in the streets of New York imagining price tags dangling from everything and everyone. Much of the urban space has been produced and is being constantly reproduced by those in power for the coldest, most opportunistic economic ends. Not only the opening of a swanky new café with frothy cappuccinos but even the construction of a pretty public park with a colorful playground can be seen as the fulfillment of very particular desires of a very particular segment of the ruling class. Every aspect of the city's vivacious culture, all its avenues of seemingly free self-expression, can also be seen by the disillusioned observer as manifestations of an amorphous "symbolic economy," which can be as influential, detrimental, and manipulative as the hard, material economy, if not more so. The metropolis is dotted with

understated signs that invite certain people and rebuff others according to their class. But as is the case with the connection between industrial development and modernity, Benjamin contends that urbanism is very much linked with but not entirely reducible to capitalism and its obvious discontents.

5. Even David Harvey, the person responsible for disseminating the merciless evaluation of the city as a sort of elaborate Ponzi scheme, concedes that it is still possible to distinguish between the city as a built form (driven by exchange value) and urbanism as a way of life (driven by use value). Benjamin is wholeheartedly committed to Harvey's call "to chart the path from an urbanism based on exploitation to an urbanism appropriate for the human species." For both, urbanism, not existentialism, is a humanism, or whatever is left of this mangled concept. For Harvey, however, this equation necessitates a neo-Marxist revolution that will transform the face of the city as we know it. Benjamin does not tend to share this communist eye for the capitalist lie. At its best, his work is an attempt to revolutionize the way we think of the city in all its microscopic intricacies and macroscopic forces. Urbanism as a way of life is not a utopia in the nebulous future but a reality that *The Manhattan Project* grasps in the messy present, alongside (not instead of) the undeniable urbanism based on exploitation that Harvey and company scrutinize so well.

6. At the heart of the Marxist urban analysis lies an unavoidable tension, best expressed in the title of Harvey's *Social Justice and the City*. Social justice is a noble and fine thing, and so is the city. The problem, of course, is the conjunction, which creates a stubborn conflict, reminiscent of the one found in the title of Arendt's "Truth and Politics." Is it possible to promote both social justice *and* the city, or is this having your cake and eating it too? This is a tricky question, because in reality states, not cities, purport to govern people through equal laws and corrective regulations (even though they often end up doing the exact opposite). Unlike the sovereign state and its vast juridical system, the city neither claims nor has the tools to ensure blind justice for all. If the goddess of the city is still depicted blindfolded, the reason is that it mimics Fortuna, not Justitia. Like nature, the city at its core is neither just *nor unjust*; it just is.

7. Herein lies the difficulty behind the attempt to condemn the modern metropolis as a "dual city" of sunshine and shadow, of privileged and underprivileged residents, separated by an unmistakable class fault line. Instead of promoting

urban solidarity, this reactionary approach ends up turning the city against it-self. Though the dream of a thoroughly equalized urban landscape is just that, Benjamin is also fully aware that a city starkly divided (from within or without) between the superrich and the rest of us is the main symptom, or even the main cause, of its own undoing. This is what informs his engagement with the discourse around the "right to the city," the main response of urban theorists since the 1960s to the diminishing access of the poor to metropolitan life. In Benjamin's view, this fight for the right to live in cities is another unfortunate confusion between the logic of the city and that of the state, like the one that lies behind the question of so-called urban justice. It has to do with the questionable assumption that the city is a sovereign body with the power to include or exclude living beings, that what the city giveth and what the city taketh away is by right rather than by chance. Blaming the city is shooting the messenger.

8. Lefebvre offers a "tripartite" account of the modern condition, presenting it as a gradual shift from a rural life to an industrial life and then—in the final stage that marks a sort of Hegelian end of history—to an urban life. The urban condition is his theoretical horizon. It is the end point of the continuum on which we pres-ently live. If a rural life revolves around need (characterized by limited produc-tion and subjection to the erratic forces of nature) and an industrial life revolves around work (characterized by fetishized production facilitated by the domination of nature and at the expense of the latter's destruction), then urbanism, Lefebvre speculates, is a completely new phase that may lead to a life that revolves around enjoyment. Yet it remains unclear what this enjoyment or *jouissance* means and what its ramifications may be, especially given its Parisian association with trans-gression. There is also no explanation about how the misery of agrarian life, which gave way to the misery of industrial life, which gave way to the misery of urban life, gets any better. In the end, the city's relationship with nature is also left unre-solved. Much of *The Manhattan Project* is an attempt to fill in these blanks.

9. Benjamin's historical perspective is even more sweeping than Lefebvre's already-bold narrative. Benjamin asks himself what the most pervasive institutions are that have dominated this civilization up to now. His unsurprising answer is the apparatus of religion and the apparatus of the state. The gradual shift of power from the first to the second—from theology to politics, from pope to sovereign, from priest to bureaucrat, from blind faith to instrumental reason—is a large part of the traditional story we like to tell ourselves about the second half of the second

millennium. Instead of dealing with this standard account, Benjamin focuses on another tectonic shift in power, one that is reshaping the world in which we currently live: the transition from states to cities. Though Benjamin can be accused of turning his urbanism into a new ideology, he insists on thinking of the city as a viable, nonvirtual reality that remains standing after all the great, lofty ideologies of the twentieth century collapsed with a thud. "More than ever," Koolhaas mused as the twentieth century was coming to an end, "the city is all we have."

10. Almost every discipline, movement, matrix of thought, and artistic outlet of the last century have employed their own ideas, methods, and convictions to come to terms with the modern city. We have history of the city and sociology of the city, geography of the city and psychology of the city, economy of the city and politics of the city; there are theories of urban architecture and urban ecology; there are films and plays and novels and poems and songs and paintings and photographs and sculptures and symphonies and choreographies and philosophies dedicated to the city. Benjamin was extremely interested in all of these, and he incorporated many of their insights into the argument of *The Manhattan Project*. But he could not help noticing that they all tend to appropriate the actual city for their own needs rather than the city's. He felt that at the end of the day, the city itself is sacrificed on the altar of its own representation.

11. For far too long we have busied ourselves with thinking about ways to change the city. It is about time that we let the city change the way we think.

NINETEENTH CHAPTER   # URBAN PHILOSOPHY

MODERN PHILOSOPHY was less than enthusiastic about the rise of the modern city. In the eighteenth century, as Paris was beginning to take shape as the grand metropolis that two centuries later would fascinate Benjamin so much, it also nurtured the person who would prove to be its most impassioned critic. Jean-Jacques Rousseau arrived in Paris as a young man with no money, status, education, or reputation to speak of. But he soon began to garner invitations to some of the most fashionable salons, where he befriended some of the most notable intellectuals of his generation. It was during the few years he lived in Paris that his philosophical star rose.

With Rousseau's fame also came his deep aversion to the city: "The manner of living in Paris amidst people of pretensions was so little to my liking. The cabals of men of letters, their little candor in their writings, and the air of importance they gave themselves in the world, were so odious to me. I found so little mildness, openness of heart, and frankness in the intercourse even of my friends. So disgusted with this life of tumult, I began ardently to wish to reside in the country." In a letter to Denis Diderot, which put an end to their friendship, Rousseau concludes: "It is in the country that men learn how to love and serve humanity; all they learn in cities is to despise it."

Everyone knew to whom Diderot was referring when he later wrote that "only the wicked lives alone." Yet it was Rousseau who had the final word, long after both men were dead. Diderot and his fellow French Enlightenment philosophes, who were inclined to cherish their burgeoning city, eventually lost the intellectual battle to the German Romantics. The latter continued Rousseau's legacy by treating the countryside as the Eden that would save humanity from the Gehenna of urban existence. "Is not a man better than a town?" Ralph Waldo Emerson could then ask his readers across the Atlantic, undeterred by his question's utter absurdity.

What was at stake in this line of thought was much more than an aesthetic choice concerning the setting for the Romantic books or paintings, or even an ethical choice concerning the preferred residence of a few hoity-toity intellectuals. The real issue was political. Beginning with Rousseau and culminating with Hegel, the critique of the city did not simply go hand in hand with an infatuation with the pastoral. The idea championed by the Romantics in opposition to the city was that of the modern sovereign nation-state.

Fast-forward a couple of centuries, and it becomes clear how the modern state on which Rousseau, Hegel, and their cohorts speculated has become our inescapable and often painful reality. It is probable that the philosophers of the state were not really making history but just predicting its future course and formulating its intricate logic by closely observing the emerging political climate of their day. Yet it is easy to see that Rousseau's two personas—the contrarian who detests the city and everything it stands for, and the authoritarian who promotes the social contract and the general will that is embodied in the sovereign—have continued to inform the way modern society thinks and acts to this day.

↳

ROUSSEAU IS THE CASE of a brilliant yet ambivalent man who was propelled by his somewhat paranoid suspicions of his Parisian friends but also by a strong longing for Geneva, the autonomous city-state where he was born and raised. With Hegel, however, the argument becomes more systematic. Humanity, Hegel claims, has gone through three distinct stages. We first found ourselves in a rural setting and our life revolved around the family. Then we moved into cities, where we became a part of civil society. But these were only the preliminary steps leading to the ultimate goal of the human race, the absolute state.

Hegel is usually a difficult writer, but his position on this matter is quite clear: "The town is the seat of civil trade and industry, of self-absorbed and divisive reflection, of individuals who mediate their own self-preservation in relation to other legal persons. The country is the seat of an ethical life based on nature and the family. Town and country—these constitute in general the two ideal moments from which the state *emerges* as their true *ground*."

Hegel believed centralized state power to be the only force that could police the egoistic life of (urban) civil society, where private individuals are moved only by economic forces, not political ones. The state, which he saw as the institutional embodiment of universal reason, is also the entity that can direct the members of the (rural) family, which is moved only by personal love. But the state is more than just an instrumental force meant to keep everyone in check. It is, first of all, the highest earthly power. It is the essential body that unites a society bent on fragmentation. It is the true end toward which all human beings must direct their entire lives. The city understood in and of itself, which is the city that does not actualize its potentiality as the kernel of the state, is but a spoiled opportunity. The state, in short, is manifest destiny.

One way to tackle Hegel's sweeping narrative is to question his assumption that the state has a monopoly on politics. Alexis de Tocqueville, for example, opposes the distinction between a civil society propelled by private interests and a political state driven by public reason. He does so by turning our attention to the emergence of what he calls a "political society" (a phrase that made Hegel spin in his freshly dug grave), which is both private and public, both economic and political. Tocqueville's firsthand knowledge of the situation at home in Europe and abroad in America made him realize that the various modes of associated life in the United States offered an interesting model that proved to be more viable than the French absolutist state that so infatuated Hegel. "Tocqueville's central idea," Jean Baudrillard explains, "is that the spirit of America is to be found in its mode of life. . . . This creates neither a new legality nor a new State, but it does create a practical legitimacy, a legitimacy grounded in the way of life."

Taking a cue from Tocqueville, Benjamin argues that the Hegelian belief in a sovereign state that can lead us toward some form of universal reason is either wishful thinking or a cruel joke. If anything, the aim of nation-states is to obscure the fact that all humans, not just those who are citizens of the same country, have much in common with one another. The divisive power of the state makes it clear that a league of nations is a contradiction in terms, because it is hopelessly trying to promote human affinities and a shared rationality that individual nations much prefer to erase. Surprisingly, Benjamin does not object here to Kant's abstract idea of a universally shared human reason. He does, however, mount a fierce attack against Hegel's attempt to realize this idea through the actual state apparatus, through his bizarre equation of rationality and nationality. Benjamin knows that the most successful way to foster the sense of a common humanity between a large group of very different people is to make them live for a while in a city. Whereas for Hegel the city is a means to a higher end, for Benjamin it is an end in itself.

BENJAMIN PLACES the idea of the city on one end of a continuum and the idea of the state on the other. He then toys with some names from the history of philosophy by situating them on this imaginary spectrum. As Isaiah Berlin divides philosophers into hedgehogs (those who are informed by one big, defining idea) and foxes (those who develop their thought from a plurality of not-necessarily-related ideas), Benjamin splits the tradition into state philosophers and city philosophers. His intention is not simply to distinguish between those who write in support of either the city or the state, or those who criticize either one, or those who physically live in metropolitan areas and those who live in the countryside.

Benjamin's deeper intention is to distinguish between philosophical works that are structured like a state organization and those that function more like a city, to discover which philosopher implements which logic into his or her actual thought. It is better not to reproduce Benjamin's sketch here, if only because it would be a shame to spoil this little game. Suffice it to say that there are more German names on the state side (where Carl Schmitt is deemed the ultimate state philosopher) and more French names on the city side (with Gilles Deleuze, who otherwise goes unmentioned in *The Manhattan Project*, representing the urban philosopher par excellence).

In popular culture, philosophy is often depicted as a solitary activity conducted in remote natural settings, such as a hut next to a fjord, a clearing in the middle of a forest, a cave on the slope of a mountain, or, these days, a rocking chair on a porch in a quaint college town. Certainly, some of the central figures in the Western tradition are responsible for promoting this ethos in their work and practicing it in their life. But even the most superficial familiarity with intellectual history reveals that the city is a necessary condition for the possibility of doing theoretical work, which may then be carried on in other, less hectic places.

It is probably enough to mention in this context the critical importance of Athens to the birth of ancient philosophy with Socrates, Plato, and Aristotle; or the way that modern philosophy got its start in Bacon's London, Descartes's Paris, and Spinoza's Amsterdam. In this light, the very expression *urban philosophy* turns out to be misleading. Philosophy is always already urban through and through. It cannot help being so. And the opposite might also be true. Perhaps cities should be viewed not only as economic and political entities but also as deeply philosophical ones.

With an unexpected nod to Martin Heidegger, Benjamin argues that our thought cannot help being *thrown* into the world. But this world, this *cosmos*—in which we find ourselves and from which we can never detach ourselves as long as we live—is not some vast and abstract universe. It is always already a *cosmopolis*, a world-city. So if Heidegger refers to the human being as a being-in-the-world, Benjamin treats human thought as thinking-in-the-city, in the *polis*, in what Arendt calls the "space for politics."

That this approach is not foreign to the philosophical tradition but hails directly from it is best expressed in the *Phaedrus*, where the titular character reproaches Socrates for failing to explore the world outside the walls of Athens. Instead of a measured reply, the father of philosophy snaps: "Landscapes and trees have nothing to teach me—only the people in the city can do that." This is one of the ways to understand the bitter quarrel the ancient philosophers had with the sophists, whose "chief sin was that they professed to be able to teach in a few short lessons, for pay, what the Hellenic city, with all its institutions co-operating, actually took a whole lifetime to give to its citizens." A city like New York, for example, has no need of an actual Socrates; it is, in itself, a very efficient Socratic device, a ruthless, ironic machine set to strip individuals of their sense of certainty and self-importance.

TWENTIETH CHAPTER **HOME RULE**

THE EVEN DISPERSION OF LIVES throughout the land is the wet dream of every nation-state. To the consternation of those who wish to control the population, we moderns tend to resist the many temptations of country life for the sake of the seemingly irrational decision to band together in the small quarters of big cities. The reason for the shift from country to city is not, as is usually assumed, solely economic. Benjamin holds that, to an equal degree, the urban revolution proves to be a genuine political move. A city is much more than a random cluster of job opportunities. The concentration of people in metropolitan centers is slowly but surely reshaping the entire web of power relations of modern life.

In the late 1960s Allen Ginsberg sent an open letter to Robert McNamara, the US secretary of defense and architect of the Vietnam War. At one point Ginsberg presents the situation in the following terms: "So we have two life forms—both brothers in their desire for life, both trapped in the dream that it is somehow 'Real,' both in separate universes of mental suspicion." Benjamin uses this quote as a lucid manifestation of the strife between city life and country life, though by country he does not mean the countryside but the homeland. Because our Benjamin is a scarred survivor of two world wars, a cynical observer of the Cold War, and a sideline supporter of the civil rights movement, there is little doubt in his mind that the notion that the state is moved by a genuine "desire for life" is a naive, untenable fantasy.

Witnessing the misery, inequality, devastation, and violence that plagued New York City during its most difficult decades, Benjamin must have had daily doubts about his theoretical commitment to the modern metropolis. Still, from his days in Paris, he never abandoned his conviction that "life in all its variety and inexhaustible wealth of permutations can thrive only among the gray cobblestones and against the gray background of despotism." Certainly, he understood that the struggle between city life and state power is here to stay, if only because these two entities have also developed deep mutual dependencies. But if the choice is between two imperfect yet concrete, nonutopian, well-established realities, he knows in which basket to put his intellectual eggs. "Compared to cities," Jane Jacobs chimes in, "nations are quite ephemeral."

The despair Benjamin felt while trying to cross the Pyrenees to escape the Nazis was not spurred only by his diminishing chances of physical survival. He was even more worried about the way his thought would survive him. It then became obvious that his long immersion in *The Arcades Project* had not allowed him to pay close enough attention to the real danger of his time. He came to realize that his elaborate literary construction, which was supposed to inform his readers (and himself) of the maladies of modernity, had turned into a kind of trap. Like the protagonist in Kafka's "The Burrow," he imagined himself to be building a shelter, when in fact he was digging his own grave.

By focusing his critique on a nineteenth-century city—the same city he was unwilling to leave until it was too late—Benjamin had not fully grasped that the clear and present danger of his generation was best exemplified by a twentieth-century state. It happened to be his own state, and it was doing its very best to exterminate an entire people, which happened to be his own people. It was heartbreaking to come to terms with the fact that his Parisian labor of love had exposed him to one kind of truth while shielding him from another. Much of his later work can be read as an attempt to mend his position by reliving in New York his years in Paris and rewriting his *Arcades Project* as *The Manhattan Project*.

AT THE TURN OF THE TWENTIETH CENTURY the majority of New York State's population lived in New York City. To accommodate the fact that the recently consolidated city was wielding far more economic and political power than the entire rest of the state, it was granted a limited autonomy called *home rule*. This act of transferring powers from a sovereign body to a local authority is called *devolution*. Juridically, the home rule of a city can be revoked by the state at any time, thus restoring the sovereign powers the state had before this devolution. Polemically, Benjamin repeatedly uses these two legal terms in his account of the urban revolution. His *Manhattan Project* can be read as a prognostic work, focused on the gradual devolution of the power of the sovereign state and the de facto establishment of the modern city's home rule.

Benjamin's redrawing of the political map is anchored in his claim that the most basic tension in modern political thought has little to do with the current dichotomy of Left versus Right but goes even deeper, to the original split between the logic of the city and that of the state. One thing that helped him elaborate this position was his rudimentary revision of the standard account of the French Revolution. He speculates that the nearly vertical rise in the population of Paris between 1600 and 1800 was a major cause of the disintegration of the monarchy, which had moved from the city to Versailles in 1682. From Benjamin's perspective (shared with Lefebvre), the Paris Commune of 1871 was a second, desperate attempt of an urban society to claim as its own a revolutionary spark that was swiftly appropriated and vigorously fanned by the nation. The basic polarity is accordingly not that of tyranny versus democracy, nor of capitalism versus communism, but of city versus state.

In 1766, as the inhabitants of Manhattan were slowly gearing up for their own little revolution, they decided to erect a liberty pole in the middle of the city hall commons. A liberty pole is essentially a flagpole without a flag. Though different versions of liberty poles have had various objects attached to their tip, what they share is precisely what they lack: a proper flag representing a specific sovereign state. In New York, for example, the pole was capped with a gilt weather vane inscribed "Liberty." The New Yorkers responsible for this makeshift monument were not necessarily trying to oppose the power of their present ruler (the British king) by pledging allegiance to another (the future American president). Like the famous medieval representations of an empty throne, the flagless pole seems to call into question the very premise of a sovereign state by subverting its most conspicuous symbol. A throne without a king. A pole without a flag. A city without a state? Instead of burning the flag or waving another flag, those New Yorkers chose to celebrate the nonflag.

ONE OF THE MORE UNEXPECTED SOURCES analyzed in *The Manhattan Project* are the letters of George Washington, where Benjamin discovered a few anecdotes that reveal an intriguing aspect of the relationship between the United States and New York City. The first is that the earliest known use of the term "New Yorker" in print appears in a letter Washington wrote in 1756. The second, more substantial anecdote is that in 1789, before Washington left Mount Vernon to go to Manhattan for his inauguration, he wrote that he felt like a "culprit . . . going to the place of his execution." The obvious question is, Why did the father of the nation feel like a criminal? Why did he equate the birth of the nation to a death sentence? His yearning to live a peaceful, rural life far from the public eye does not seem to warrant such a strong pronouncement. Maybe his retreat from New York City at the beginning of the Revolutionary War made him uncomfortable about this return. Although, when the battles subsided, it became clear that his early decision to save his troops rather than confront the superior British army was a strategic cornerstone of his eventual triumph. What, then, other than a psychological motive, could have led Washington to compare the first capital of the United States to a scaffold?

Perhaps the answer has something to do with the fact that New York was only a temporary capital and that the future sovereign seat, established a year after

Washington's inauguration and named in his honor, was about to set a precedent in Western history: a country with "two centers, one governmental, the other economic." This unofficial but most significant physical separation of powers destabilizes the position of the traditional capital city as the focal point not just of politics and business but also of culture and religion. The case of Moscow and St. Petersburg is remotely comparable to the American situation, though more recent examples (such as Jerusalem and Tel Aviv) were to follow. New York is still the best example of a city that secures its position as the most important in the nation despite its sundering from the apparatus of state power. Historians even speculate that the fact that it was not a national capital is what enabled it to become the capital of the world.

From the religious ideal of Puritan New England to the enlightened ideal of Jeffersonian Virginia, the ability to accommodate difference, to make place for the other, has never been a given in the American scene. The Puritan model is that of the little town where everyone is supposed to live in "concord." If you wish to live differently, be our guest, but please build your own separate settlement. To a great extent, the suburbs and gated communities of the twentieth century are direct extensions of this model.

The enlightened model is based not on the convergence of like-minded individuals in a single small space but on the grander aspiration to achieve hegemony throughout the land. It is the dream that everybody can reach some elementary, rational, national agreement. Thomas Jefferson, however, had little faith that former slaves and slave owners could ever live together in the same country. He also opposed emigration from foreign countries and supported territorial expansion, because he believed that these moves would enhance his anti-agonistic democratic vision, which depended on the avoidance of internal or external conflict at almost any cost. This explains why he was so suspicious of big, heterogeneous cities. A space of difference like New York is, through Jeffersonian eyes, a clear threat to the perfection of the American union.

TRIVIA QUESTION: Out of the forty-some US presidents, how many were born in one of the major forty-some cities in America? A clue: One hand is more than enough. Benjamin lived in New York when the polarization between the city and the rest of the country was at its strongest. Unlike today, his was a time when the power of the United States seemed to be growing in direct correlation to his city's decline. In such an environment, one might mistakenly presume his

Manhattan Project to be full of antigovernmental, down-with-the-state demagogy. Even worse, one might be led to cast Benjamin as a conservative weary of any federal intervention.

If the previous considerations lead to such impressions, then let me just say that as far as national and international politics is concerned, Benjamin was fairly agnostic. He was so focused on the development of his analysis of the city that he left to other thinkers the trouble of engaging in a detailed critique of the state. Sovereign nations (such as the United States, Israel, East and West Germany) are merely background noise in *The Manhattan Project*. It was far from his intention to turn the city into another state, complete with its elaborate military and governmental apparatuses. He was evidently unimpressed by Norman Mailer's proposition during his 1969 botched mayoral campaign to secede from Albany and turn New York City into the fifty-first state in the Union. To explain Benjamin's position in the most unequivocal, minimal terms, one could say that his hope is that one day we will learn to *see like a city* instead of "seeing like a state."

TWENTY-FIRST CHAPTER   CITY OF REFUGE

IT WOULD BE DIFFICULT to understand the spirit of ancient Athens without reading Homer's *Odyssey*. It would be just as difficult to comprehend the ethos of modern New York without taking into account Herman Melville's *Moby-Dick*. Although the publication of this novel falls outside the historical purview of Benjamin's investigation into twentieth-century New York, there was no way he could have avoided analyzing this urtext. The only other exception he allows himself to make is Walt Whitman's *Leaves of Grass*, which carries a similar foundational status in his *Manhattan Project*.

Influenced by his early study of baroque theater, Benjamin decides to approach *Moby-Dick* as an allegorical work. The only trouble is that he offers two, somewhat conflicting, interpretations of the same book. According to the first, the *Pequod*, the ship at the center of Melville's story, stands for the nation. Moby-Dick, the white whale vainly pursued across oceans by the *Pequod*, stands for the city. Ahab—the monomaniacal captain of the whaler who forgoes the charter of the expedition (to hunt for as many whales as possible and extract the precious oil from their blubber) in an attempt to get his revenge on Moby-Dick (who previously bit off his leg)—stands for the sovereign. Ishmael—the narrator (but not necessarily the protagonist) of the story, who leaves his "insular city of the Manhattoes" and joins the disastrous voyage—stands for the city dweller who learns, as the story progresses, the inner workings of the mighty state.

There are many intertextual clues that may have led Benjamin to this rather straightforward reading. But the most obvious one comes from an external source, a sentence written by Thomas Hobbes: "For by art is created that great *Leviathan*, called a *Commonwealth* or *State*, in Latin, *civitas*, which is but an artificial man." Hobbes refers to the state as the *Leviathan*, after a mystical sea monster often depicted as a whale. The clear difference is that in Hobbes's political philosophy a state is considered an artificial man, and in Melville's allegorical novel a ship is understood as an artificial whale. Like the state and the ship, *Moby-Dick* (the book, not the whale) is itself a colossal work created "by art" and told by an "artificial man" ("Call me Ishmael," the book begins, as if it were a hypothesis).

But Melville himself, the flesh-and-blood author, along with the city of his birth and death, are not artificial, fictional constructions. And as the real whale is not just any whale but a singular one, with a name and even a persona, New York is not an abstraction, interchangeable with any other city. While the general opinion in the nineteenth and twentieth centuries was that the impersonal and uncontrollable urban beast must somehow be stopped, Melville uses *Moby-Dick* as a coded counterargument. He claims that it is actually the commonwealth/*Pequod*, under the direction of its sovereign/Ahab, that is the real threat. It is a threat not merely to the city/whale but to the safety and well-being of all its citizens/sailors, or anyone else who stands in its way. Still, the city outlives the nation, as, by the novel's end, the whale survives the ship and everyone on board, save Ishmael, who lives to tell this edifying tale.

Moby-Dick teaches us a simple historical truth with a surprisingly happy ending. All empires and tyrants, as powerful and evil as they may be, eventually wither away. Cities, for some reason, more often than not just don't. There is probably no better example of this than Benjamin's hometown. Berlin, which could have easily been the capital of the twentieth century, will be remembered as its sacrificial victim. But just imagine Benjamin's ghost strolling today, in the twenty-first century, alongside the tourists, from Potsdamer Platz toward Brandenburg Gate, where the wall used to be, passing on the way the nondescript parking lot under which Hitler's bunker still lies, crossing Hannah-Arendt-Straße to the concrete slabs of the Holocaust memorial (which most people see as tombs, though Benjamin would probably notice their resemblance to an aerial view of Manhattan). Then, turning left, he would wander the winding paths of the green Tiergarten, exiting by the zoo, and arriving finally at the familiar streets of Charlottenburg, his childhood neighborhood. As Melville signs off, "The drama's done."

BENJAMIN'S OTHER INTERPRETATION of *Moby-Dick* can be found in just a single question written at the end of his pages devoted to Melville's novel. What if, Benjamin wonders, the *Pequod* is a modern version of Noah's ark and New York is the modern incarnation of the biblical city of refuge? I may be completely off base here, but it seems that this idea is rooted in a gnostic view of history, according to which the world in which we live exists in a perpetually flooded state. But there are always also arks that can save us from drowning. Great cities function like such arks. Redemption, in other words, is not an event in time but in space. It is, however, not a simple geographic location. In Melville's own words, "it is not down in any map; true places never are."

History is an endless body of water with no land in sight. The way to be saved is to climb aboard one of the ships adrift in its liquid infinity. When the exception becomes the rule, when the catastrophe is in no way special but rather quotidian, when the world exists in a state of "petrified unrest," when the apocalypse is not behind us or ahead of us but never ending (and thus usually unnoticed or at least bearable), it is still possible to create a place that will function as an exception to the exception. A city like New York is such a place. Benjamin calls it a "real state of exception," though a *city of exception* sounds better. This is not so far off from what Hegel calls the end of history but much closer to what may be called the end of geography.

Moby-Dick begins where the *Odyssey* ends: at home. These opposite journeys represent a simple way to distinguish between modernism and classicism. Despite what some adventurers may believe, a ship is not exactly a home. And if New York is a city of refuge from the perpetual flood, then it cannot be considered a proper home either. It is, rather, where one goes when one loses the protection of one's home. Let me explain. In biblical times, cities of refuge were established to protect those who were accused of accidental manslaughter and thus feared retribution from their victim's family. Within the boundaries of the city of refuge the offenders were protected from any harm. Anywhere else, though, it was permitted to kill them with impunity. The inhabitants of the cities of refuge were all pardoned on the day the High Priest in Jerusalem died. Then they were free to return to their original homes. An amusing consequence of this strange legal arrangement was that the priest's mother would frequently bring gifts to the residents of the cities of refuge in an attempt to dissuade them from praying for her son's premature death.

The serious point here has to do with the convoluted status of the city of refuge in biblical jurisprudence. Normally, killing a person was a grave transgression first proscribed in God's covenant with Noah and then by the Sixth Commandment. But the Israelites also created an exception, suspending the commandment's application to those who committed manslaughter. The next logical step was therefore the establishment of a city of refuge. This city functioned as a shelter that offered an exception to the exception. It protected within a prescribed space those living beings who were anywhere else forsaken. For Benjamin, every city is a city of refuge, or an exception to the exception. But because the position of the High Priest has remained vacant for millennia (following the destruction of the Temple in Jerusalem), no one can be pardoned anymore; no one can return home.

FOR MANY TWENTY-FIRST-CENTURY NEW YORKERS, visiting Times Square feels like visiting the parents. A sense of antagonistic, almost Oedipal unease arises when one confronts the fact that one is much more similar to a tourist than one is willing to admit. Similarly, the overwhelming presence of foreign-born residents makes it difficult to call New York an American city. By now it is as American as it is European, as Asian as it is African, as Caribbean as it is Russian, as Jewish as it is Christian. Hence, Henry James challenges the assumption that immigrants who arrive in New York are under an unspoken obligation to comply with the established form of life of the local residents. On the contrary. The natives, like James himself, must constantly adjust to newcomers: "To recover confidence and regain lost ground," he writes in *The American Scene*, "we, not they, must make the surrender and accept the orientation. We must go, in other words, *more* than half way to meet them; which is all the difference, for us, between possession and dispossession."

The sense of dispossession, of "alienism" as James calls it, or *refugism* as Benjamin dubs the same condition, is so deeply ingrained in the ethos of New York that the experience of immigrants and even tourists upon their arrival in the city is often its exact opposite. They tend to feel immediately at home in this place where everybody is, to some extent, homeless. The early twentieth-century novelist Thomas Wolfe can claim in this spirit that "one belongs to New York instantly, one belongs to it as much in five minutes as in five years," which sounds optimistic to the newcomer but vaguely pessimistic to the local. It takes some time to realize that this comfortable feeling of instant acceptance is not the result of the city's motherly embrace but of its motherlessness. Like in Neverland, the parents are missing in action. Every New Yorker possesses this sense of dispossession within this place of displacement. Every New Yorker is an Ishmael. New York is not a metropolis (mother city); it is an *orbapolis* (orphan city).

TWENTY-SECOND CHAPTER   ARENDT'S CITY

HANNAH ARENDT'S work in political philosophy draws much of its inspiration from her unique understanding of the constellation of ideas and practices, persons and institutions, artifacts and especially texts that we usually group together into the catch-all category of ancient Greece. She is particularly fascinated by the political culture of Athens, its central city-state. Like Heidegger, her teacher back in Germany, she assumes that our comprehension of the world in which we live now depends on our ability to decipher the world in which the Greeks lived then. Failing to come to terms with this primordial force that presumably propelled the Western tradition into being renders the present, not just the past, illegible.

But Athens is not the only exemplary city for Arendt's thought. There are at least two other places that help us understand where she is coming from, figuratively speaking. The first is New York, the city where she spent the second half of her life, after leaving her former country and teacher to their disastrous national-socialist adventure. The second is Rome. As a close reader of Augustine, Arendt must have noticed the parallels between the former's experience of the sack of Rome and her experience of the decline of New York. Like Rome, New York was an imperial city that seemed to be losing its sense of direction. One of New York's many maladies was that it basically went bankrupt. As a last resort, City Hall had turned to the White House for financial backing, but at the end of October 1975, only a month before Arendt's death, the president flatly denied the request. The *Daily News* crystallized this dismal moment with a pitch-perfect headline: "*Ford to City: Drop Dead.*"

Augustine, of course, couldn't have cared less whether Rome dropped dead or not. Arendt explains that the fall of Rome "was interpreted by Christians and pagans alike as a decisive event, and it was to the refutation of this belief that Augustine devoted thirteen years of his life." (It took Augustine the same number of years to write *City of God* as it took Benjamin to compose his *Arcades Project*.)

Augustine's point, Arendt continues, "was that no purely secular event could or should ever be of central import to man." Thus, he insisted that beyond the concrete yet temporary city of man lay the immaterial yet eternal city of God.

As a good Athenian, or a good New Yorker, Arendt must reject this Augustinian logic. She does her best to upend Augustine's report on the banality of the political city, as well as his homily on the radicality, depth, and goodness of the theological city. Instead, she holds on to the Greek belief that the only immortality to which humans can and should aspire does not await them in some heavenly realm. Only if they speak and act in ways that remain engraved in the hearts and minds of others do they stand a chance of attaining a semblance of eternity. Warhol calls this human achievement fame. Benjamin calls it profane redemption. Yet Arendt laments that today we tend to treat this aspiration as a mark of vanity.

AS WE HAVE SEEN, Benjamin understands Auschwitz as the place that realized "the most absolute *conditio inhumana* that has ever existed on earth." Arendt's philosophy is clearly behind his corollary attempt to show that, despite all evidence to the contrary, New York remains an exemplary expression of *The Human Condition*, the title of her masterpiece. As an aside, Benjamin adds that Augustine's *City of God* might aptly be renamed *The Divine Condition*.

In many of the pages he devotes to Arendt, Benjamin depicts New York as an efficient machine set to generate certain conditions for being human. Rather than deduce the meaning of the city from its human inhabitants, he asks himself what politico-economic structure makes it possible for human beings to live in it? He does not regard his paradigm case—twentieth-century New York—as a historical fact that belongs to our past. What he seeks is the hidden matrix of political and economic forces that informs the cities in which we are still living today.

The point of the exercise is not to discover our human nature but only to describe a context of, or to analyze conditions for, possible human existence. We will soon see how Benjamin comes to appreciate the economic structure of the city through his close reading of Jane Jacobs. But as long as the political matrix of the city is at stake, he is guided by the strange belief that although Arendt almost never discusses New York, almost all her descriptions of the political realm of ancient Greece are essentially allegories for her present. Guided by his earlier realization that the Parisian crowd was so crucial for Baudelaire that the poet rarely described it in explicit terms, Benjamin became convinced that whenever *The Human Condition* mentions Athens, it really means New York.

Consider, for example, the section in which Arendt claims that, for the Athenians, "the laws, like the wall around the city, were not results of action but products of making. Before men began to act, a definite space had to be secured and a structure built where all subsequent actions could take place, the space being the public realm of the *polis* and its structure the law: legislator and architect belonged in the same categories. But these tangible entities in and of themselves were not the content of politics (not Athens, but the Athenians, were the *polis*)." This passage is the source for some of Benjamin's major themes in *The Manhattan Project*: the dual critique of the legal form propagated by the state and the built form propagated by architecture, along with his underlying interest in what he sees as the city's lived form.

Laws and buildings may be important, but they are not a part of the *polis*; they are *prepolitical* in their very nature; they are merely two conditions (among many others) that must usually (but not necessarily) be met before we can begin to share our lives with one another. The space of a city like New York has less to do with its physical location than some might assume. In essence, the city "lies between people living together." Whenever we act and speak with one another, "we insert ourselves into the human world, and this insertion is like a second birth, in which we confirm and take upon ourselves the naked fact of our original physical appearance." Understood as this place of rebirth, the city is irreducible to a set of written rules, or an arrangement of physical structures, or a conglomerate of bare lives. Instead, the city is defined as a space for politics, as "the space where I appear to others as others appear to me."

In another example from *The Human Condition*, we can simply swap the names of the two cities: "One, if not the chief reason for the incredible development of gift and genius in New York, as well as for the hardly less surprising swift decline of the city, was precisely that from beginning to end its foremost aim was to make the extraordinary an ordinary occurrence of everyday life." As was the case in Athens, New York's public sphere—the space where people mutually display their gifts and values, their character and nerve—is ephemeral and fragile. It depends on the perpetuation of the extraordinary, without which it quickly collapses and ceases to exist.

As the writer Fran Lebowitz puts it in her *Metropolitan Life*, "the common good is not my cup of tea—it is the uncommon good in which I am interested." Although, physically speaking, Athens and Rome, Paris and New York are still standing, and although, for millions of people, these cities still function as a home, workplace, or tourist attraction, all of this means very little to Arendt. Once a metropolis is no longer an *uncommonplace*, it loses its political raison d'être.

Benjamin links this observation to the main, twofold lesson Arendt drew from seeing Eichmann in Jerusalem. She realized then that evil in modern times had lost its "quality of temptation"; it was no longer a diabolical desire that external society and our inner conscience must keep in check. But her more disturbing insight, though much less discussed, is that the good became a temptation instead. The target of prohibition has been shifting from doing wrong to doing right, and the subject of repression has gone from being wicked to being exceptional. In this atmosphere of stifling mediocrity, Arendt's city is supposed to be a source of political oxygen, an exception to the humdrum of our rule-driven society.

In the twenty-first century many people seem to come to New York less in order to appear and more, like Benjamin, in order to disappear. Seeing and hearing take priority over being seen and being heard. Blending in is appreciated; sticking out is less so. This does not change the fact that what happened during a city's golden age is here to stay: it is "in the very nature of things human that every act that has once made its appearance and has been recorded in the history of mankind stays with mankind as a potentiality long after its actuality has become a thing of the past." Cities, for Arendt, are not "holes of oblivion." They are memory bombs.

WHAT DISTINGUISHES Athens from New York and antiquity from modernity has something to do with the fact that today we use two words—*city* and *state*—to designate two very different entities. This distinction did not exist in ancient Greek, which explains why the word *polis* is usually translated as "city-state." The signature gesture in Arendt's philosophy is to show that our understanding of the present is muddled by our inability to make a conceptual differentiation that, for the ancients, was as clear as day. Above all, she claims that the Greeks' stark separation between their public and their private spheres, between their *polis* and their *oikos*, between politics and economy, has been losing its force in modernity.

Benjamin notes that we can just as easily claim the inverse. The citizens of the *polis* lacked a linguistic tool to fully comprehend a simple distinction of which we are well aware: the city and the state are only rarely conflated today. Nevertheless, Max Weber argues that "even in Antiquity the concept of the 'community' began its differentiation from that of the 'state.' To be sure, this only occurred with incorporation into the large Hellenistic and Roman states which robbed the city communities of their political independence." When the empire strikes, the city begins to murmur.

Because Arendt's thought was still very much caught up in the Athenian experience, the dual meaning of the *polis* does not receive the explicit attention it deserves. Still, Benjamin surmises that this is the implicit impetus behind her complex philosophical project. Arendt aimed to salvage the political from politics, to show why the empty speeches and camera-ready actions of professional politicians on TV have little to do with the deeds and words of those who occupy a true public sphere. This failure to incorporate a direct, continuous involvement of regular citizens in the decision-making process through their participation in city-hall councils is a tragedy that Arendt saw as the "lost treasure" of our revolutionary tradition.

Like Arendt, Benjamin also strove to "emphasize how the spirit of representative political discourse has conformed to that of empty chatter and civic gossip." It was this state-sanctioned, spectacular politics that Arendt strove to dismantle, and it was the city-nurtured public space for radical human interactions that she wished to see rise again. Modernity for her was a struggle between the *vita activa* and acts of state. She must have witnessed intimations of this during her years in New York, for example, in her friendship with W. H. Auden, who once wrote, "Private faces in public places are wiser and nicer than public faces in private places."

Such considerations enable Benjamin to structure the history of political thought as three leaps, each ushered in by the establishment of a new dualistic differentiation, by a new contrast between the city and its opposite. Ancient politics is based on the Aristotelian distinction between *polis* and *oikos*; medieval politics is grounded in the Augustinian separation of *civitate Dei* and *civitate hominum*; modern politics is defined by the Arendtian chasm between city and state. Although the city and the state are mutually dependent and are therefore complicit in the instigation and perpetuation of a myriad of modern ills, lumping the two together would be both analytically and strategically foolish. For both Benjamin and Arendt, the city is the alpha and omega of the coming politics.

TWENTY-THIRD CHAPTER   HERE COMES EVERYBODY

IN *THE NOTEBOOKS OF MALTE LAURIDS BRIGGE*, Rainer Maria Rilke offers a tested method for camouflaging, even for only a few hours, the unmistakable stain of poverty. Like Rilke himself (and like Benjamin a few years later), the semiautobiographical Malte comes to Paris in pursuit of his dream of literary success, which soon gives way to the reality of material destitution. In the streets, Malte's worn-out clothes do not fool the other poor, who instantly recognize him as one of their own. But because entrance to the French National Library is granted only to the holders of a special card, it also serves as a temporary shield, protecting those who can get in from the miseries of the outside world. Once the privileged patrons have passed the glass door and entered the grand reading hall, they are able to separate themselves from the less privileged crowd, from those "husks of people spat out by fate," take a seat next to Malte, or Rilke, or Benjamin, and read their book of choice in respectable silence.

In New York Benjamin experienced a very different situation. The Public Library's main branch, where he worked almost every day for the last thirty years of his life, does not require an identification card for entry or even for the use of its vast, noncirculating holdings. The building is truly open to the public. Its unadorned stacks are sacred after a fashion, in that the only people authorized to enter them are the library workers. But most of the rest of the sacrosanct building is designated for the free use of all and sundry.

Though the library is a public space, it also remains an unusually private place where people can think their own thoughts and write their own notes. With skyscrapers peeking through the huge windows of the main reading room and white clouds painted on its fifty-foot-high ceiling, its interior resembles an exterior. Despite this simulation of the outdoors, it gives its patrons a very intimate sense of being indoors, sometimes even more so than in their apartments, where small desks abut warm beds.

Part of the reason Benjamin is so intrigued by the library has to do with his odd belief that it is a model of Manhattan in miniature. The two rows of long tables in the main reading room on the third floor, one to the east and one to the west, represent for him the numbered streets. The walls of reference books on both sides stand for the Hudson and East Rivers. The red-tiled walkway in the middle is Fifth Avenue. And the book delivery desk at the very center of the hall is like the location of the library itself—a microcosm within a microcosm, within the microcosm that is Manhattan as a whole.

Free associations aside, Benjamin is mainly concerned here with the type of institution the Public Library embodies, which secretly sets the tone for the entire city. Hence the contrast with Malte's Parisian library. It is also instructive to think of the contrast between the Public Library and the university—another institution dedicated to higher learning, though one where Benjamin never found his proper place. The library, like the city, accepts you when you come and releases you when you go. There is no admissions committee as you arrive, no program during your stay, and no diploma ceremony as you depart. Once you enter, it is as if you have always been there; once you exit, it is as if you never have.

These considerations lead Benjamin to proffer a simple contrast between the logic of the city and that of the state. On the one hand, we have the idea of the modern nation-state as shell and shield, as an apparatus meant not only to include and protect within its borders certain elements, called citizens, but also to exclude and forsake others, who have no rights and little political significance. This is poignantly illustrated in Rilke's account of those who cannot enter the French National Library. On the other hand, Benjamin positions New York City (and its Public Library as its embryonic model) as a possible and viable alternative to this basic state logic. The city is a zone that facilitates the interconnection of different elements and the disconnection of others. The city is not a container for lives but their meeting point (not to be confused with a melting pot). Who you are is decided by whom you meet. By facilitating associations and interactions, the city also produces separations and isolations. In connecting certain lives, it disconnects others. Separation and disconnection are to the city what exclusion and forsaking are to the state: collateral damage.

The philosophical experiment Benjamin conducted in the Public Library led him to suspend, though not ignore, the ways in which we define different lives. He brackets off or passes over, without canceling or transcending, the ways by which we categorize various human beings. This position is surprisingly similar to the one he could have arrived at through "contacts"—sexual or otherwise, random or not—in and around the pornographic movie theaters a few blocks to the west on Forty-Second Street. It explains the near absence of direct engagement in his *Manhattan Project* with, for example, Jewish New York, or Working-Class New York, or Bohemian New York, or Gay New York, or any other representative ethnicity or gender, class or creed, borough or neighborhood, cultural milieu or political identity. His project is a search for neither human universality nor particularity but for a kind of "whatever singularity." To imagine a city is to imagine its sheer life both before and after, but not instead of, its different forms of life.

The Manhattan Project offers a new *raison de ville* as an alternative to the *raison d'état*. As a result, Benjamin can distance himself from the old saw that in New York, "everything is possible." As Arendt shows, that expression is actually a very good encapsulation of the logic of the totalitarian state, in which actions once unimaginable under lawful rule become the new, arbitrary state of affairs. Instead,

Benjamin sides here with E. B. White, who suggests that "in New York everything is optional." One can even opt out of the whole darn thing at any given moment.

DURING THE 1970s AND 1980s, as the surface of the city was gradually covered with graffiti, Benjamin noticed that the library's walls remained conspicuously untouched. How perplexing, he notes, given that the building seems to have only a limited security detail and that the adjacent Bryant Park is a rather dangerous place dominated by drug pushers and hobos. What better place to immortalize one's name (at least until the cleaning crew arrives) than this monumental building? Why did the graffiti writers decide to spare the library's white marble walls?

Benjamin, who had been fascinated by graffiti since its early days, when no one thought of this emerging practice as art, appears to offer one explanation by writing that, if he were once again a young man, he would try to climb to the library's roof and spray three letters over each of the three marble plaques above the main entrance that commemorate its principle founders: *H. C. E.* This is a clear enough reference to the protagonist of James Joyce's *Finnegans Wake*: Here Comes Everybody.

Benjamin knows that such radical democracy, reminiscent of the sentiment promoted by Walt Whitman, as simple as it is terrifying, is more wishful dream than concrete reality. For this reason it is usually pushed to the margins of his thought. "Today," Whitman writes in 1882, "I should say—defiant of cynics and pessimists, and with a full knowledge of all their exceptions—an appreciative and perceptive study of the current humanity of New York gives the directest proof yet of successful Democracy, and of the solution of that paradox, the eligibility of the free and fully developed individual with the paramount aggregate." With this logic in mind, Benjamin maintains that even though the random strangers who share the library's communal tables rarely utter a single word, as if each were encased in an impenetrable bubble, the sight of them would cause Whitman's ghost to flash one of his signature smiles.

A basic formulation of New York's logic can be found in Whitman's "Crossing Brooklyn Ferry." Its general form can be rendered as follows: Just as you *x*, I also *x*. A few examples: "Just as you feel when you look on the river and sky, so I felt. . . . It is not upon you alone the dark patches fall, the dark threw its patches down upon me also. . . . Nor is it you alone who know what it is to be evil, I am he who knew what it was to be evil." The interesting thing about these propositions is that they do not assume an equality between you and me, that you and

I have the same capabilities or opportunities. We are disintegrated and radically different from each other, and even from ourselves. A century and a half is only one of a thousand factors separating Whitman from you, and you from me, and me from me.

But in the end, those differences "avail not." Whitman feels closer to his speculative future readers, wherever they are, than he does to his sweaty fellow ferry travelers. Although his identity and destiny, his essence and existence, have everything to do with his own particular body, something, somehow, also "pours my meaning into you." This logic is not to be confused with empathy. Arendt claims that empathy is politically unadvisable and, in any case, that it is philosophically impossible to think or feel or be like someone else ("I can feel your pain," the candidate tells the crowd). Still, just as you can represent to yourself that which you do not perceive with your own eyes, just as you can enlarge your mentality by considering someone else's position, just as you can make present to yourself something that is otherwise absent, just as you can imagine a form of life that is not your own, so can I.

THIRD THRESHOLD   ECOPOLIS

NEW YORK IS A MULTISTABLE FIGURE, like that drawing reproduced in Ludwig Wittgenstein's *Philosophical Investigations* of a duck that can also be seen as a rabbit. We look at a multistable figure and see one thing, until it suddenly dawns on us that we can look at it in a completely different way. One perception of the duck-rabbit is not truer than the other, though we cannot see the two at the same time, and we do not get the full picture until we account for both.

Today, economy and politics can no longer be treated as two distinct phenomena. What Arendt was the first to notice and Benjamin the first to develop to its logical conclusion is that the modern erosion of the boundary line that used to divide *oikos* and *polis*, home and city, private and public, requires a completely new way of approaching the space in which we currently live. Benjamin calls this new spatial configuration an *ecopolis*.

An ecopolis can be defined as the field of tensions generated by the confluence of economic and political forces within a single place. It is a hybrid of the statist leviathan and the corporate behemoth, or the merging of biopower and biocapital. To appropriate Warhol's definition of pop, we could say that the birth of the ecopolis happened on the day that modernity "took the inside and put it outside, took the outside and put it inside," which is the same day Benjamin alluded to when he observed that "the street becomes room and the room becomes street."

New York can be seen as a living, breathing, multistable figure. This does not seem to mean much, because it is still possible to analyze the city by looking at it either as a *polis* (which was the goal of the third part of this book) or as an *oikos* (which is the aim of the next). But in reality, these two conceptual schemes through which we approach the urban space do not operate side by side, like two independent and incongruous systems, or like two giants trying not to step on each other's toes. It does not even make sense to speak here of synergy once we acknowledge that economics and politics are two complementary ways of looking at the very same city. A relativist approach is equally unhelpful because, as with a coin, both sides demand to be seen, even though they cannot see each other.

It is unclear whether Benjamin is inspired here by Spinoza's claim that thought and extension are two attributes of the same monistic substance. Maybe he is even influenced by Niels Bohr's claim that the famous double-slit experiment, in which light is measured either as a wave or as a particle, is not contradictory but complementary. But what is certain is that Benjamin is not offering policies concerning the right balance between political and economic forces, or strategies for either meshing or separating the two. Instead, he is looking for a new way of understanding and coping with this given urban parallax.

Modernity's schizophrenia could be said to stem not from the duality of church and state but from its inability to reconcile power and capital, public and private considerations, or political and economic interests, which often pretend to be sundered from one another. Unsurprisingly, neither of the two conflicting demands can ever be satisfied. There is a creeping, unshakable sense that politics is essentially a means to economic ends and that the opposite is no less true. This schizophrenia is not the consequence of an inability to embrace one path and jettison the other but the culmination of our failure to come to terms with the fact that these two paths are parallel tunnels leading to the same city.

NEW YORK BEGAN as New Amsterdam, an outpost of the West India Company. Its first inhabitants were employees of this international megacorporation, which was driven by one basic goal: to turn a profit for its shareholders back home. But it would be inaccurate to portray the origin of the city as a strictly private, economic enterprise. The West India Company was also one of the earliest examples of what we call today, with the ascent of China, state capitalism. New Amsterdam was a body politic as much as it was a body corporate. It was a company town as much as a Dutch colony. Its 1621 charter covers issues that have to do with signing contracts and trading goods as well as building castles and waging wars. The question of revenue and the question of sovereignty have been so intermingled since Gotham's earliest days that it is fair to say it has always been an ecopolis.

On the one hand, virtually every political issue today is an economic problem in disguise. State sovereigns are essentially governors of out-of-proportion households, and political actors cannot get off the ground without a direct hookup to big piles of cash. On the other, the private sphere has become a political battleground vying for public approval, and capitalist ventures cannot survive without persistent political lobbying and the occasional governmental bailout. It appears that no side is capable of letting the other go. One of the conspicuous results of this interpenetration of private and public is that the billionaire and the mayor end up being (quite conveniently) the very same person. But this is far from just a local phenomenon. When corporations act like governments and governments act like corporations, the whole planet can best be described not as a cosmopolis but as an ecopolis.

For clarity's sake, I have chosen to divide Benjamin's approach to the subject between the third and fourth parts of this book. But in *The Manhattan Project* private and public spheres are treated as if they were one and the same. One can still go to the trouble to distinguish throughout the manuscript between the traces of Arendt's theory of the urban polity and those of Jacobs's theory of the urban economy. Their texts clearly function as Benjamin's two, complementary handbooks for the twentieth-century city.

Since the nineteenth century, radical thought has been dominated by two basic options: communists wish to do away with the prevalent economic system (capitalism), and anarchists wish to do away with the prevalent political system (the sovereign nation-state). Instead of crushing either one, or even both, to pieces, Benjamin holds that today's true radical option is to find a way to penetrate both.

Which is not to say that we should accept the way things are. Not in the least. What it means is that "economic and political changes are inextricably intertwined and must be studied together"; that only those who can "hold two opposed ideas in the mind at the same time, and still retain the ability to function" effectively and differently in today's ecopolitical climate are capable of leading the urban revolution in the right direction.

BECAUSE OF AN ONGOING copyright dispute between the Walter Benjamin Archive in Berlin and the Public Library in New York, the present book includes no substantial quotations from the manuscript of *The Manhattan Project*. The sole exception is the following list, reproduced here with permission and without alterations. It shows how many of the main topics that occupied Benjamin during his years in Paris were transformed into his final work. But it denotes a tension rather than a progression. If the early project looks like a duck, the later project looks like a rabbit. They are basically two aspects of the same ecopolis. Needless to add, this simple list barely begins to express what Benjamin himself saw as the "contradictory and mobile whole that his convictions represent in their multiplicity."

The Arcades Project	*The Manhattan Project*
Karl Marx	Hannah Arendt
The Flâneur	The Homeless
Charles Fourier	Jane Jacobs
Jugendstil	Minimalism
Baron Haussmann	Robert Moses
The Collector	The Hoarder
The Interior	The Street
Dandyism	Punk
Iron Construction	Concrete Construction
Honoré Daumier	Woody Allen
Fashion	Architecture
Louis Auguste Blanqui	Joseph Ferdinand Gould
Gamblers, Prostitutes	Traders, Sandwich Men
The Arcade	The Shopping Mall
Louis Daguerre, Félix Nadar	Helen Levitt, Diane Arbus
Dream City, Freud, Jung	Suburban Dreams, Tafuri, Koolhaas
Honoré de Balzac	Henry Miller
Gaslight	Neon
The Commune	The Urban Revolution
Grandville	Steinberg
Social Movement	Art Movement
Baudelaire	Warhol/W. B.
Saint-Somonianism	Pragmatism

École Polytechnique	The New School
Hashish, Opium	Heroin, Crack
Hugo	Fitzgerald
The Doll, The Automaton	The Fashion Model, The Celebrity
The Capitalist City	The Nation-State
Advertising	Graffiti
The Panorama	Sheep Meadow
Nietzsche's Eternal Return	Spinoza's Substance
Bibliothèque Nationale de France	The New York Public Library
Modernism	Urbanism

FOURTH PART

It is more important to affirm the least sincere.

—FRANK O'HARA

THE LIBRARY

JUST AS THE CITY where Benjamin lived became the supreme object of his thought, the library where he worked took on mythical proportions. It is not a coincidence, he reasons, that the library's central building is located at the site of the old Croton Distributing Reservoir, on the corner of Forty-Second Street and Fifth Avenue. In the same place where librarians and readers have been browsing book-lined shelves for the past hundred years, there was once a nineteenth-century structure of similar size that contained more than twenty million gallons of potable water.

Today people think of Central Park as an exemplary model of a public initiative. Back then, the multitude of downtown residents saw the park as out of reach (the ride was too long and too expensive) and saw its function as out of touch with their everyday pressing needs. Their assessment becomes even more understandable once we compare Central Park with the necessity and vitality of the reservoir. The city's new water system was by far the most momentous civic enterprise of its time, replacing a spotty and shoddy network of unsanitary wells. It would be surpassed only at the beginning of the twentieth century by another system of underground tunnels, this time designed to transport not water but people.

Though the water system was forty-five miles long, from the Croton Dam in upstate New York to the city center in lower Manhattan, its truly powerful, most visible manifestation was the reservoir's Egyptian-style building on Fifth Avenue. Completed in 1842, it was strategically located on the summit of Murray Hill, the highest point overlooking the dense city to the south. In a landscape still dominated by natural elevation rather than an artificial skyline, a stroll along the parapet atop the reservoir's massive granite walls gave New Yorkers a commanding vista of "the whole city to the Battery; with a large portion of the harbor, and long reaches of the Hudson and East Rivers," as Edgar Allan Poe reports. For the city inhabitants in the streets below, the reservoir seemed to be the closest thing they had to the Athenian Parthenon.

THE AURA of the imposing reservoir began to fade as the nineteenth century came to a close, and tall new buildings rose up in the adjacent blocks. But for minds with even rudimentary mythical sensibilities, the source of water is always associated with the source of life. In this way, the reservoir can be approached as the rarely acknowledged heart of the city. A sacred place does not necessarily lose its force once a sacred structure on its grounds is demolished (think of the Temple Mount in Jerusalem). As New York became the center of the known universe in the twentieth century, the semisecret aura of this particular site only intensified, even though its original function was all but forgotten.

Located between Grand Central and Times Square (that is to say, between the hub of daily work and the hub of nightly leisure) or, by the end of Benjamin's life, between the headquarters of the United Nations on the East River and the military Intrepid Museum on the Hudson (that is to say, between a place of wishful peace and a place of wishful war), the library stands at the precise center of the capital of the twentieth century. For this reason, Benjamin regards its grounds as the very navel of the earth. This was a crucial realization for him, both philosophically and personally. Sitting in the magnificent main reading room, the holy of holies of the templelike edifice, he reflected on the significance of the wooden enclosure at the center of the hall—an area accessible only to the elect employees, where books are delivered to readers from the unfathomable depths of the stacks—and dubbed it the inner sanctum.

At the epicenter of the twentieth-century world stood nothing more, but nothing less, than a library. Not a temple, not a palace, not a market, not a square, not a monument, not a tower, not a park. A library. In the calm eye of modernity's storm sat an anonymous old man, working undisturbed for three decades on a strange book that might never be read. Our fantastic tale notwithstanding, it is still impossible to deny the concrete fact of the library's position at this precise point on earth. For Benjamin, it was the fountain that constantly refreshed his faith in the city's concealed truth: when stripped of all the distractions, all the things that people usually take to be the essence of this place (the power, the glory, the money, the spectacle, the architecture, the masses), at the city's (and hence the world's) center lies that odd thing called *thought*. New York, Zelda Fitzgerald once commented, is "more full of reflections than of itself."

But this thought, this life of the mind, is not a specific thought about a specific thing. Nor is it the accumulation of particular thoughts over time. A library is not just a container of knowledge or a depository of information, a mere facilitator and corroborator in the service of thinking. Just as a water well is not life but only a condition of life, the dumbwaiter that carries the books to the center of the reading room is not to be confused with the library's essence. The building's exterior and interior transmit the unequivocal message that before being a home for printed documents (which are mostly concealed from the eye and are by now almost superfluous), it is a functional monument to the potentiality of thought.

The central building in Rockefeller Center, in the shifting heart of Midtown Manhattan, is located eight blocks north of the library. If the focal point of the second half of the twentieth century's economic activity should be located any-where, this would be another good spot. The building has two main entrances. The famous one from the pedestrian plaza to the east is topped with a frieze de-picting the bearded god Wisdom. Above the opposite entrance on Sixth Avenue is a partially hidden, quite beautiful mosaic. At its center stands the goddess Thought. Some will object that this is just capitalist lip service. But for Benjamin it is another proof that philosophy is not necessarily a foreign body in the urban landscape, not just a Socratic gadfly that is supposed, at best, to disturb the peace of conceited city dwellers. His meditations on this subject imply that abstract thought may occupy the very nucleus of New York.

IN A CLOSELY RELATED fragment that at first seems rather bizarre, Benjamin recounts a dream he had in which the library's expansive main reading room was transformed into a gigantic public swimming pool, with bathers instead of readers jumping from the second floor's balconies into the deep, warm water. Presiding over the surreal scene from an elevated chair at the center of the hall was the chief lifeguard, identified by Benjamin as Thales of Miletus.

My interpretation of this dream is informed by the fact that the origin of Western philosophy is traditionally traced back to Thales, whose main claim to fame was his assertion that the entire universe is made out of water. Legend has it that one day, Thales was wandering alone while gazing at the stars, which caused him to trip and fall into a well. This story came to be understood as a metaphor for the perils of the life of the mind. But this interpretation contradicts another famous water-related anecdote about Thales. Having predicted that the ideal weather in the year to come would yield a bountiful olive crop, the philosopher bought on the cheap every olive press in Miletus and cornered the local oil market. This clever business venture was hardly at odds with Thales's lofty metaphysical work. In fact, both were based on the very same activity, *speculation*. Though his ideas and actions were based to some extent on certain facts or clues, Thales had no way of being sure that water was the elementary substance of the world or that the branches of the olive trees would be heavy with fruit that season (indeed, he happened to be wrong about the former).

In other words, there is nothing anomalous about the position of a library at the center of the capital of capitalism. Philosophers and businesspeople are both speculators who may trip or fall by investing their minds or funds in the wrong venture. As such, they can both be accused of engaging in speculative activities that either harm or contribute nothing to the reality in which we live. If we take Thales to be the patron saint not only of philosophy but also of economy, then *liquidity* could be said to be their shared mantra. Ideas, like things, are fungible. They flow from hand to hand, from mind to mind, from speculator to speculator. Thoughts, like commodities, are assessed less according to their use value than according to their exchange value. The consequence is that theory, like labor, can be a source of alienation rather than satisfaction.

THE SECOND FLOOR of the Public Library used to house an economics department, complete with up-to-date information about stocks, bonds, and other investment opportunities. Before the big Wall Street crash, the place was abuzz with men and women poring over the comprehensive reference volumes for long hours. Occasionally, someone would rush to the public telephones at the end of the hall, from which an order could be communicated to a downtown broker. "No one knows or is willing to state that the market is actually played from the quiet seclusion of the Library," an anonymous *New Yorker* scribe opined in 1926, "but it is easy to imagine so."

TWENTY-FIFTH CHAPTER # THE ECONOMY OF PHILOSOPHY

ONE DAY A GROUP OF ADMIRERS came to see Heraclitus at his home in Ephesus. To their consternation, they found the great philosopher hunched over the hearth, warming his old bones. Since they were hesitant to enter his intimate abode, Heraclitus implored them not to be afraid and invited them in by saying that "even in the kitchen divinities are present."

For Aristotle this anecdote is meant to show that everything in nature can provoke wonder, even the least developed forms of life. Another interpretation of Heraclitus's gesture is that it eliminates the threshold between inside and outside, between *oikos* and *polis*. Philosophy, he seems to be telling his visitors, has a place not only in the agora but also by the stove. Remember in this context that modern philosophy begins when Descartes, dressed in a nightgown, invites the readers of his *Meditations* into his home. He too is sitting next to a fireplace, wondering if it is all just a dream.

Whereas Thales believed the universe to be made of water, Heraclitus was convinced that it was made of fire. This idea probably had to do with the fact that the fireplace carried a very special meaning for the Greeks. They maintained a public hearth with an eternal flame (not a water reservoir) at the center of every city. They also considered the hearth to be the sacred center of every home.

The hearth had its own goddess, Hestia. She was considered the protector of the household and, by extension, the patron of economy (*oikonomia* designated for the Greeks, as it often does for Benjamin, all matters pertaining to the home). According to mythology, Hestia gave up her seat in the assembly of the twelve Olympian gods to Dionysus, presumably to avoid conflict. This detail reflects the Greek hyperpolitical, public mind-set that tended to undermine the importance of the home, the home that Hestia was unwilling to leave. When the gods followed Zeus on an excursion, she was the only one who had to stay behind. Hestia is thus rarely mentioned in the texts of the ancient Greeks and only scantly represented in their surviving artifacts.

But it was impossible for the Greeks to simply let go of the goddess who gave stability to their very homes and cities. For this reason she still received the first part of every sacrifice and was often invoked first in prayers and oaths. Relying on the scholarly work of Jean-Pierre Vernant, Benjamin claims that Hestia even makes a cameo appearance at the end of Plato's *Republic*, where she is disguised as the goddess Necessity. There she is depicted enthroned at the center of the universe in the middle of a vertical shaft of light, holding on her knees a spindle "whose movement controls the rotation of all the celestial spheres." She herself may be immobile, but she is the principle of motion of everything around her. This duality is present in Hestia's very name, which, as Plato explains elsewhere, derives not only from *ousia*, "immutable and permanent essence," but also from *osia*, "the impetus of movement." Hestia, in short, represents what Aristotle will later call the unmoved mover.

GIVEN THIS RICH CLASSICAL TRADITION, Benjamin wonders how political thought came to be such an integral part of Western philosophy, while serious economic thought is almost always pushed to its margins. To this day, material considerations are usually deemed unworthy of the philosophical sanctuary. Even Marx, who ridiculed this intellectual bias better than any other great philosopher, once confessed in a letter to Engels that he was exasperated with his ongoing research into the entire "economic shit" (*ökonomische Scheiße*). He said that he wanted to be done with it in five weeks. It took him another thirty years.

Benjamin's own philosophy of economy begins with a short meditation on something that is called "the economy of philosophy." He claims that the most abstract philosophical work is still precisely that: a kind of work, labor, drudgery even. It is less a matter of inspired good ideas than of acquired good skills. A profound philosophical thought has to be scrupulously governed, directed, and organized. The economy of a good argument determines whether it will thrive or go bust. Notions and ideas must be repeatedly ordered and reordered, dusted off and polished up. Philosophers are essentially housekeepers, though they will rarely admit this humbling truth. Wittgenstein did, at least when he likened his method to "the tidying up of a room where you have to move the same object several times before you can get the room really tidy."

The myth of Sisyphus is the myth of the philosopher, and the search for the good life begins in the kitchen: "Happiness," Benjamin writes in *The Arcades Project*, "has its recipes like any pudding. It is realized on the basis of precise measuring out of different ingredients. It is an effect." The result is that any viable economy, including that of true philosophy, can have no end. This is not to say that it is an impractical endeavor. "My father," Wittgenstein confessed, "was a businessman and I am a businessman too: I want my philosophy to be business-like, to get something done, to get something settled."

HERE IS A GOOD EXAMPLE of the interpenetration of philosophy and economy. Consider one of the most basic questions imaginable, the one that stands at the foundation of every ethics: "What should I do?" Benjamin claims that the real ethos (Greek for "dwelling place") of New York makes sense only once we employ two complementary categorical imperatives, which, in their almost embarrassing simplicity, dramatically depart from the famous one proposed by Kant ("Act only according to that maxim whereby you can at the same time will that it should become a universal law"). Benjamin's first, philosophical imperative is that one ought to "always do the right thing." The second, economic imperative is that, while you're at it, also make sure that you "get paid." These elementary demands, neither of which makes much sense independently of the other, generate the basic tension that drives Spike Lee's *Do the Right Thing*, a film released two years after Benjamin's death. There is also a third, political imperative that literally plays in the background of the entire film, which is that "we've got to fight the powers that be." But this is another issue.

A masterpiece of New York cinema, the film treats two questions that were rarely conflated in ancient Athens but are inseparable in modern New York: how to live and how to make a living. The dual concerns are in no way particular to Mookie, the film's protagonist, whose life revolves around a single block in Brooklyn where he lives and works as a delivery boy at Sal's Pizzeria. The philosophical and economic imperatives, explicitly cited in key moments throughout the film, apply to worlds far beyond the microcosm it depicts.

Most of us do our best to reconcile the need to do the right thing with the need to get paid. Though we meet with varying degrees of success or failure, we belong to the same group. A second, smaller group consists of those who decide to live in accordance with only one of these basic competing demands and neglect the other. Whether one dedicates one's entire existence solely to the philosophical imperative or solely to the economic one, such monomania invariably leads to ruin. A third, even smaller group consists of those who live their whole lives unbothered by both material and spiritual questions. It consists of children who die at a very young age.

If there is such a thing as an afterlife, the first group will end up in heaven, the second in hell, and the third in limbo. Of those born with a silver spoon in their mouths Dorothy Parker once remarked, "If you want to know what the Lord God thinks of money, you have only to look at those to whom he gives it." Of those who obey the divine word and thus never have to ask whether they are doing the right thing, Woody Allen remarks, "God is a luxury I can't afford."

TWENTY-SIXTH CHAPTER   **BUSINESS ART**

THE PHILOSOPHY OF ANDY WARHOL begins with a transcript of a phone conversation between A (Warhol) and B (his friend Brigid Berlin). They have both just gotten out of bed. A casual chat revolves around subjects ranging from ways to deal with pimples ("If someone asked me, 'What's your problem?' I'd have to say, 'Skin'"), to tricks for falling asleep ("The thing is to think of nothing, B. Look, nothing is exciting, nothing is sexy, nothing is not embarrassing. The only time I ever want to be something is outside a party so I can get in"), and back to cosmetics ("I don't really use makeup, but I buy it and I think about it a lot. Makeup is so well-advertised you can't ignore it completely"). The book ends with A and B shopping at Macy's, during which Warhol says, "I think buying underwear is the most personal thing you can do, and if you could watch a person buying underwear you would really get to know them. I mean, I would rather watch somebody buy their underwear than read a book they wrote."

What does Warhol's book have to do with philosophy? In the same way Truman Capote describes Holly Golightly as a "*real* phony," Warhol claims that his goal is to do things "*exactly* wrong," because then "you always turn up something." It is hard to imagine a more wrong way of doing philosophy than Warhol's. But instead of saying that it is not philosophy, let us try to rethink what philosophy is. Why do we assume that all those private, intimate, domestic, or economic issues that occupy his mind should be excluded from the philosophical discourse? And why did we once think that the same issues should be excluded from art—until Warhol entered the scene? And is there some truth behind Wallace Stevens's suggestion that "money is a kind of poetry"?

Art in the classical world was inseparable from the public realm of politics. Art in the medieval world was inseparable from the spiritual realm of religion. Art in the modern world is inseparable from the private realm of economy. Nobody understood the last proposition better than Warhol. Modernity did all that it could to resist this linkage and pretend that art occupies an autonomous field. From Kant's idea of disinterested beauty, through the nineteenth-century Parisian movement of *l'art pour l'art*, to Clement Greenberg's distinction between avant-garde and kitsch (the latter, he wrote, "pretends to demand nothing of its customers except their money—not even their time"), the attempt to fend off the economic onslaught on art seemed to be working. With Warhol, the two spheres collapse into one:

> Business art is the step that comes after Art. I started as a commercial artist, and I want to finish as a business artist. After I did the thing called "art" or whatever it's called, I went into business art. I wanted to be an Art Business-man or a Business Artist. Being good in business is the most fascinating kind of art. During the hippie era people put down the idea of business—they'd say, "Money is bad," and "Working is bad," but making money is art and working is art and good business is the best art.

But Warhol was only running a tongue-in-cheek business. His so-called Factory of the 1960s, like the corporate office he ran during the 1970s and 1980s, was a queer and crude version of the genuine article. He was a most peculiar boss, and the people in his studio made for a weird workforce. In such a factory, it is impossible to speak of an assembly line or a business strategy with a straight face. Compared with the ultracapitalist phase of our economy—streamlined and sleek, technocratic and global, hands-free and out of hand—everything Warhol did seems so amateurish, and probably intentionally so. The do-it-yourself feel was present throughout: from his early commercial illustrations from the 1950s with their delicate blotted lines, all the way to his TV shows from the 1980s, which look anything but professional, often in the most hilarious, campy ways.

It is as much a mistake to blame Warhol for the mingling of art and economy as it is to praise him for inventing it. He merely comprehended this fundamental modern truth and brought it to its logical conclusion at the moment when it could no longer be ignored. He discovered that one of the best ways to resist the "aestheticization of the commodity," which happens mainly through advertisement, was by means of the complete and utter commodification of art. Taking his cue from Warhol's observation that "department stores are kind of like museums,"

Benjamin has no qualms about his (accurate) prediction that museums will soon turn into department stores. No wonder that the array of artworks in a museum, like the array of commodities in a bazaar, often triggers in the visitor "the notion that some part of this should fall to him as well."

Warhol's approach is more honest than we might assume. When asked by a TV reporter why he bothered to copy a common item that was readily available instead of creating something new, he replied that it was easier to do so. Other artists, he explained, work so hard to resist things that anyone can notice. It is not a coincidence that many of the overlooked themes he took up in his art are economic in nature: from foodstuffs to cleaning products, from advertisements to celebrities, from dollar bills to corporate logos. Ease can be extremely deceptive. It is not easy to notice that which is hidden as a consequence of its simplicity and familiarity (Wittgenstein would say that this is the very task of philosophy). Benjamin argues that once Warhol "got a glimpse of the field of debris left behind by capitalist development," he used his art as "the object of a research no less impassioned than that which the humanists of the Renaissance conducted on the remnants of classical antiquity." For Warhol, however, antiquity was yesterday.

BENJAMIN CONSIDERS SIX of the films Warhol made in the 1960s as the testament to the artist's unique ability to do away with fine art's anti-economic defense mechanism. These films can be seen as a pair of trilogies: The first consists of *Sleep*, *Eat*, and *Drink*; the second, of *Kiss*, *Blow Job*, and *Fuck* (later renamed *Blue Movie*). Each film depicts exactly what the title advertises and almost nothing else, with no embellishments, and for a boringly long time. *Sleep* is more than five hours of a shirtless man snoozing, *Eat* is more than forty minutes of a guy in a fedora slowly consuming a mushroom, and so forth. These mundane or intimate activities, these domestic and thus deeply economic moments, which are traditionally kept out of public sight, are nonchalantly placed on the pedestal of high art. As does his later book of philosophy, his art films take the elements of our bare life, the necessities of life that we usually take care of within the privacy of our *oikos*, and put them at the center of the *polis*. "Our movies may have looked like home movies," he once commented, "but then our *home* wasn't like anybody else's."

Benjamin is surprised by how easily one can make the opposite move: Warhol not only took the inside and put it outside. He also took the outside and put it inside. Think, for example, of his Mao portraits, which he reproduced in stark colors as a wallpaper, over which more proper paintings could be hung. Here street propaganda turns into interior design. Think also of his silk screens of newspaper clippings, celebrity shots, and other mass-produced images. How odd it must be to live in a house with one of those works hanging on the wall—with all those public faces in private places. Yet the point of all these exercises, Benjamin clarifies, is not the exposure of "the economic origins of culture" but the discovery of "the expression of the economy in its culture."

Perhaps the most interesting example of this process of economization is Warhol's approach to his own fame. His first work as a commercial artist was for the magazine article "Success Is a Job in New York." Traditionally, exposure to the public eye, the multitudes' admiration for one's acts or words or works, is considered a quintessentially political phenomenon. But Warhol transforms fame into just another economic function. He insists, for example, that there is nothing special about being a famous artist in a city like New York. It is just another job: "Bianca [Jagger] was driving me crazy," he writes in his (private?) diary, "saying how she's researching my days in Pittsburgh for her book on Great Men, and she went on and on about how I broke the system, broke the system, broke the system, and I felt like saying, 'Look, Bianca, I'm just *here*. I'm just a working person. How did I break the system?' God, she's dumb."

When Warhol became famous, he began to receive many invitations to give lectures in colleges around the country. Instead of bothering to leave New York, he asked an actor named Allen Midgette to impersonate him on one of those tours. The hoax lasted until the day Midgette decided not to put on his usual makeup. Until that point, the actor was for all intents and purposes a human silk screen, a copy of the man who copied images and called them art. This makes sense, especially as there is no other visual artist whose own image and likeness are as well known as his works. Marcel Duchamp is the only notable precedent, though he was not nearly as prolific as Warhol. Should we say then that Warhol's life was his greatest masterpiece? Or was he an artifact of sorts? But if life is a work of art, and art is a business, was his life then just a commodity?

To answer these questions, we need to take a short detour. In Christianity, the words *Christ* and *Messiah* are synonyms. Yet "Jesus Christ" is usually misunderstood as a proper name, like "Walter Benjamin." The reason is that "Jesus Christ" is a very strange formulation, first introduced by Paul of Tarsus, which really means, "Jesus Messiah." The more grammatically sound construction would be "Jesus is the Messiah." Yet for Paul the meaning of faith is not to believe that *messiah* is an attribute attached to the subject *Jesus*, in the same way that we say that the sky is blue or that Socrates is wise. The meaning of faith is that one believes in "Jesus Messiah," and the lack of space between the two words keeps any contingency from creeping in (maybe he is, but maybe he isn't).

This is how Benjamin understands the formulation "Andy Warhol Enterprises." The name of the company that handled all his art business from 1957 until his death is not called "Andy Warhol's Enterprises." It is impossible to distinguish between Warhol the man and Warhol the business, between the life and the art. The space between *Andy* and *Warhol* is as insubstantial as that between *Warhol* and *Enterprises*. Benjamin did not believe that Warhol was a string of different enterprises. He believed in Andy Warhol Enterprises.

TWENTY-SEVENTH CHAPTER   # MODES OF ASSOCIATED LIFE

THE PHILOSOPHY OF ECONOMY has a name, and no, it is not Objectivism. Benjamin never even bothered to criticize Ayn Rand. Instead, *The Manhattan Project*'s position can be characterized as a brand of pragmatism. Pragmatism is a philosophical movement with deep roots in New York, the city where William James spent the first years of his life as a curious child, where John Dewey spent the last years of his life as a revered professor, and where Charles Sanders Peirce spent the saddest years of his life as an occasionally homeless person on the lam (after being charged with the "aggravated assault and battery" of his servant). These biographical notes about the fathers of pragmatism are not entirely inconsequential, especially if we remember that one of their basic beliefs is that ideas do not operate in a void. Ideas respond to and depend on human beings in their particular situations. They are embedded in what Dewey calls "modes of associated life." Ideas prevail not because they have an immutable inner logic but because they adapt to the social environment at hand.

To elaborate, consider the rationale for upholding free speech. This, the pragmatist will argue, has little to do with the individual's right to express his or her private opinions. Free speech is much more securely grounded in the communal responsibility to allow all sorts of ideas to compete with one another in an open intellectual market. Truth can be approximated only if we allow many different people to exchange many contradictory ideas, some of them foolish, bad, or extremely harmful. We have to let these ideas run their natural course in the public square, which at times seems more like a jungle. We can then witness which ones survive and which ones fail—an outcome that often leads anyone other than a staunch pragmatist to lose faith in such a delicate process.

The "marketplace of ideas," a notion credited to Oliver Wendell Holmes Jr. (the Supreme Court justice who was an old friend of Peirce and James), is only one among many pragmatist ideas based on analogies drawn from economics. James, for example, speaks of the need to attend to the "cash-value" of our conceptions by insisting that sooner or later ideas must be "cashed in." He even claims that truth is based on a "credit system," by which he means that "our thoughts and be-liefs 'pass,' so long as nothing challenges them, just as bank-notes pass so long as nobody refuses them. But this all points to direct face-to-face verifications some-where, without which the fabric of truth collapses like a financial system with no cash-basis whatever. You accept my verification of one thing, I yours of another. We trade on each other's truth." Curiously, while the New York Stock Exchange, in a colossal show of mutual mistrust, has crashed more than once since James wrote these lines, the truth exchange in this city, though certainly fluctuating, is arguably much less fragile than the financial one.

🐦

"WE ARE FREE," Dewey writes, "not because of what we statically are, but insofar as we are becoming different from what we have been." This means that liberty is the harbinger of insecurity and uncertainty. It is a gamble. Given Peirce's claim that our beliefs are essentially bets, we cannot know for sure that we have placed our chips on the right square in this pragmatist roulette. If beliefs, as James elabo-rates, "are really rules for action" and if "thinking is but one step in the produc-tion of habits of action," then the philosophical quest for an unshakable certainty seems quixotic at best. In a pragmatist world, life is conceived as a continuous experiment. Yet no individual experiment (my life, your life) exists or matters in and of itself. The odds of the society as a whole decide, and are decided by, the individual bets each of us makes as we live the lives we live and hold the beliefs we hold among a sea of other gamblers.

A city, like a life, tends to unfold as a constant process of trial and error, winning and losing. Though rules and habits do get formed along the way, our attachment to them is not one of conviction but of convenience, like it or not. A pragmatist city, therefore, can have no specific goals in mind other than the shifting goals that converge with those of life itself, which is always multiple. A city is less a place to realize or express what you are. It is more a place you go to become what you are not, maybe what you never even thought that you could or should be, by discovering things you do not even seek. "Each thought, each day, each life lies here as on a laboratory table," Benjamin writes about the city. "And as if it were a metal from which an unknown substance is by every means to be extracted, it must endure experimentation to the point of exhaustion. No organism, no organization, can escape this process."

Benjamin's interpolation of Peirce's pragmatic maxim becomes a basic analytic tool in his urban philosophy: "Consider what effects, which might conceivably have practical bearings, we conceive New York to have. Then, our conception of these effects is the whole of our conception of this city." If New York is the sum of its effects, then there can be no a priori theory of New York. Pragmatism, after all, is less a theory than a method to "unstiffen" our various theories, to use another of James's quirky terms. It enables Benjamin to guide his *Manhattan Project* through a closer receptiveness and larger responsibility to the concrete object of his investigation.

Whatever ideas we may have of the city can only arise from our experience of actually living in it. "Concepts," Dewey writes, "are so clear; it takes so little time to develop their implications; experiences," however, "are so confused, and it requires so much time and energy to lay hold of them." Benjamin admits that his limited, conceptual approach to New York can only scratch the metropolitan surface. It can neither change nor rectify the place. But like a guidebook, his philosophy can also orient readers as they experience, or experiment with, the city, themselves, and each other.

THINK OF THE PRAGMATIST METHOD as a city street with different entrances to a variety of old and new edifices, residential and municipal buildings, small shops and large department stores, fine restaurants and sleazy bars. Like the street and the city as a whole, pragmatists tend to be "completely genial" toward these different enterprises, disparate activities, and mixed uses. Like entrepreneurs, they are willing to take anything, to entertain contradictory possibilities, without losing sight of the profit (not necessarily monetary) that may be gained from taking this rather than that route. But this is not utilitarianism. This is ethics. Its basic assumption is that reality, not hell, is other people.

A pragmatist life is consequently the exact opposite of a monomaniacal existence, like that of *Moby-Dick*'s Ahab. And a pragmatist city is the exact opposite of a universe. It is, rather, closer to what James calls a "pluriverse." During his visit to New York, Jean-Paul Sartre wrote, "Nowhere more than here can you feel the simultaneity of human lives." Benjamin takes this a step further by calling simultaneity "the basis of the new style of living." But as much as this simultaneous experience of multiple lives in New York City must have informed the first pragmatists' vision, Louis Menand argues in *The Metaphysical Club* that the gruesome experience of the American Civil War gave these thinkers a clear picture of what they were trying to avoid. The main problem with abstract metaphysical convictions or unwavering ultimate truths, with fixations on certain principles or ideals, is not necessarily that they are wrong or even nonsensical but that they are just plain dangerous. There is no light at the end of tunnel vision.

Ever since the disturbing experience of the Industrial Revolution set the argument of *Capital* in motion, a similar ideological fervor has informed our approach to economics. Dewey follows Marx in admitting that material means determine our human ends. Yet he does not join those who push "industry and its material phase out into a region remote from human values." He senses that there is a secret alliance between those who distance themselves from the inhuman economic field for the sake of personal dignity and those who use the economic order for selfish monetary gain. So he avoids this convenient separation of politics and economics, democracy and industry, ethics and business. Instead, he delineates a more transparent alliance between the public and private spheres, one that tries to sidestep the traps of cruel individualistic capitalism and ruthless collectivist statism. For this reason Benjamin crowns Dewey the secret philosopher-king of ecopolis.

🐦

THERE IS MORE, but the bottom line is that no one really knows what needs to be done or what is right, or true, or good. Those who claim otherwise are simply trying to bend reality to their own arbitrary will. We are all shooting in the dark, which means that we usually, unknowingly, end up shooting one another. But some of us, by sheer chance, end up hitting an unseen target. What the pragmatist cares about is not those rare flickers (or flukes) of so-called great (or privileged) men who leave behind them so-called immortal (or hegemonic) legacies. The pragmatist's aim, instead, is to figure out ways to intensify, magnify, and, most important, *complexify* the conditions by which more people, and different people, take part in this gigantic human experiment.

This is what a city like New York does best. Jacobs's epigraph for *The Death and Life of Great American Cities*, which she borrows from Holmes, says precisely this: "The chief worth of civilization is just that it makes the means of living more complex; that it calls for great and combined intellectual efforts, instead of simple, uncoordinated ones." This is desirable, Holmes argues, because "more complex and intense intellectual efforts mean a fuller and richer life. They mean more life. Life is an end in itself, and the only question as to whether it is worth living is whether you have enough of it."

TWENTY-EIGHTH CHAPTER   JACOBS'S CITY

IT WOULD BE DIFFICULT to overstate the impact of Jane Jacobs's urban trilogy on the overarching argument of *The Manhattan Project*: not only her canonical *The Death and Life of Great American Cities* (1961) but also, or mainly, her much neglected sequels, *The Economy of Cities* (1969) and *Cities and the Wealth of Nations* (1984). One can trace the most dramatic swerves in Benjamin's later thought to the date of these publications.

There is a textbook method to defuse a powerful philosophy that threatens to reshape the world. All one needs to do is extract from it a simple and convenient single idea. This catchy idea should be potent enough to bring about some exciting change. But because it is isolated from the context in which it was meant to be understood, its impoverished realization—which can be easily manipulated by those already in power, those who avoid making the smallest adjustment to the status quo—appears to prove that the original thought was a dud.

It is thus that a sanitized version of Jacobs's revolutionary theory, based on a simplistic and selective reading of only certain sections from her first book, was enough to completely alter the way we have perceived, built, and lived in cities for the past fifty years. But her most famous idea is also one of her most problematic ones, especially when it stands alone, isolated from the rest of her urban philosophy. As is often the case, Saint Jane was beatified for the wrong reasons.

Jacobs's philosophy is often reduced to her celebrated city-as-choreography metaphor. The modernist planners that preceded her, so the argument goes, perceived the urban landscape as a "simple-minded precision dance with everyone kicking up at the same time, twirling in unison and bowing off en masse." Jacobs, instead, envisioned the city as this "intricate ballet in which the individual dancers and ensembles all have distinctive parts which miraculously reinforce each other and compose an orderly whole."

The consensus before Jacobs entered the scene was that, in the name of so-called urban renewal, old neighborhoods, perceived as slums, must be replaced by efficient and monotonous new housing projects that eliminate the street grid. Jacobs did not buy the solution of winding paths for pedestrians and fast highways for cars. She believed in the power of short, lively, existing streets with their healthy mix of buildings from different periods, designed in different styles, which lend themselves to a variety of uses and users, all of which intermingle to form an "organized complexity."

A city is not a work of art. Jacobs argues that treating the urban landscape as a disciplined artwork "is to make the mistake of attempting to substitute art for life. The results of such profound confusion . . . are neither life nor art. They are taxidermy." One of the greatest compliments Jacobs accords a building, street, neighborhood, or a city as a whole is that it is "unselfconscious." The ego of the architect, engineer, and planner, those who fix their ideas in iron and concrete, must dissolve in the fluid bloodstream of city life. The streets that Descartes snubbed ("it is chance rather than the will of some men using reason that has arranged them thus") are the ones Jacobs taught us to cherish.

The problem is that all our big plans to overhaul our great modernistic cities end up producing a space so self-conscious that it is either awkward or perverse. Even more problematically, these plans "render us unadaptable. We can't adjust to the changes they did not foresee. We can hardly even acknowledge the changes as they become evident." Life, Jacobs continues, is an "ad hoc affair. It has to be improvised all the time because of the hard fact that everything we do changes what is." These are the sorts of statements that led Benjamin to declare Jacobs the heiress apparent to the pragmatist throne.

For those who prefer to see things beautifully planned out and settled once and for all, the wild shifts and organic flows of big cities can be very distressing. "What is responsible for their present emptiness," Lewis Mumford writes in his condescending review of *The Death and Life*, "is something Mrs. Jacobs disregards: the increasing pathology of the whole mode of life in the great metropolis, a pathology that is directly proportionate to its overgrowth, its purposeless materialism, its congestion, and its insensate disorder—the very conditions she vehemently upholds as marks of urban vitality."

Benjamin was a great admirer of Mumford's bleak urban view until he experienced a conversion while reading Jacobs's first book. "I had my doubts about him," Jacobs reminisced about Mumford in a late interview, "because we rode into the city together in a car. And I watched how he acted as soon as he began to get into the city. And he had been talking and all pleasant but as soon as he began to get into the city he got grim, withdrawn, and distressed. And it was just so clear that he just hated the city and hated being in it. And I was thinking, you know, this is the most interesting part!"

BUT HERE'S THE CATCH. The problematic outcome of this Jacobsian approach, the direct result of her way of looking at cities, is the rise of today's gentrified neighborhoods, with their cute little boutiques, artisanal restaurants, and high-end mom-and-pop shops. "Just as nature heals the wounds of old castles with greenery," Benjamin writes with Paris on his mind, "so here a bustling bourgeoisie has settled down and calmed the strife of the metropolis." Rather than function as safe havens for regular folk (as Jacobs hoped), gentrified neighborhoods turn one by one into exclusive spaces of luxury living.

In the hands of savvy real estate brokers the jargon of authenticity is a marketing ploy, transforming larger and larger swaths of the city into pure fetish (the names alone are enough to evoke their aura: Greenwich Village, SoHo, Williamsburg). The irresistible attraction of certain neighborhoods is in many ways their undoing. This may explain how Jacobs's modest home, at 555 Hudson Street in the West Village, where she raised three children and wrote two books until 1968, became a multimillion-dollar asset currently occupied by a retailer of one-of-a-kind, hand-crafted cups that cost fifty bucks a pop. There was simply no way that during the last years of her life, at the beginning of the twenty-first century, Jacobs could have afforded to live in the very neighborhood she helped transform into a precious gem.

Jacobs knew that there is very little one can do to fight gentrification. Grieving the good-old neighborhood as it vanishes from one month to the next was not for her. New York, at any rate, is always vanishing. As soon as the first espresso bar opens, it is possible to move to the next new urban frontier, though this strategy seems only to perpetuate the problem rather than solve it. As thrifty development gives way to stagnant opulence, even those who can still somehow afford the neighborhood tend to find it stultifying. "When a place gets boring," Jacobs joked not long before her death, "even the rich people leave."

The fashionable twentieth-century attitude toward a city like New York was to sigh at its decay. Today, the fashionable attitude is to sigh at its revitalization. Neither comportment helps us even begin to understand how cities really work. To do that, we will need to approach Jacobs's theory in a less superficial way. We must move from the microlevel of a neighborhood block to first account for the city as a whole and then zoom out even more in order to see its place within the overall economic system.

This move, which becomes possible in the two sequels to *The Death and Life*, is what enabled Benjamin to finally let go of the ready-made economic theories that are all too often the lens through which we observe how cities work. Rather than investigate the material conditions of urban development, Jacobs dedicates her work to the urban conditions of any possible material development. Picking up where Smith and Marx left off, she inaugurates nothing less than a paradigm shift in the field of economics.

TWENTY-NINTH CHAPTER   # HOW NEW WORK BEGINS

POLITICAL ECONOMY, just like political philosophy, begins with a myth of origins. Remember Hobbes's story about the state of nature and Rousseau's story about the noble savage. Every prehistoric tale about the birth of politics from where the wild things were is a hypothetical construct. No one knows for sure how humans first banded together in organized communities or how they lived beforehand. But when philosophers develop theories of our shared existence, the attempt to explain how things turned out the way they did is irresistible, almost inevitable. The theory then feeds the myth, as the myth feeds the theory. This is true of *The Manhattan Project* as well.

The crucial piece of the economic myth of prehistoric origins was made famous by Adam Smith in the eighteenth century, taken up without much modification by Marx in the nineteenth, and accepted as a given by intellectuals from a variety of disciplines and ideological schools in the twentieth. Until, that is, Jacobs called the mythology into question in the opening chapter of *The Economy of Cities*.

Smith and company consider the invention of agriculture to be the major leap in the development of *homo economicus*. Beforehand, the story goes, our food supply was dependent on seasonal hunting and gathering. Agriculture allowed us to produce our own sustenance in a more organized and predictable manner and made us less dependent on Mother Nature. We ceased to roam the land and became peasants. We settled in small, rural villages. We used our primitive technologies to produce more food than we cared to consume, so we began to trade the surplus with other villagers. The rest is economic history.

A related assumption is that before rural agriculture jump-started our civilization, we were a bunch of scattered, primitive, unruly hunter-gatherers, with an economic life no more complex than that of many other animals. This part of the myth is surely false. Twentieth-century archeology demonstrated that pre-agrarian humans were much, much more than hunters and gatherers. They manufactured elaborate artifacts using various raw materials; they built sturdy homes and astonishing sacred monuments; they adorned themselves with long necklaces; they painted magnificent murals; they engaged in extensive trade, long before the emergence of the first peasants. And there is one more thing: there is now solid proof that many of them built and lived in big cities.

How can a city come to be, the skeptic asks, without the supply of great quantities of food, first produced in agricultural villages? Jacobs employs a clever analogy to show how this is possible. Present-day cities are so dependent on electricity that their economies would almost instantly collapse without it. But the massive power plants are usually located in less densely populated areas, far away from the city center. For a future archeologist who knows nothing about life predating these twentieth-century findings, it may thus appear as if the use of electric power originated in the countryside and was a precondition of the rise of modern cities. But what is true about electricity might also be true about agriculture. The fallacy, Jacobs explains, "is to mistake the results of city economic development" for its preconditions. Cities come first. They grow as they develop knowledge, science, technology, skill, art, and industry. These novelties can be exported to the hinterlands as well, but only because they depend on the mother cities.

Another counterintuitive line of thought that has a similar effect is Jacobs's suggestion that the seemingly "pristine economies" of tribes that anthropologists love to discover on remote islands and in impenetrable jungles tell us less about the dawn of civilization than about its decline. Rather than innocent communities untouched by modern culture, such tribes can be understood as the scattered remnants of ancient societies that used to be highly developed. The economic conditions of these tribes deteriorated to their current primitive state because of their isolation, because their ties to the city were lost, or because the city was destroyed. Such tribes should therefore evoke the Apocalypse more than the Garden of Eden; they say less about how we were and more about how we might end up.

When he surveyed the Europe of his time, Smith noticed that backward agriculture was often found in countries that lack well-developed cities. He also knew that more advanced agricultural methods existed in areas closest to major cities. He admitted that developments in agriculture did not precede developments in industry and commerce but rather quite the contrary (England was a ready example). Yet he was living in an age when the average educated person believed that man was born in a garden. He was therefore incapable of taking a logical step that required a huge leap of faith. He was unable to see that rural life depends on urban life and not vice versa.

That an iconoclast like Marx was also convinced that industry and commerce arise subsequent to agriculture and the domestication of animals, and that generations of intellectuals continue to accept this upside-down causality uncritically, is far more scandalous. Jacobs was one of the first to suggest that agricultural techniques were most likely first developed in cities and only then exported to the countryside. In the same way, we should remember that the twentieth-century commuter suburb, as well as large-scale industrial and agricultural production, was first developed in nineteenth-century America by families and businesses that moved out of Manhattan to settle in Brooklyn, Queens, and the Bronx.

Admittedly, the claim that economic life began in prehistoric cities may be just another origin myth that Jacobs employs to introduce her own theory of economic development. She even invented an imaginary city, New Obsidian, as a thought experiment to help further her argument. Nevertheless, her story is based on James Mallaart's discovery, in 1958, of Çatalhöyük, a neolithic city more than nine thousand years old, located in present-day Turkey, which was the home of up to ten thousand residents at a time when most people were still hunting and gathering. Ian Hodder's recent dig at the same site has helped advance the emerging narrative of complex cities predating small agricultural settlements. For example, Hodder concludes that the combination of barren land and unpredictable floods meant that agriculture in this particular area "was probably risky and prone to failure."

PREHISTORY OR MYTHOLOGY ASIDE, Jacobs's theory goes something like this. A belief in economic development without vigorous cities is like a belief in immaculate conception. Only urban centers can spark prosperity. Their absence or stagnation points to an impending dark age and death. Thus, the first responsibility of a city is to itself. A metropolis grows like an embryo: not through expansion but through diversification. This process is organic and cannot be preordained by planners or governments. It takes shape as new types of work break away from established types of work. A small city imports everything: raw materials and finished goods, services and skills, capital and people, but also novels and paintings, fashion trends and philosophical ideas, different lifestyles and moral values. As the city grows, it replaces these material and immaterial imported goods by developing new local equivalents. This process of internal differentiation is the most crucial factor for guaranteeing the city's future success.

What emerges from an urban center influences its periphery and beyond. The rural, less populated, inert regions depend on the city. They supply the city with what it demands, and they do the work (agricultural or otherwise) that it no longer cares to handle within its cramped quarters, where such work originated. In addition to this colonial relationship between city and country, Jacobs emphasizes the even greater importance of other, older urban centers, which enable young hubs to develop through mutual trade. Oftentimes, faraway cities are more intimately linked to each other than a single city is to its immediate vicinity. New York needed nineteenth-century Paris just as today Shanghai needs New York. When a city stagnates and grows old, when its work stops diversifying at the same rapid pace, it can still facilitate the rise of other, budding cities and thus still contribute to economic growth.

SMITH'S MOST IMPORTANT REVELATION, which had such a decisive impact on modern economics, was the division of labor: a single type of work becomes much more efficient once it is divided between different persons. His eureka moment came when he realized that one worker could make, say, twenty pins a day, but ten workers could churn out about twelve pounds of perfectly formed units. Jacobs, however, points out that *"division of labor, in itself, creates nothing."* The decisive event in economic growth was not the day the pin maker decided to divide a single task into more specialized, smaller tasks. It came when the people who were making bristles for use in the textile industry decided for the first time to produce pins as well. These people, Jacobs writes, were not "further dividing the labor of making bristles. They were not dividing at all. They were adding a new complexity, pin making, to an older simplicity, bristle making." They invented a new product, which created a new need, which generated new work, which required new skills. It is not the quantity of the same thing but the quantity of different things that Jacobs considers a vital sign of urban economy.

Although Smith in particular and modern economy in general are obsessed with efficiency, Jacobs claims that inefficiency is one of the most important things about powerful cities. Efficiency is not necessarily conducive to economic growth, which depends on the repeated splintering of one work into new types of work, new skills, and the constant crossbreeding between different, usually small enterprises, which in turn leads to more breakaway innovation. If, at the beginning of the twentieth century the birth rate of new, competing enterprises in a city like Detroit was off the charts, with small companies manufacturing different parts of every car, by the same century's end, there were essentially only three big companies. They were indeed very efficient, but they were consequently also moribund, as was the city.

Development always operates within a web of interdependent co-developments. Jacobs thus never conflates the urban and the industrial revolutions. She shows that the big factory with its ordered assembly line and unskilled laborers, along with today's behemoth corporations and big-box retailers, may be the emblems of our efficient and soulless modern economy, but they are also its kiss of death. Monopolies can be resisted not only through strict legislation but also through the growth of vibrant and diverse big cities. The messy-yet-blessed competition between an urban cluster of skillful individuals cannot be easily eliminated and replaced with more of the same.

Marx teaches that the basic conflict of interest is that between the business owner and the worker. Jacobs holds that the primary economic conflict is between a new kind of work and an outdated one, that is, "between people whose interests are with already well-established economic activities [whether employers or employees], and those whose interests are with the emergence of new economic activities. This is a conflict that can never be put to rest except by economic stagnation." And a city in stasis is a dying city.

For Marx, the division of labor leads to "the separation of industrial and commercial from agricultural labor, and hence to the separation of *town* and *country* and to the conflict of their interests." Jacobsian economics is equally agonistic. The difference is that, in her theory, the crucial struggle is neither between the bourgeoisie and the working class nor between urban and rural societies, but rather between the *status quo ante* and the *status quo post*. As in Arendt's political theory, Jacobs's economic theory is predicated on valorizing the proliferation of unexpected new beginnings.

THIRTIETH CHAPTER **TRANSACTIONS OF DECLINE**

THE QUESTION OF HOW the other half lives, the urban poor and disenfranchised, must take into account this provocative quote from Jacobs, which for some reason Benjamin copied twice: "Poverty has no causes. Only prosperity has causes. Analogically, heat is a result of active processes; it has causes. But cold is not a result of any processes; it is only the absence of heat. Just so, the great cold of poverty and economic stagnation is the absence of economic development." Only a viable city, Jacobs shows, with all its functions and populations, with all the pushes and pulls of its multiple power relations, with all its chaotic inefficiencies, even with some of its inequalities and injustices, can function as a sustained source of heat and postpone for a bit what she predicts to be the dark age ahead.

The complex causes of prosperity are invariably elusive and divisive. But when nations, not cities, come to consider this issue, they usually end up seeing things as a binary choice and follow either John Maynard Keynes or Milton Friedman. The two most influential economists of the twentieth century appear to offer contradictory guidelines. It is not easy for policy makers to decide which of these theories should be put into practice, because both boast spectacular success stories and repress their miserable failures. Each had a few solid decades to test its hypothesis—not in isolated labs but in actual markets on national and international scales. "Never has a science, or supposed science," Jacobs writes about the discipline of macroeconomics that was shaped by Keynes and Friedman, "been so generously indulged. And never have experiments left in their wakes more wreckage, unpleasant surprises, blasted hopes and confusion, to the point that the question seriously arises whether the wreckage is reparable; if it is, certainly not with more of the same."

A crash course on the subject may begin with the first question most economists ask themselves: What drives economic growth? Practically put, they wonder who should have more money in their pockets in order to stimulate economic expansion. Demand-side economists such as Keynes (and Marx) say that the money should go to the consumer. Supply-side economists such as Friedman (and Smith) claim that no growth is possible unless more money lands in the hands of the producer. Think about the Big Bang of present-day economic theory, the Wall Street crash of 1929, and the Great Depression that followed on its heels. This chain of events is understood in two distinct ways. Keynesians see people as having spent as little as possible, as having held on to their wallets even though their savings evaporated in the bear market. Friedman and the other Chicago school economists see a sudden decline in supply. The problem was not that people suddenly decided to buy, for example, fewer cars but that the car companies decided to produce fewer of them, because their line of credit was cut off.

Keynes's solution was to make the government act like a superrich consumer on a frivolous shopping spree. By injecting huge sums of money into the market through various investments, expenditures, and tax adjustments, the government did its best to defrost the economy. Friedman's solution was to make the government act like a giant, careless bank, granting low-interest loans and guaranteeing the loans given by commercial banks. The sovereign state would then drastically expand the national credit line by (in Friedman's own words) acting like a helicopter that is dropping bills "from the sky."

ON CLOSER INSPECTION, the differences fall away. Despite attempts to use Friedman's argument against the sort of governmental intervention in the free market that Keynes supports, neither can imagine eschewing the pivotal role of the state in the inner workings of world economy. Both theories stipulate that even in times of relative prosperity the subtle regulation of the market must never stop. Why is it, then, that this fiscal (*pace* Keynes) or monetary (*pace* Friedman) fine-tuning that the two schools championed whenever their men were in charge failed to create even the semblance of long-lasting economic stability?

Jacobs's answer is that despite their sharp disagreements and claims to the contrary, Keynes and Friedman, following Smith and Marx, share one crucial assumption: the sovereign state is the supreme economic arbiter; the civil servants and elected officials in finance ministries and central banks who watch over the national and international markets are true economic angels. Jacobs asks us to stop thinking in these terms of state economies (what Smith calls the wealth of nations) and begin thinking in terms of city economies.

"Choosing among the existing schools of thought is bootless. We are on our own." This is how Jacobs concludes the opening chapter of *Cities and the Wealth of Nations*, the final installment in her urban trilogy. We take leave of this fool's paradise, as she calls it, as soon as we acknowledge that the city, not the nation, must function as the basic economic unit. In this respect, Friedman and Marx may form here an unexpected alliance, on the grounds of their vague dreams of the day when states will wither away and economic life will no longer be restricted by national considerations. Keynes and Smith, in contrast, did not care for this stateless, utopian vision, which communists call a classless society and neoliberals call globalization.

"Nobody," Jacobs writes in 1984, "places more faith in the nation as the suitable entity for analyzing economic life and its prospects than the rulers of communist and socialist countries." Yet during the same years capitalist countries, no matter how laissez-faire they aspired to be (like the one Friedman was shaping as a top adviser to Ronald Reagan), continued to think in the same nationalistic terms. Only anarchists deny the validity of the state, but Jacobs is not impressed by those who "have been preoccupied with their conception of how economic life ought to work and dismiss how it actually does work, which is in ways they reject out of hand, as it were."

ONE SIMPLE WAY economic life works is through the corrective feedback of its currency. Once the exchange rate of a certain legal tender falls, export is cheap and import gets expensive. Once the rate rises, the opposite occurs. This fluctuation can be healthy, unless it happens overnight. Currency gives the system reliable feedback information, of the kind we get from our body: we breathe faster when the heart rate goes up while running, slower when it goes down while sleeping; we get closer to a source of heat when it is cold, and distance ourselves from it when it gets too hot. Currency does the same thing by encouraging either import or export.

The problem, Jacobs demonstrates, is that a national currency (not to speak of a continental one, like the euro) ends up giving the economy "faulty feedback." It is like a single brain that tells different lungs in different bodies to inhale and exhale at the same rate. A nation is a fictive economic unit. The United States, for example, is, politically speaking, a union of fifty states. But economically speaking it remains a loose agglomeration of no more than a handful of concentrated city regions with feverish activity, despite the federal government's epic endeavor in the twentieth century to create a more balanced distribution of people and businesses throughout its vast territories.

A big nation is like an "elephant hooked up with three sheep, two puppy dogs and a rabbit," all controlled by the same brain stem that collectively decides on the operation of these different lungs. In such an arrangement, it is naturally the elephant, the metropolis, that dictates how rapid the breathing will be. The less powerful areas away from the city centers are bound to get faulty feedback information from the national economic system, no matter how much the government tries to offset this predicament by pouring its tax revenues—the overwhelming majority of which come from the earnings of city inhabitants—into those depressed regions. In this awkward arrangement, even big-city regions get faulty feedback from the centralized, national economy, which makes them react in ways that betray their own condition. For example, in the postwar era, New York was an obvious victim of the federal government's suburban economic policies, which affected the city's poorest neighborhoods the most.

Jacobs saves the punch line for the last pages of *Cities and the Wealth of Nations*. She begins by talking about this "dog that realizes he is the object of an approaching hostile advance. The dog is just standing around at the time, but the one thing he can't continue to do is just stand around. He must do something radically different: prepare to attack, or run." She then explains that "this is the situation of a nation in which instabilities and stresses have reached a point demanding action. The one thing the nation cannot do is stand around and do nothing."

So one option is to attack. This amounts to the prescribed methods of coping with mounting economic difficulties by means of what Jacobs calls "transactions of decline." The governmental implementation of economic adjustments, from fiscal stimulus to austerity measures, about which we occasionally read in the daily papers and which are directed by the acolytes of either Keynes or Friedman, tend to bring about some temporary relief, as well as a sense that everything is under control and heading in the right direction. But Jacobs demonstrates that ultimately they slowly drag the nation further down in an overall, inevitable slump.

But the dog also has another option. "We are taught," Jacobs writes, "that running away from a problem doesn't solve it. However, in real life it occasionally does, as the metaphor of the dog suggests." For the sovereign state, this means that it must acknowledge its ingrained ineptitude in economic matters, "resist the temptation of engaging in transactions of decline," stop "trying to hold itself together," and implode.

THIRTY-FIRST CHAPTER   EMINENT DOMAIN

THOUGH PARIS FIGURES in Benjamin's thought as New York's doppelgänger, the singular elements of both cities, which seem to mirror each other so well, undergo a very significant transformation. As Benjamin translates one city from one century into another place and another time, what is most interesting is not how his two seemingly different subjects are actually the same. Rather, it is more intriguing to account for the metamorphosis they come to represent.

There is one notable exception to this rule of thumb: the almost perfectly symmetrical roles played by Baron Haussmann in nineteenth-century Paris and Robert Moses in twentieth-century New York. Haussmann is best known for building the straight, expansive boulevards that cut through the crooked and narrow medieval streets. Moses will probably be remembered as the person responsible for laying out the main vehicular arteries that gave the growing swarm of cars better access to a city designed with carriages and trains in mind.

Moses made his mark on New York not only by ramming numerous highways through what he saw as its dilapidated neighborhoods. He also stands behind such a staggering list of construction projects in the city and its environs—from beaches to public pools, from parks to housing complexes, from bridges to dams, from the World's Fair to the UN headquarters to Lincoln Center—that he is easily the single most influential person in the entire history of New York. He serves as an excellent example of what happens when one tries to change the city instead of understand it.

Like Haussmann, Moses was faced with a metropolis that appeared to be ungovernable. Both Paris and New York were perceived as labyrinths that only the most experienced local residents knew how to navigate. Instead of adding new structures to the urban cacophony, the two men preferred to engage in constructive destruction, seeing themselves as "demolition artists." By clearing out strategic parts of the maze, they believed that they were making the city less insular, less messy, less resistant and more porous, manageable, and open to external forces.

Their emphases may have been different, but Haussmann's and Moses's secret agendas seem quite similar. On the one hand, there is the need to reconfigure the city in such a way that its radical, public nature (as described by Arendt) will no longer pose a political threat to the nation so that it will thereafter become a more integral part of the state's growing dominion. On the other, there is an attempt to untangle the knot of urban economy (as described by Jacobs) so that it can submit to the very different logic that governs sovereign economy.

Just as Haussmann's expansive boulevards were designed to be barricade-proof in an age scarred by revolutions and civil wars, Moses's plethora of projects, constructed during the age of suburban sprawl and large-scale industrial expansion, were devised to control or simply disperse the urban crowd, which would otherwise clutter the inefficiently chaotic city. By vivisecting neighborhoods populated by lower- to middle-class residents (the very same neighborhoods that Jacobs believed should be saved), the two men reconfigured the modern city as a streamlined space geared toward luxury living, conspicuous consumption, and international trade, all of which stand at the center of the urban experience as we know it today. Of course, the poor and the working class are not eradicated completely from the face of the city. Instead, they are gradually contained within the circumscribed ghettoes of housing projects (which Mumford lauded as "Versailles for the Millions"), where they are much less disruptive, or at least less visible, in the urban spectacle of late capitalism.

It is important to note that Haussmann only wished for something that Moses never had to fight for: that a Parisian boulevard be as wide and as straight as a standard New York avenue. Nevertheless, the identical outcome of the Haussmannization of Paris and the Mosesization of New York is that the relatively small, organic neighborhoods of which both cities were composed had to forgo their distinctive physiognomy and way of life. They became a part of the somewhat artificial and inhuman modern metropolis, where it is much more difficult to feel at home. Benjamin reproduces in *The Arcades Project* the following poem, written as a lamentation against Haussmann, though it could have been easily written with Moses in mind: "You will live to see the city grown desolate and bleak. Your glory will be great in the eyes of future archeologists, but your last days will be sad and bitter . . . And the heart of the city will slowly freeze . . . And loneliness, the tedious goddess of deserts, will come and settle upon this new empire."

MOSES'S STORY is a crucial one not just because of what he managed to do but mainly because of how he did it. By accumulating multiple titles in every significant junction in New York's elaborate governmental apparatus, Moses, who began his career as a progressive civil servant, transformed himself over the years into a master operator, brilliantly bending virtually anyone in the political and economic establishments to his will. And he did it all without ever being elected to public office. Ultimately, not only the mayor of the city and the governor of the state were merely rubber-stamping his various projects but even President Roosevelt had to back off from his attempt to fire Moses from a key position.

All of Moses's projects were supposed to benefit the people and be built in their name. But the reality was that whenever actual persons, independently of those great amorphous masses, tried to voice their own opinions, Moses treated them as nothing more than pointless hurdles on the path to the realization of his grandiose plans. The public had to be bathed, aired, housed, transported, entertained, and so on. As Frances Perkins, the US secretary of labor discovered with "shock," Moses—who grew up in the "snug luxury" of a private home on Forty-Sixth Street just off Fifth Avenue—was secretly driven by a deep-seated distaste for the sort of people who were using his public projects to improve their welfare. To his mind, the masses of New York were a problem awaiting a solution. And only he knew what that was.

When people turn into populations, when democracy turns into demography, when conversation turns into control, the city is reduced to the sort of aerial map on which Moses made his sweeping marks. One day, a visitor to Moses's office was about to leave when two men entered the room, but Moses told him to stay. "There was an exchange of questions and answers," the visitor reported, "a very brief exchange—after which the two men quickly departed." Asking who they were, the visitor was told that he had just sat through a monthly board meeting of the Triborough Bridge Authority, the umbrella legal entity through which Moses controlled his multitude of projects.

This anecdote illustrates the flip side of the dreaded bureaucratic system that Kafka taught us to disdain. Without red tape, a civil servant can easily transform into an urban tyrant. Moses maneuvered the legal system in such a way that he became the de facto sovereign of a city that he treated as a war zone. He constructed his projects and destroyed what stood in their way by executing his exceptional powers, while minimizing the need to adhere to either public or private interests, to political or economic pressures.

NORMALLY, PRIVATE PROPERTY can be sold whenever a buyer and a seller are in agreement. I cannot force you to sell me your house just as you cannot force me to buy yours. Nevertheless, this simple rule does not apply to those vested with sovereign power. The state can be, at least potentially, the owner of whatever lies within its jurisdiction. The government can appropriate what it desires by using an exceptional measure called "eminent domain." The lawful owners do not need to agree to sell their property once the state decides to use its power of eminent domain. The state is only required to give the rightful owners reasonable compensation for what it forced them to sell. It also must guarantee that the expropriated property will benefit that amorphous entity called the public.

Moses elevated the sovereign power of eminent domain to a veritable art form. In the beginning he made use of it to build his parkways right through the lush estates of the robber barons on Long Island. In later years it was almost always large swaths of poor and middle-class inner-city neighborhoods that he expropriated to make way for his ever-growing roster of construction projects. Whether those projects were indeed in the public interest (as if the public could ever be thought of as a single body with a single will) was never clear.

Eminent domain is the public card that trumps anyone trying to play the private card. Moses, however, also used a very interesting private card with which he was able to trump anyone trying to play the public card, which was based on a neat legal twist. Under the Constitution, states are prohibited from passing any law "impairing the obligation of contracts." Only the parties involved can change or cancel a signed contract. With this clause in mind, Moses formed a new entity, called "public authority." The ultimate amalgam of body politic and body corporate, a public authority is able to make contracts, like any private company. But it also has something that every private company can only dream of: the public power of eminent domain.

In the 1930s and 1940s Moses got most of the funding for his projects from the federal government. Once this well dried up in the 1950s and 1960s, he began to depend on money generated from selling bonds, issued by his public authority. Since a bond is a contract, no one was able to scrutinize the financial agreement he made with the private bankers, who in turn were very happy to invest in a developer who was capable of building pretty much whatever he wanted wherever he wanted, as well as generating very substantial revenues from the resulting operations (a toll bridge, for example, turned out to be an extremely lucrative cash cow). This special arrangement allowed Moses to operate in the twilight zone between politics and economy, in a space above the ecopolis, where many of the rules that normally apply to these realms were effectively suspended.

But politics, like economics, "is a thieves' game. Those who stay in it long enough are invariably robbed." During Moses's final years, in the late 1970s and early 1980s, it became clear that his seemingly benevolent and enlightened projects, projects that modernized the city and even made it greener, were what brought it to the edge of the abyss. The Bronx, in the heart of which he built a monumental expressway, suffered from his fiats more than any other part of town. Thanks to *The Power Broker*, Robert Caro's most detailed and most condemning biography of Moses, New York's legendary master builder was revealed as the city demolisher he in large part was. Caro's thousand-page tome defines to this day Moses's legacy better than anything the latter ever built. Although Moses's deed was done and the physical city was altered almost beyond recognition, a line from Hugo could have been the perfect motto for Caro's well-crafted hatchet job: "This will destroy that. The book will destroy the edifice."

IN 1964 WARHOL WAS COMMISSIONED to create a mural for the upcoming World's Fair in Flushing Meadows. His submission consisted of large, black-and-white silk-screened plates, reproducing mug shots of the thirteen most-wanted men on the FBI list. Just before opening day, an order came from on high, presumably from Moses, who served as the fair's director, to promptly and completely alter the artwork. Warhol complied by offering to paint on top of each plate identical portraits of Moses himself, an idea that was also swiftly rejected. Instead, Warhol covered the whole piece with a reflective silvery paint, thus destroying the original.

"Encompassing both Warhol and Moses," Benjamin writes in what is probably a rephrasing of a point he made in *The Arcades Project*, "would mean drawing the spirit of contemporary New York like a bow, with which knowledge shoots the moment in the heart." The story behind Warhol's *Thirteen Most Wanted Men* can easily be interpreted as suggesting that the real Public Enemy Number One is Moses himself. But treating Moses as an actor with either diabolical intentions or a moral flaw would make sense only if this were the script for a Hollywood biopic. Within the context of our theoretical investigation, it is better to view his actions as the tragically effective execution of a new way of thinking to which Moses, like many others at the time, uncritically subscribed. Since this way of thinking stands in diametric opposition to Jacobs's, to understand what he got wrong is to understand what she got right.

As a community activist, Jacobs had a positive, transformative impact on her neighborhood. But today, in the twenty-first century, when her derivative fingerprints are scattered all over cities worldwide, it is she, perhaps even more than Moses, who appears to be on the run from the urban crime scene. We may conclude then that present-day New York would not be able to function and dysfunction without the complementary implementation of the philosophies of both Moses and Jacobs. This odd couple represents not only the two basic visions of twentieth-century New York, not only the two cardinal approaches to the modern city, but also the two elementary spirits of modernity as such. Moses's is called high modernism; Jacobs's just got out of rehab.

FOURTH THRESHOLD   DEAD-END STREET

THE PRESENT BOOK is supposed to make Benjamin's many disparate ideas more or less cohere into concise arguments. This approach naturally oversimplifies the original text at many points. What follows are but a few of the leftover notes

I jotted down on the question of economy while reading *The Manhattan Project*. It is not exactly clear to me how to make perfect sense of them all, but someone else may figure it out.

A COMPARATIVE READING of Jacobs's and Arendt's books reveals many striking similarities. But even more striking is a comment made by their mutual friend, the editor Jason Epstein, who believes that the paths of these remarkable women who lived and worked in midcentury Manhattan probably never crossed: "Hannah was part of a worldly coterie which would not have interested Jane. Hannah was an intellectual. Jane was self-educated. Hannah was chic. Jane didn't care what she wore. They may have been kindred spirits but they occupied different worlds. I can't imagine a conversation between them." And yet this imaginary conversation constitutes the central argument of Benjamin's later work.

THE EXPERIENCE OF BENJAMIN'S GENERATION, as he summed it up in *The Arcades Project*, was "that capitalism will not die a natural death." The realization of every generation since has been that capitalism will not die an unnatural death either.

ONE OF THE MOST BASIC economic lessons to be learned from twentieth-century New York can be taught with the help of a short episode from *The Bonfire of the Vanities*. Imagine that you are the proud owner of a boiler (the kind that heats entire buildings in New York). If you do not know how to operate it and how to control the steam, then your property is completely worthless. "So you think capital is owning things. But you are mistaken. Capital is controlling things." You could be the landlord of an entire tenement building in the Lower East Side in the late 1970s, but because part of that neighborhood was a dangerous no-man's land, it was often more lucrative to burn your property to the ground than to collect the rent. Once the area got safer, once the steam was under control, the neighborhood also turned into a real estate bonanza. In short, control is one of the best capital investments imaginable. Put differently, the rhetorical question is this: "What are all the limestone facades of Fifth Avenue and all the marble halls and stuffed-leather libraries and all the riches of Wall Street in the face of *my* control of *your* destiny and your helplessness in the face of the Power?"

"LOOK AT THOSE PEOPLE who live in the immediate neighborhood of the Church of Rome, which is the head of our religion, and see how there is less religion among them than elsewhere." Machiavelli's observation makes sense not only in the religious field but also in the economic one. New York, the capital of capitalism, is the eye of the storm, where the weather tends to be eerily pleasant.

SOMEHOW BENJAMIN MANAGED to obtain the tapes of Foucault's lectures at the Collège de France from 1979. He quotes from them extensively and approvingly, especially from the sections that try to show how *homo economicus* becomes the figure in modernity that defies the logic of state sovereignty. Economic man can do so not because he says to the state sovereign, "Listen, I have rights, I have entrusted some of them to you, the others you must not touch." This is the sort of thing that *homo juridicus* would typically say. *Homo economicus* explains to the sovereign something else: "You must not touch me simply because you cannot, in the sense that you are powerless. And you are powerless because you can neither know nor control everything that is going on in the realm of economy." In other words, there can be no economic sovereign. The invisible hand is a refutation, a disqualification, of the state and its sovereignty. Political economy is a biting critique of governmental reason.

IN HIS LAST, posthumously published article, A. J. Liebling comes close to summarizing his view of New York City in a single sentence: "Behind each of those windows, a man is awake, scheming to take somebody else's money."

AN EARLY *NEW YORKER* CARTOON shows a man trying to commit suicide by jumping off the Brooklyn Bridge with a rock tied to his neck. But he is not alone. Right after him a taxi is also leaping into the East River with the hope of soliciting the despairing potential costumer for a last ride. Capitalism will hunt for life all the way unto death if there is profit to be had. It might even convince us that dying makes better economic sense than living. After visiting New York for the first and only time, Freud penned a slogan for an undertaker that he considered the epitome of American publicity: "Why live, if you can be buried for ten dollars?" Marx explains this rationale in the following devastating terms: "The less you eat, drink, and read books; the less you go to the theater, the dance hall, the public house; the less you think, love, theorize, sing, paint, fence, etc. the more you *save*—the *greater* becomes your treasure which neither moths nor dust will devour—your *capital.* The less you *are*, the more you *have*; the less you express your own life, the greater is your *alienated* life."

MOST OF THE TIME as we go about our everyday lives, our existence can be unproblematically reduced to a simple economic unit. From this perspective, Heidegger sneers, "'Life' is a 'business,' whether or not it covers its costs." To this we should add a famous line from Villiers de L'Isle-Adam's *Axël*, conspicuously absent from *The Arcades Project*, which surfaces in Benjamin's later work to convey the decisive attitude that twentieth-century New Yorkers were unwilling or unable to share with nineteenth-century Parisians: "Living? Our servants will do that for us."

IN HER LAST BOOK, from 2004, Jacobs writes, "Just to keep itself going, life makes demands on energy, supplied from inside and outside a living being, that are voracious compared with the undemanding thriftiness of death and decay." There is no institution that understands this simple equation better than the modern state, though it uses this piece of information in two seemingly contradictory ways. On the one hand, the state sees as its primary task the care and governance of almost every aspect of its citizens' lives from infancy to old age. On the other, life's seemingly exorbitant demands on its limited resources often lead the modern state to renounce the task it originally took upon itself. At these moments, instead of continuing its colossal management of lives, the state treats certain people as redundant and hence disposable. But the city operates according to a completely different logic. Benjamin argues that, unlike the state, the city should not be understood as a power *over* life but as the manifestation of the power *of* life itself. It does not invest *in* but is invested *with* lives.

WHAT IS ECONOMY? Jacobs's straightforward definition is that "it is what people do to make their livings." Another early *New Yorker* cartoon deals with the same question by depicting a wife knitting and a husband ironing just before going to bed. The caption reads: "Economy is idealism in its most practical form." Yet it is Elizabeth Hardwick's utterance in the first issue of the *New York Review of Books* that can dissolve this conversation into an uncomfortable silence: "Making a living is nothing; the great difficulty is making a point."

AS EARLY AS THE END of the eighteenth century, well-to-do New Yorkers began separating their businesses from their residences. Originally, economic enterprises were located on the ground floor of buildings, while the living quarters were on the floor above, though there was no clear-cut separation between private and public, between labor and life. As the city evolved, those who could afford to do so began to erect their homes uptown. Over the years, they moved farther and farther away from their downtown workplace. By the 1820s, respectable ladies were a rare sight in the business district, and gentlemen were resigned to the notion of commuting from their relatively secluded abodes. This new breed of New Yorkers immediately felt the need to be intellectually and artistically cultured, because they were no longer comfortable with being seen as mere merchants or moneyed men. They also aspired to appear benevolent and compassionate rather than self-interested and hard-nosed. These "philosophes and philanthropists" of the nineteenth century gave rise to liberal sentiment, not to speak of sentimentalism. Their domestic frenzy, which extended well into the twentieth century's suburban culture, was meant to create and protect a dream house where an individual can hold on to his or her traces of humanity rather than be just another drop in the sea of the undistinguishable, alienated, ruthless masses. If there is a social project that Benjamin felt the urgent need to dismantle by means of his intellectual project, then this is the one.

AN UNUSUAL SOURCE quoted in *The Manhattan Project* is a sentence tattooed on the upper back of a man Benjamin once saw washing himself in the Public Library's restrooms: "Fex urbis, lex orbis" (dregs of the city, law of the world).

I WAS WALKING with a friend through Central Park on New Year's Eve in 1999. Somewhere around the pond at the southeast corner I overheard a homeless man telling his friend: "Can you imagine God bothering to go person by person, or even people by people, choosing which one to save? The Day of Judgment must be the same for all humans throughout history. As a whole, we probably deserve to be doomed. In our defense, I guess, we still got this city."

ONE TEMPTING PIECE of biographical information that I would rather not divulge is Benjamin's New York address, or else the erection of another monument in his honor, like the one in Portbou, would be regrettably inevitable and inevitably regrettable. I can say, however, that, symbolically or ironically, he lived on the top floor in the last building on a dead-end street.

FIFTH PART

Stand clear of the closing doors, please.

—SUBWAY ANNOUNCEMENT

"AT NIGHT," Henry Miller wrote in the late 1930s, "the streets of New York reflect the crucifixion and death of Christ. When the snow is on the ground and there is the utmost silence, there comes out of the hideous buildings of New York a music of such sullen despair and bankruptcy as to make the flesh shrivel. No stone was laid upon another with love or reverence; no street was laid for dance or joy."

"At night," Luc Sante wrote in the early 1990s, the same New York streets present "the city as a living ruin." For him the night is "the corridor of history, not the history of famous people or great events, but that of the marginal, the ignored, the suppressed, the unacknowledged; the history of vice, of error, of confusion, of fear, of want; the history of intoxication, of vainglory, of delusion, of dissipation, of delirium. It strips off the city's veneer of progress and modernity and civilization and reveals the wilderness." This, Sante concludes, is not an illusion:

> It is the daytime that is a chimera, that pretends New York is anyplace, maybe with bigger buildings, but just as workaday, with a population that goes about its business and then goes to sleep, a great machine humming away for the benefit of the world. Night reveals this to be a pantomime. In the streets at night, everything kept hidden comes forth, everything is subject to the rules of chance, everyone is potentially both murderer and victim, everyone is afraid, just as anyone who sets his or her mind to it can inspire fear in others. At night, everyone is naked.

It is the same "naked city" that led Arthur Fellig, the New York photographer better known as Weegee, to carry with him every night a camera and a portable police radio, searching for whatever crimes and misdemeanors might come his way. While the cops were looking for culprits, Weegee was looking for fresh relics. Consider in this respect how little his "Corpse with Revolver" leaves to the imagination. It is as if not the man but the phantasmic urban order was shot in the face. The use, exchange, and exhibition values of the photo are negligible in comparison to its shock value. Such pictures of the gritty, filthy, naughty city certainly cater to a voyeuristic fascination with low life. But they also act like clandestine postcards addressed specifically to those who may be versed in the clean, affluent, and safe side of the urban landscape but are ignorant of the dark corners of its past and dead ends of its present, of its underbellies and empty bellies.

The easy way out is to treat these questionable urban elements as enchanting lures or as the subject of trite morality lessons and occasions for pity. But Benjamin senses that he faces here more than a problem to which good society ought to find a solution, as it eliminates the downtrodden from the whitewashed cityscape. Back in the day, when a street was cordoned off, people didn't have to ask. They knew that someone had been shot and that the area had been declared a crime scene. At present, we instinctively assume that someone is shooting yet another movie scene. Violence and deviance are more often fabricated than documented.

IN MUCH THE SAME WAY that the printing press was a turning point for both writers and readers, the invention of photography was a turning point for both lawbreakers and law enforcers. The mug shot allowed Alphonse Bertillon to revolutionize police work in late nineteenth-century Paris. For the first time, every arrest led to a positive identification of a certain individual, singled out from the urban masses, and cataloged either as a new offender or as a recidivist. The passport photo may connote freedom of movement instead of confinement, but we need to remember that it is nothing other than an application of a measure originally used against criminals to the entire population.

At the same time, the ability to save a permanent record of a human being and capture his or her traces was not only used as a device to criminalize or control the population. It also turned into a tool that enabled the less powerful to become more visible. The story the archive told began to include other characters besides those of the ruling class. Every police record turned into a miniature biography of an infamous life. People got their fifteen milliseconds of dubious fame long before

Warhol came onto the scene, though it is not a coincidence that he was one of the first to use passport-sized self-portraits from photo booths in his art, as well as original mug shots of wanted criminals.

When Jacob Riis, a police reporter turned social reformer, published in 1890 a book called *How the Other Half Lives*, it wasn't his stereotypical accounts of the New York slums that made it such a sensation ("Money is their God," he writes in a chapter titled "Jewtown." "Life itself is of little value compared with even the leanest bank account"). The text presents the poor as victims worthy, at most, of the genteel readers' benevolent compassion, but not their respect. It was, instead, the accompanying photos he took in those miserable neighborhoods that completely transformed the way people perceived the city's destitute dwellers.

Riis was one of the first to utilize a portable flash to take his photos in dark alleyways and cramped tenements that were blocked from the sun. Sometimes he stealthily surprised his subjects in their corners or attics and then disappeared, long before they even realized that it was not lightning that just hit them and protested this intrusion of their privacy. One time his primitive flash lamp even set a tenement he visited on fire. The resulting images of slum life ushered in a new era, as every inch of the city transformed into a potential spectacle. Nothing was hidden or veiled anymore, not even the poor elderly woman he photographed in the Eldridge Street Police Lodger. Notice the wooden plank at her side, which was used as a makeshift bed, and the hand holding a needle on the right. Three things are conspicuously missing from this photo: a rich man, a camel, and the heavenly kingdom.

RIIS'S PHOTOS, not his prose, reveal more than a problem of welfare, sanitation, or policing. Without romanticizing or patronizing his subjects too much, his camera manages to give a sense of a life lived. A photo, however, can take us only so far. So from Stephen Crane's 1893 fictional account of Maggie, the poor Bowery girl, to Mitchell Duneier's 1999 sociological account of Hakim Hasan and the other sidewalk booksellers on Sixth Avenue, New York also produced a penetrating range of texts whose aim was not to theorize "the subject's voice" and the subaltern's ability to speak but to demonstrate a willingness to just listen to otherwise marginalized city inhabitants.

Sante claims that one aspect of this "increasing fascination with urban low life was a phenomenon that is distinctly of the twentieth century." Unlike in Dickens's London and Hugo's Paris, in New York there was a "wish to enter the slums and actually settle there, via a complicated concatenation of motives that include the old allure of exotica and frisson, the wish to cleanse oneself, the pioneer spirit, the search for the mythical simple life, rebellion against the established order, and, of course, the search for a bargain." But if we were to temporarily turn a blind eye to the buoyant spirit of gentrification and orientalist fascination with the wretched of the city, we would see that the engagement with what the novelist Theodore Dreiser calls "the antithesis of what life would prefer to be" goes even deeper.

The Manhattan Project, as the name suggests, is very Manhattan-centric. The other four boroughs usually squeeze their way into the manuscript only as a backdrop, and the rest of the world is only a horizon. But Benjamin also brushes history against the grain by zooming in on those New Yorkers who were left in the shadows of the big, cruel, power-hungry metropolis, those crumbs of the economic cake whose recipe was outlined in the previous part of this book. He knows more than well that every document of civilization is a document of barbarism. He certainly does not identify with the aggressor. He only rarely empathizes with the victor. And he registers his respect for those who give an account of the vanquished. But it is unhelpful to read his manuscript as an attempt to speak in the name of any outsider other than himself.

🕊

BENJAMIN'S INTEREST in low life arises from his sense that "innocence from sin" also entails that one is "innocent of it." It therefore makes little sense to divide the inhabitants of a place like New York according to their different classes, races, or nationalities, because in the end, everyone is "united under the single standard of greed." Once we step into this urban zone of indeterminacy that blurs the already thin line separating success story from gangster story, business from racket, parade from riot, chance from con, virtue from vice, sheer life from pure violence, it becomes necessary to pay closer attention to those who are at least honest about it all.

"I do not know that I have any code of ethics," Richard Canfield, the great New York gambling mogul, declared at the turn of the century. "I do not care a rap about what other people think about me. I never did. As morals are considered by most people, I have no more than a cat." While the Rockefellers and Vanderbilts and Astors and the other robber barons did everything within their considerable power to persuade the public that they were guiltless and righteous at heart, Canfield saw no reason to even pretend.

It is important to recall that New York is a city where every other church was built with the proceeds of gambling; where policemen used to tell each other that "there is more law in the end of their nightstick than in a decision of the supreme court"; where elected officials practiced "honest graft" and believed that the greatest political crime is ingratitude; where gangs distributed printed takeout menus with a detailed price list of their violent services; where most inhabitants used to be able to point the disoriented visitor not only in the direction of the flower or garment districts but also of the crime district.

In such a place, the very knowledge of good and evil turns into a useless moralistic tool or a dangerously cynical weapon in the hands of postlapsarian humanity. In a city where the best hit men were for all intents and purposes unionized under the name "Murder Inc.," one had to look up to gangsters as the only people who had the audacity to demonstrate "their mingled respect and derision for the world outside their turf." Sante's astute argument in *Low Life* is that they did so not simply through lawbreaking but through parody: "parody of order, parody of law, parody of commerce, parody of progress."

THE MORALITY OF A PERSON or legitimacy of a thing did not inform life in twentieth-century New York as much as the potential memory of them. No human creation is more resilient to the forces of oblivion than a city. But even though "everybody remembers the city," chances are that it will fail to remember us. To leave a mark on one's family and friends is one thing; to leave a mark on a big city is quite another. By way of analogy, think of all the flora and fauna that ever existed in prehistoric times, and then think of those that calcified into immutable stones.

It might be interesting to ask a paleontologist why it is that certain lives petrify into fossils and others disintegrate without leaving a trace. But this question can also be reformulated to address a fundamental urban predicament that informs a novel by Richard Price called *Lush Life*. In a moment of grief and rage, one of the characters demands to know what it really takes, other than dumb luck, to survive in a city like New York. Who is allowed to stay and leave a mark? "The already half-dead? The unconscious? . . . Do you survive because of what is *in* you? Or because of what *isn't*?" Benjamin, our urban paleontologist, registers a similar sentiment when he writes: "Do I need to live like a fossil to become one after I die?"

THIRTY-THIRD CHAPTER   GARBAGE STUDIES

WHEN BENJAMIN introduced himself to new acquaintances in the 1920s, he often refrained from saying that he was a philosopher or a literary critic. Half in jest, this self-conscious young bourgeois presented himself as a collector of books. During the 1930s, as his deteriorating financial and political status made it impossible to hold on to his impressive library, he began to think of himself as a collector of quotations. There was something sad about the way he read to his friends snippets from *The Arcades Project*, eagerly sharing odd lines pillaged from the obscure holdings of the French National Library. As volumes of beautifully bound first editions gave way to small scribbles on random scraps of paper lifted from Parisian cafés, he could not imagine himself a collector of any kind without a bitter tinge of irony.

It was only on the day Benjamin copied Charles Baudelaire's description of the Parisian ragpicker that he managed to redefine his compromised condition: "Here we have a man whose job it is to pick up the day's rubbish in the capital. He collects and catalogues everything that the great city has cast off, everything it has lost, and discarded, and broken. He goes through the archives of debauchery, and the jumbled array of refuse. He makes a selection, an intelligent choice; like a miser hoarding treasure, he collects the garbage that will become objects of utility or pleasure when refurbished by Industrial magic."

"The rags, the refuse," Benjamin writes about his *Arcades Project*, "these I will not describe but put on display." In his eyes, the dustbin of history always calls for a treasure hunt, and philosophy is a form of dumpster diving. His *Arcades*, however, is a fairly well-organized collection of fragments, cataloged according to well-defined themes. *The Manhattan Project* is a more chaotic jumble of quotations and notations, with seemingly random clusters of records about certain ideas, people, events, and places. There is something obsessive about the way he fills in page after page with repetitive formulations, without necessarily saying anything new. At one point in the surviving manuscript he becomes aware of this, referring to himself as a literary hoarder.

Benjamin's fascination with collectors, ragpickers, and later, in what became the ultimate mutation of this social type, with hoarders, was not merely the result of personal identification. The figure of the hoarder occupies one of his most fruitful lines of investigation during his New York years, mainly because it illuminated for him some of the basic forces that shape our modern life. Hoarding becomes a meaningful (rather than merely pathological) activity once it is understood within the context of contemporary capitalist society. But it is hardly a new phenomenon. Already in the fourteenth century Dante noticed that hoarders and squanderers are the two sides of the same coin, which explains why he relegated both, with their "squinting minds," to the fourth circle of hell.

Hoarding objects, like hoarding capital, is a symptom of an economic system in a state of exception. Normally, currencies and commodities circulate freely. The flow is channeled and monitored but never blocked. As a society, we must spend money to make money; we must jettison the old to make room for the new. In other words, prosperity is predicated on waste. When, in moments of economic crisis, people decide not to let go of the goods and funds they already possess, the system goes into paralyzing shock. So is the flip side of consumer society necessarily a producer society, or rather a hoarder society? Isn't garbage a surplus of sorts? And what is this pile of debris that grows skyward before Benjamin's angel of history? Could that wasteland be a scene from the house of a hoarder? Is the accumulation of junk precisely what capitalists call "progress"?

IT IS DIFFICULT TO UNDERSTAND the hoarder without comparing him to his historical predecessor: the collector. "Perhaps the most deeply hidden motive of the person who collects," Benjamin writes in *The Arcades Project*, "can be described this way: he takes up the struggle against dispersion. Right from the start, the great collector is struck by the confusion, by the scatter, in which the things of the world are found." It might be assumed that whereas collectors fastidiously organize and catalog their inventory, hoarders just keep their things in disarray. But the truth is that many hoarders have elaborate mental maps that enable them, and them alone, to make sense of their continuously mounting piles of possessions.

Nevertheless, hoarding is not a reaction to the disorder of things. It is not a struggle against *dispersion* but against *dispossession*. Although dispossession conventionally denotes a compulsory act perpetuated by one person against another (I seize something you currently own), Benjamin uses this word to refer to a voluntary act of release (I rid myself of something that is presently mine). In this sense, to hoard is neither an attempt to possess things nor an attempt to dispossess things. Rather, it is an act of *dis-dispossession*.

Today people seem to be more interested in curating than in collecting. Either way, Benjamin claims that what is decisive in such activities "is that the object is detached from all its original functions in order to enter into the closest conceivable relation to things of the same kind. This relation is the diametric opposite of any utility, and falls into the peculiar category of completeness." He goes so far as to claim that collectors redeem the object by refusing to treat it as a means to an end and, in this way, reveal its intrinsic worth.

For the hoarder, though, the moment an object loses its use value is not a moment of redemption but one of impossible mourning, simply because he cannot let it go. Hoarding is not driven by the dream of completing a collection; the hoarder knows no such end. Most hoarders are less interested in tracing all the exemplars of a specific series than in piling up more of the same. They are attracted to abundance more than to rarity. Paraphrasing Marx's observation about misers and capitalists, Benjamin claims that whereas the hoarder is a collector "gone mad," the collector is nothing but a rational hoarder. The hoarder may also be defined as a "collector of nothing."

But the hoarder is also propelled by a powerful dream that, like the collector's dream of completeness, is rarely if ever realized. The hoarder's basic fantasy is the fantasy of *reuse*. It is his hope that the lost use value of an empty plastic bottle or an old magazine will one day, in the unknown future, be restored. An object that the good consumer considers dead is kept by the hoarder in anticipation of what may be called its materialistic resurrection. Think of the hoarder as a modern pharaoh and of his home as a pyramid. Whereas the treasures in Egyptian tombs were intended for the comfort of the sovereign in the afterlife, the hoarder's own domain, of which he is no longer master, is primarily dedicated to the hereafter of things, not persons.

ANOTHER WAY TO APPROACH HOARDING is to contrast it with ragpicking. Like the collector, the ragpicker can estimate what every object is worth. Collectors renounce the use value of the object (try to read an actual copy of a first-edition Spiderman comic book), but they do so in order to solidify its exchange value (a value recognized by other collectors, who are all potential buyers). To use a similar logic, ragpickers are often oblivious to the precise utility of whatever they rummage from the metropolitan bins because their primary concern is how much they can get for it. Yet most hoarders could not care less about the exchange value of their stuff. To an outsider, a pile belonging to a hoarder and another to a ragpicker might look indistinguishable, but in the hoarder's eyes his junk has a personal value and an intricate history that only he can comprehend.

This is what prevents the hoarder from letting go, no matter how useless or worthless the contents of his pile might seem to an outsider. It is, after all, not *just* stuff but *his* stuff, his *own* dis-dispossession (notice, however, that it is not exactly correct to say that the hoarder is the *owner* of his hoard). "Between what a man calls *me* and what he simply calls *mine*," William James argues, "the line is difficult to draw. We feel and act about certain things that are ours very much as we feel and act about ourselves." Most of us buy and dispose of things with neither end nor remorse. Hoarders try to save, to spare, not only things but also, in a sense, themselves. The secret of hoarding, Benjamin explains, is to receive "things into our space. We don't displace our being into theirs; they step into our life."

Warhol was a notorious hoarder who filled six hundred brown cardboard boxes—known as "time capsules," and now considered part of his artistic oeuvre—with a mélange of his industrious life's detritus, which otherwise just piled up on his desk. They contain among other things taxi receipts, dress shoes, pizza boxes, and old toupees. Of course, his more conventional artworks also show his deep understanding of the rapid process, inherent in late capitalism, through which commodities lose both their use and exchange values. He was therefore well aware of the problem that this situation poses for the hoarder. Because the commodities' perverse, fading fetish still lingers in the hoarder's mind, he cannot help serving as their "tribal sorcerer." The problem is that no one cares about his magic powers, unless, again, his name is Andy.

While billions of mass-produced, identical objects are quickly used and then nonchalantly discarded without a second thought, the hoarder imbues these trivial pieces of trash with deep meaning and eternal significance. Or maybe the hoarder does not impose his ideas on inanimate things. Maybe hoarders are even capable of listening to what things say in their own language. For the hoarder, this urban Mowgli, nothing is too unimportant or too low to be dis-dispossessed, to be worthy of being listened to. Even the waste of the human body—nails, hair, and even excrement—is sometimes hoarded with enigmatic dedication.

THE COLLYER BROTHERS are the most famous case of compulsive hoarding. Born to an upper-class family with deep roots in the New York aristocracy (their father was a doctor; their mother, an opera singer), Homer and Langley Collyer both attended Columbia University, but they never moved out of their parents' Fifth Avenue brownstone, which they eventually inherited in 1929. By the time of their death, a couple of decades later, they had managed to amass no less than 120 tons of various items, including fourteen pianos and enough other musical instruments to equip an entire orchestra; massive collections of bowling balls, potato peelers, baby carriages, and guns; thousands of empty bottles and cans; countless stacks of books and newspapers; a clunky X-ray machine; and a dismantled Model T Ford automobile, which Langley tried to reconfigure as an electrical generator after their house was disconnected from the grid.

Homer, who gradually became both paralyzed and blind, never left the house. Langley made only nightly excursions, searching throughout the city for water, food, and whatever else he either scavenged or bought with the brothers' substantial (yet dwindling) funds. To avert intruders both real and imagined, he boarded up the windows and set up ingenious booby traps in every room. When, in 1942, a curious reporter asked him to explain the stacks of old newspapers, he said that he was saving them for the day his brother would regain his eyesight, so he could "catch up on the news."

Following an anonymous tip, the police arrived at the Collyers' dilapidated mansion on March 21, 1947. After long hours spent trying to clear out one of the blocked entryways, a single patrolman managed to crawl in. Homer was found dead, though still slightly warm, seated with his head resting on his knees. Langley was still at large, so he became the quarry of an elaborate manhunt across multiple states. Seventeen days later, after workers had removed tons of garbage from the brother's home, they discovered Langley's body ten feet from where Homer was found. The detectives reasoned that he had been caught in one of his own booby traps while getting food for his brother, who starved to death a few days later.

"How can you make an ontological distinction between outside and inside?" E. L. Doctorow asks in his fictional retelling of the Collyers' true story. "On the basis of staying dry when it rains? Warm when it's cold? What after all can be said about having a roof over your head that is philosophically meaningful? The inside is the outside and the outside is the inside. Call it God's inescapable world." In Doctorow's novel hoarding seems less a sign of weakness than the manifestation of a radical power. The hoarder is the only one who is capable of inviting the whole world in, who is not driven by the fear that leads most of us to protect the sacred indoors from the profane filth that lies outside. For the hoarder, the home's interiority is no longer a place to escape from the harsh world without but a place into which all the world's lowly forms are welcome with a motto that contradicts the naysayers: In My Back Yard. If Saint Francis of Assisi were alive today, he would not rid himself of all his earthly possessions. He would prefer, like the hoarder, to let go, or dispossess himself, of nothing.

One of the greatest paradoxes at the heart of liberalism now becomes clear. As an example, think about the actions we personally take, or consider taking, to help the homeless. It hardly occurs to us to invite one of them over for dinner. Liberal benevolence usually stops at the doorstep. Dewey criticizes this tendency by echoing Voltaire: "Each of us needs to cultivate his own garden. But there is no fence about this garden: it is not sharply marked-off enclosure. Our garden is the world." Would it be possible to use the hoarder's exceptional hospitality toward objects as a basic model for a new kind of hospitality directed at persons? This is not as far-fetched as it seems. Imagine that New York is one big Collyer mansion and all its inhabitants are but disposable human waste. Emma Lazarus's "New Colossus" can then be read as a hoarder's plea: "Give me your tired, your poor, your huddled masses yearning to breathe free, the wretched refuse of your teeming shore."

THIRTY-FOURTH CHAPTER   JUNK

IN WHAT WAS PROBABLY one of his last long strolls around town, Benjamin found himself in Alphabet City, a section of the Lower East Side that in the mid-1980s looked more like a war zone than a residential neighborhood, complete with burnt-out buildings and sporadic gunfire. Miraculously, no one even bothered to rob this scruffy old man. But he was still offered every type of drug under the sun by a handful of enthusiastic dealers. Back then, people liked to say that those who went to Avenue A were Adventurous, those who went down to B were Bold, those who went all the way to C were Crazy, and those who ventured to Avenue D were just Dead. At the corner of C and Eighth Benjamin noticed to his delight the graffiti on the exterior wall of a squatted building. It read, "Opium is the religion of the people." When he got back to his apartment, he copied this obvious quip as the epigraph for a section in *The Manhattan Project* called "Down and Out," which I will now analyze.

Between 1927 and 1934 Benjamin composed detailed protocols to chart his repeated experimentations with hashish. Some of these notes even found their way into the pages of *The Arcades Project*. In other texts written during the same period under the influence, it seems as if the hashish adventures and the impact of surrealism merge into one. Famously, he refers to both experiences as "profane illuminations." These were his prime examples of moments in which an illumination is triggered by an encounter with the everyday rather than the holy, by experiences that are rooted in material conditions rather than spiritual ones. They constitute, in a sense, an irreligious religion.

There are a few other ways to explain this key notion in Benjamin's thought. A profane illumination often involves pleasurable practices instead of ascetic ones. The light tends to emanate not from what society looks up to and consecrates but precisely from what it neglects or casts aside. Whereas sacred illumination tries to open the gate to the other world, profane illumination tries to open our minds to a different life. While religious illumination is heliotropic, forcing all living beings to grow in the direction of a single source of light, profane illumination is rhizomatic, in that it encourages a multiplicity of roots and shoots to develop underground in every which way. It now becomes apparent that one of the best profane illuminations can come to those who go to the trouble of reading *The Arcades Project* itself.

🐦

UNDERSTANDING THE SHIFT in Benjamin's approach to this issue as he worked on *The Manhattan Project* requires no pharmacological assistance. It takes only a measure of basic sociological and literary insight. Think, in this context, of a man like Henry James, who was convinced that "character is so lost in quantity," who received "through almost any accident of vision more impressions than he knew what to do with." The infinite commotion caused by the masses living in twentieth-century New York—this "tremendous *muchness*," as his brother William called it—was therefore perceived by Henry as a deadly Sahara, as a place where his delicate art of profane illuminations and convoluted observations stood no chance of survival. For the average twentieth-century New Yorker, however, reading James's novels can lead to the assumption that the man was *on* something.

This makes sense once we realize that James was unwilling or unable to embrace an attitude that he felt to be an artificial, altered state of consciousness. This attitude was what Georg Simmel, one of Benjamin's teachers, called urban blasé, which he defined as an "indifference toward the distinctions between things." This is not to suggest that the average twentieth-century New Yorker thought that, say, the dignitary who just passed by in a motorcade on the way to the United Nations was identical to the unhinged homeless person loitering on the corner. The nerves of the urban dweller are neither numb nor exhausted but very receptive and constantly alert, not only to the palpable differences between the sovereign and the beggar but also to the minutest distinctions to which out-of-towners can be impervious (the cut of a jacket, a look in the eye, the scent in the air). City dwellers are very attuned to the fact that everything is different from everything else, but they also assume that almost nothing should be a cause for either excitement or alarm, let alone a literary treatment.

If James was overdosing on the city, then Simmel got high off its fumes. Informed by this dual observation during the time his life in New York began to take shape, Benjamin realized that hashish could only be a gateway to a much deeper, or darker, experience fueled by heroin. At his advanced age, he was wise enough, or timid enough, to forgo the required fieldwork. Instead of developing a habit as a user, he settled for developing a theory as a scholar, one dedicated to what he considered the definitive drug of twentieth-century New York.

Admittedly, Benjamin's encounters with heroin culture were few and far between. His main sources of information on the subject were a couple of slim books: William Burroughs's *Junky* and, to a lesser extent, Jim Carroll's *The Basketball Diaries*. The yellowish copies of these titles at the Public Library contain numerous notations in Benjamin's handwriting. His reflections on heroin are consequently not so edifying for those seriously interested in this subject. Yet they still require at least the minimal attention of this short chapter for the disruptive force they have on his own evolving thought.

In a nutshell, Benjamin argues that a heroin habit gives the junky an introductory lesson in what he calls *profane darkness*. This not-too-clever wordplay is effective in stressing the point that the addict is not inspired, that he is not among the illuminati. It is not that he can see something the others cannot. The point is that he can *not* see this something that others cannot *not* see, and that this something is what we call *the light*.

Profane darkness, however, has little to do with religious sin or punishment. Though Burroughs claims that "if God made anything better, He kept it for

Himself," Benjamin does his best to clear the experience of heroin use of any theological overtones. This is possibly what he has in mind when he mentions that instead of speaking of heaven or hell (depending on how much time has passed since a last hit), New York addicts prefer to talk about going "uptown" or "downtown."

Burroughs argues that unlike alcohol and cannabis, which may increase the enjoyment of life, heroin "is not a kick. It is a way of life." This is one of the better ways to explain the difficulty in overcoming this drug habit. The problem is not that heroin, also known as junk, is so addictive, or that it is so good, or that the withdrawal sickness is so horrible to bear. The main problem is that "when you give up junk, you give up a way of life." Hashish may open up the floodgates of experience that modern society has dried out, but heroin is capable of demolishing its entire mode of being to such an extent that, in comparison, religious conversion seems like make-believe. It is reality, not fantasy, that presents itself to the junky as an impossible pipe dream. The days turn dark.

Benjamin suggests that shooting heroin is like pulling the emergency brake of a subway car in the middle of the tunnel during rush hour. Burroughs's formulation is even more evocative: "Junk is the inoculation of death that keeps the body in a condition of emergency." Unless you overdose, heroin is not going to kill you; it is just going to submerge your existence into a profane darkness, a blackout, that will render the normal life of all the clean people around you not only indecipherable but outright unlivable.

Rather than try to listen to what junkies have to say about our deeply problematic modern society, we tend to dismiss them as a societal problem or even threat. "Many policemen and narcotics agents," Burroughs argues, "are precisely addicted to power, to exercising a certain nasty kind of power over people who are helpless. The nasty sort of power: white junk, I call it—rightness; they're right, right, right—and if they lost that power, they would suffer excruciating withdrawal symptoms." The junky knows that even those who pretend to be clean are secretly hooked on what Benjamin believes to be the "most terrible drug—ourselves—which we take in solitude." Compared to this drug, heroin is benign.

🐦

BENJAMIN DID NOT USUALLY date his *Manhattan Project* entries. He made an exception as he was copying a well-known line from *Thus Spoke Zarathustra*, uttered as the townspeople await the tightrope walker to begin his soon-to-be-disastrous stunt:

"I love those who do not know how to live, except by going under, for they are the ones who cross over." Just below this line Benjamin added: August 7, 1974. This is the day he happened to see with his own eyes Philippe Petit successfully balanced on a wire stretched between the just-completed Twin Towers.

THIRTY-FIFTH CHAPTER   **LOST**

"IF YOU'RE A ROCKEFELLER, New York is really your town." One may wonder whether this line from Warhol is correct in its assumption that even the Rockefellers could claim for themselves such a privileged position. Either way, the important question is where does this assessment leave everybody else? Why does it feel slightly strange to treat New York as *your* city, no matter how long you have been living in it?

The phrase *my city* rarely appears in the literature on New York. It could very well be that the last time it was written without raising the critical reader's eyebrow is sometime in the second half of the nineteenth century, around the time Whitman made use of it in "Mannahatta" ("I was asking for something specific and perfect for my city, whereupon lo! upsprang the aboriginal name!"). Of course, even this case is quite problematic, given that Whitman was from Brooklyn, which was a separate city back then.

Once old New York grew into the immense metropolis of the twentieth century, the fact that someone, anyone, chose to claim possession of such a complex place was not so much wrong as it was a marker of bad taste. For example, Lewis Mumford, who developed a deeply antagonistic relationship with New York (while spending most of his days in a picturesque little hamlet upstate), repeatedly refers to it as "my city" throughout his voluminous publications.

The most intriguing case of this philological oddity will not show up in a typical database phrase search. The reason is that, in this case, there is a third word wedged between *my* and *city*. Benjamin shows that this little word transforms the phrase beyond recognition: "Thus I take leave of my lost city," Fitzgerald writes. "Seen from the ferry boat in the early morning, it no longer whispers of fantastic success and eternal youth." In other words, the city can be mine only after it is already lost, only after it is no longer mine. In other words, only the dispossessed can possess New York. But like my dead language, my lost city is slightly more than just a contradiction in terms.

"My Lost City" is an essay in which Fitzgerald recounts his personal rise and fall through the lens of his oscillating relationship with New York. It begins with his first encounter with Manhattan as a teenager, when he viewed the island as a place of romance and triumph and splendor, followed by a description of his first days living in a small Bronx apartment after he had dropped out of college, when the city still "had all the iridescence of the beginning of the world." Then comes the requisite account of the first hard years leading up to his meteoric literary success as the voice of his generation and "archetype of what New York wanted."

Nevertheless, Fitzgerald claims that it was *after* he left the city (for the Midwest and then for Europe) that he began to "see New York whole" and to treat it as his home whenever he happened to be back. He first returned just before the Wall Street crash, when "the city was bloated, glutted, stupid with cake and circuses." But it was only when he returned a second time, after the Great Depression had taken its toll, that his scattered view of the city crystallized into these iconic lines:

> From the ruins, lonely and inexplicable as the sphinx, rose the Empire State Building and, just as it had been a tradition of mine to climb to the Plaza Roof to take leave of the beautiful city, extending as far as eyes could reach, so now I went to the roof of the last and most magnificent of towers. Then I understood—everything was explained: I had discovered the crowning error of the city, its Pandora's box. Full of vaunting pride the New Yorker had climbed here and seen with dismay what he had never suspected, that the city was not the endless succession of canyons that he had supposed but that *it had limits*—from the tallest structure he saw for the first time that it faded out into the country on all sides, into an expanse of green and blue that alone was limitless. And with the awful realization that New York was a city after all and not a universe, the whole shining edifice that he had reared in his imagination came crashing to the ground.

When, immediately after this passage, Fitzgerald calls New York "my lost city," it is unclear whether the loss hinges on the word *my* or on the word *city*, whether it is the author or the place (or both) that exudes, at the essay's conclusion, a sense of failure or defeat. Wittgenstein argues that "*the limits of my language* mean the limits of my world." Fitzgerald suggests that the limits of his city must also mean the limits of his life, that neither he nor it is the endless field of possibilities that his young self took for granted. He manages to blur the lines between the prodigal city and its prodigal son, between the lost generation and the lost hope of its poster child, drinking away his life.

Benjamin, however, does not interpret this finale as a projection of a state of mind onto a state of affairs, or an introjection of a state of affairs into a state of mind. Rather, he sees it as the constitution of a special zone, called literature, where place and self cannot be thought of independently of each other. This feat is not achieved at the moment when Fitzgerald takes possession of New York, or at the moment when New York takes possession of Fitzgerald, but, improbably, at the very moment when they lose each other, when they let each other go.

This moment is less tragic than it first appears. As Fitzgerald demonstrates in *The Great Gatsby*, real tragedy befalls the titular character because he "sprang from his Platonic conception of himself." Jay Gatsby is a self-made man in more than one sense. He is impelled by his unattainable conception of love as he sits in his suburban conception of a home. When Fitzgerald's image of the city, but also his own self-image, comes crashing to the ground, at least the risk that either he or it will suffer the devastating consequences of such a Platonic or unrealistic ideal of greatness has been averted.

FITZGERALD WAS ONE of the first to realize that all significant concepts in modern economic thought are monetized psychological concepts. Setting aside some obvious examples (depression and depreciation, trust and risk, incentive and demand, equity and liability, credit and debt), as well as Fitzgerald's own meditation in *Gatsby* on the complex relationship between being rich and being happy, Benjamin focuses on the novelist's consistent view of failure as a "mark of spiritual bankruptcy" or "emotional bankruptcy."

Fitzgerald was convinced that people have a certain amount of emotional capital and that reckless spending of this special, irreplaceable fund can make a person go bust and crack up. This, he came to realize around the time he wrote "My Lost City," was the best way to describe his own predicament. He was, in short, going under. Once, when a friend tried to warn the Fitzgeralds about their erratic behavior, Zelda replied, "But Sara, didn't you know? We don't believe in conservation."

Living is traditionally understood either as a striving for growth (what Nietzsche calls the will to power) or, at the very least, for perseverance (what Spinoza calls *conatus*). With this in mind, Benjamin wants to dispel the assumption that Fitzgerald wrote "The Crack-Up," a sequel of sorts to "My Lost City," as merely an autobiographical exposé. Echoing Ernest Hemingway's unsurprisingly virile reaction to this "whining in public," Maxwell Perkins, the legendary editor of both writers, describes Fitzgerald's text as "an indecent invasion of his own privacy." For Benjamin, however, "The Crack-Up" is so much more. He approaches the essay as a first-rate philosophical treatise whose aim is to stand the established view of life on its head.

"Of course," Fitzgerald asserts in the first sentence, "all life is a process of breaking down." To be sure, until one reaches a certain age, life may have presented itself as a process of creative discoveries and edifying growth, as "something you dominated if you were any good," something that "yielded easily to intelligence and effort." But this is just the illusory preamble to the long process of falling apart, which is what life turns out to be really about. Fitzgerald's essay is mapping the varieties of destructive experience. The question is not whether, but when, and how, and to what extent, each of us is going to crack:

> The blows that do the dramatic side of the work—the big sudden blows that come, or seem to come, from outside—the ones you remember and blame things on and, in moments of weakness, tell your friends about, don't show their effect all at once. There is another sort of blow that comes from within—that you don't feel until it's too late to do anything about it, until you realize with finality that in some regard you will never be as good a man again. The first sort of breakage seems to happen quick—the second kind happens almost without your knowing it but is realized suddenly indeed.

Things would have been much simpler if the crack-up had either come from an external force or simply meant death. But Fitzgerald treats this breakage as the very thing that defines life as such. The crack-up does not give form to my life but deforms it, as in an anti-bildungsroman. Blow by blow, it shatters whatever values and meanings I used to have. But for some reason, I keep on going, like a cracked plate kept in the pantry.

This crack-up, according to Fitzgerald, constitutes the true meaning and value of our existence. Life is like a restaurant where almost everyone is getting a different dish from the one ordered. Fitzgerald adds another culinary allegory, borrowed from the Gospels: It is one thing to imagine that everything that we eat is completely bland because it lacks even a pinch of salt. It is quite another to imagine that salt itself lost its taste, so that even the hope of anything ever being salted becomes impossible. The crack-up means that life itself is lifeless in the same way that this cursed salt is saltless.

Even though there are no second acts in American lives, Fitzgerald predicts that "there was certainly to be a second act to New York's boom days." Published in 1945, five years after Fitzgerald's death, the personal essays in *The Crack-Up* struck the wrong chord in a city celebrating the victorious end of the Second

World War. Yet prescient New Yorkers like Benjamin soon realized that the war's end was also the moment when the tables turned and the small cracks throughout the city began to show.

The slow disintegration that began around 1945 petered out only after Benjamin's last days, in the late 1980s. From then on there arose the cautious sense that New York was slowly getting back on its feet. It was as if the city had indeed gotten its promised second act. Even the tragedy of 2001 did not manage to shut down the "lush and liquid garden parties" that Fitzgerald remembered from his first giddy New York days. Still, all cities, prosperous or ailing, break down the lives of their inhabitants. To imagine a city means to imagine a fractured life.

THIRTY-SIXTH CHAPTER **PERFECT DAY**

THIS SHORT ADDENDUM to the last chapter can begin with the observation that Fitzgerald narrates the city from without. He is that "young boy arriving from the Corn Belt with a manuscript in his suitcase and a pain in his heart," as typified by E. B. White's description of the urban settler who "embraces New York with the intense excitement of first love," absorbs it "with the fresh eyes of an adventurer," and then "generates heat and light to dwarf the Consolidated Edison Company." J. D. Salinger, in contrast, narrates the city from within. He uses his Manhattan childhood as source material for the young New Yorkers who populate many of the stories he published before he withdrew in seclusion to New Hampshire.

Salinger is not so interested in urban narratives drenched in motifs of rebirth and the hereafter, second comings and second acts, promised lands and New Jerusalems. His city is not the destiny of triumphant arrival but a trap to be escaped, where nearly everyone is phony, where "everything everybody does is so—I don't know—not *wrong*, or even mean, or even stupid necessarily. But just so tiny and meaningless and—sad-making." This, however, does not change the fact that the island of Manhattan remains the geographic anchor of his fiction. It is the only place that feels real. It is the place where his brilliant-yet-troubled characters spend their formative years. It is also the place to which they often return, though without a shred of enchantment.

The word *naive* is related to the word *native* (and both are relatives of the word *nation*). Nevertheless, in Salinger's universe naiveté is something that his native New Yorkers are completely unfamiliar with, even as children. Consider

"Hapworth 16, 1924," the last piece he ever published. It is a story in the form of a letter, written by Seymour Glass, a seven-year-old wunderkind at summer camp who shows levels of intelligence and maturity that feel more freakish and alarming than impressive. The letter is so elaborate and so long that it filled an entire issue of the *New Yorker* magazine. It is Salinger's most radical attempt to do something that seems to be theologically impossible: to imagine a life that eats from the Tree of Knowledge but remains innocent.

Salinger's young characters, many of whom make up his Glass family saga, may not lead happy lives. But they are very much alive. Their attitude toward the city is hardly blasé. They are not desensitized but rather hypersensitized by New York's muchness. This is not the life of well-protected suburban kids, the life of the naive nonnatives. Salinger's not-naive natives were even exposed to the merciless public eye from a very early age. The seven Glass children were the stars of the radio show *It's a Wise Child* (an allusion to Telemachus, Penelope's son, expressing skepticism that Odysseus is indeed his father). Benjamin therefore speculates that if the siblings of the James family (not only William and Henry but also Alice, Bob, and Wilkie) had grown up in twentieth-century New York instead of in the more manageable nineteenth-century city, they would probably have ended up like the Glass family.

The openness, absorption, and intensity with which Salinger's characters face their surroundings—but also their own existence—is nothing short of mesmerizing. Yet it is also obviously self-destructive. If mental health requires a certain level of mental deprivation, then they would rather go unhinged. They tend not to crack like plates but to shatter like glass. Salinger's "A Perfect Day for Bananafish" concludes (in the same way as Fitzgerald's "May Day") when the main character, the same Seymour Glass (the unhappy camper from Hapworth), now thirty-one years old, suddenly shoots himself in the head.

Seymour exemplifies a person "not deprived of, but rather surfeited with, the joys of life." He is a kind of "paranoiac in reverse," always suspecting that others are plotting to make him happy. We should note this before mentioning Alfred Kazin's accusation that Salinger is fixated on the sort of individuals "who have been released by our society to think of themselves as endlessly sensitive, spiritually alone, gifted, and whose suffering lies in the narrowing of their consciousness to themselves, in the withdrawal of their curiosity from a society which they think they understand all too well, in the drying up of their hope, their trust, and their wonder at the great world itself."

A more generous reading would be to say that Salinger's precocious characters suffer not because they are self-absorbed but because they are environment-absorbed;

because they are captivated by the world; because they embrace the abundance of city life, taking it all in, filtering and concealing and withholding almost nothing, for which reason they fail to protect their own fragile selves. Benjamin surmises that this might also explain why Salinger chose to leave the city at the height of his success. For Salinger, New York was the banana hole into which the bananafish swims to eat so many bananas that it gets fat, gets stuck, gets banana fever, and dies.

THIRTY-SEVENTH CHAPTER   # A THEORY OF THE HOMELESS

THE MODERN NATION-STATE is a political machine whose operation consists of constant management and occasional disposal of vast quantities of human waste. The excluded individuals who find themselves in the latter predicament cannot expect to be protected by the same laws, or granted the same rights, that regular citizens take for granted. During the 1930s Benjamin was relegated to the status of refuse by the German body politic. Luckily, he had only a limited firsthand experience of the network of ghettos and camps into which millions of others were herded. There he would have met those human beings who were stripped of their political existence in the most extreme ways imaginable. Those bare lives whose worth was close to zero exposed the true horror of modern politics.

During the same twentieth century the operation of the economic system was also pushing hordes of human beings to the periphery of irrelevance. Those individuals had little chance to be anything more than fodder for the capitalist machine. They were, and still are, disposable. Big cities, the engines of economic expansion, tried to cope with their growing shantytowns, slums, or ghettos by constructing massive housing projects. One could say, after making all the necessary qualifications, that the logic that once led progressive policy makers and modernistic architects to consider these drab housing projects the rational cure for urban blight was not completely dissimilar to the logic that made the camps look like a more advanced and efficient solution to the Jewish problem than the chaotic ghettos from the beginning of the war had proven to be. Cloaked in layers of moralistic and technocratic benevolence, all too many public housing projects cannot hide the fact that they are social concentration camps.

Surveying the urban economic spectrum that extends from opulence to wretchedness, Benjamin focuses on those who have truly touched bottom. He looks for those city inhabitants separated from their economic existence in the most extreme form imaginable, the limit cases for whom even public housing would be considered a dream come true. Enter the homeless, the only figure that deserves to be called the protagonist of *The Manhattan Project*.

The refugee is politically homeless, because he has no homeland, or he has no access to it. A refugee camp is a space designed to contain the anomalies who fail to fit the Western tradition's definition of man as *homo politicus* in the same way that a homeless shelter is a space that is supposed to keep tabs on the aberrations who fail to fit the definition of man as *homo economicus*. These architectonic receptacles for those who question with their very being the idea that all humans are equally and fully both political and economic animals are not merely practical solutions to exigent problems. They are also precisely what allow this deceitful idea to perpetuate itself.

Modern society sometimes looks for ways to care for the superfluous individuals who are excluded from the political and economic systems. At other times, it simply forsakes them. Benjamin knew of Marx's claim that Henry VIII ordered the systematic hanging of seventy-two thousand vagrants in sixteenth-century England. After the colonization of North America many British vagrants avoided punishment for their nonexistent crimes by opting to be shipped to New York. Benjamin was also aware that in late nineteenth-century Paris "between one-third and one-half of all arrests fell under vagrancy laws." He also cites a few clippings from the *New York Times* about the various anti-homeless policies implemented in the 1980s. Though no solution to the homeless problem was in sight by the time of his death, the mere possibility filled him with understandable dread.

Benjamin does not delude himself that the constant oscillation between the two patronizing gestures toward the homeless—inclusion and exclusion, looking after and looking away—can ever be stopped. The stakes for him are different. He chooses to consider the homeless person as a historical figure that requires a theoretical understanding rather than as a social problem that demands a practical solution. On the heels of his original approach to the flâneur, who aimlessly strolled through the streets of Paris, he tried to think of homelessness as an ideal type of New York life. He knew that the homeless were the key to his decoding of a crucial segment in the DNA not only of the city but of modernity.

His approach is based on his observation, first formulated in the 1920s, that the persistence of beggars "in front of our noses is as justified as a scholar's before a difficult text." In *The Arcades Project*, the flâneur takes the role of the scholar, scrupulously "reading" the streets of Paris as if they were verses in a sacred manuscript.

In *The Manhattan Project*, however, the beggar and the homeless do not appear necessarily to be engaged in a close reading of the city. Their persistence, their scrupulousness, is directed at *us*.

WANDERING THE CITY STREETS while lost in reverie, or strolling while being receptive to whatever reaches your senses, is a somewhat privileged experience. It is hard to be a flâneur when you are in a hurry or when there are things on your mind. Most important, most of us have to have a home to fall back on, someplace, even just a couch in a friend's apartment, where we can crash at the end of our meandering. The homeless person's perception of the city must therefore be radically different, also because, in New York, there is something further that prevents most people from observing the city through the eyes of the flâneur.

With Berlin on his mind, Benjamin writes about the importance of losing oneself in one's own city, because only then do "signboards and street names, passers-by, roofs, kiosks, and bars . . . speak to the wanderer like a twig snapping under his feet in the forest, like the startling call of a bittern in the distance, like the sudden stillness of a clearing with a lily standing erect at its center." But thanks to New York's gridiron street plan, it is much more difficult to truly get lost there. The young Benjamin's romantic vision of cities is rendered obsolete by the ninety-degree intersections of numbered streets and avenues. His New York years were mostly informed by the imminent danger of getting mugged rather than getting lost.

Pedestrians rarely feel at home in the streets of New York, at least not in the same way the flâneur felt that the Parisian boulevards and arcades were closing in on him as if they were his personal living room. But as we replace this Parisian character with his emblematic New York heir, we must maintain our approach to the homeless person as the true inhabitant of the street, as the figure who can best bear witness to the nonarchitectonic city, to the city that lacks insidedness, even if his testimony is rarely heard. There remains an understandable temptation to transplant wholesale the experience of the nineteenth-century flâneur into twentieth-century New York. Here is one such attempt, taken from Paul Auster's *New York Trilogy*, which Benjamin quotes in its entirety:

> New York was an inexhaustible space, a labyrinth of endless steps, and no matter how far he walked, no matter how well he came to know its neighborhoods and streets, it always left him with the feeling of being lost. Lost, not only in the city, but within himself as well. Each time he took a walk he felt as

though he were leaving himself behind, and by giving himself up to the movement of the streets, by reducing himself to a seeing eye, he was able to escape the obligation to think, and this, more than anything else, brought him a measure of peace, a salutary emptiness within. The world was outside of him, around him, before him, and the speed with which it kept changing made it impossible for him to dwell on any one thing for very long. Motion was of the essence, the act of putting one foot in front of the other and allowing himself to follow the drift of his own body. By wandering aimlessly, all places became equal, and it no longer mattered where he was. On his best walks, he was able to feel that he was nowhere. New York was the nowhere he had built around himself, and he realized that he had no intention of ever leaving it again.

It is no surprise that Quinn, the main character presented to the reader on the second page of the book as a certified flâneur, will metamorphose by the end of the story into a hopeless homeless person, stranded on a street corner, unable or unwilling to keep going. It is as if in the figure of the homeless the constant movement of the flâneur comes to a standstill. The city itself comes to a standstill. The homeless person, Benjamin therefore argues, is an *exhausted flâneur*. He usually sits or lies down. He could walk around, but what for? What is there to see, or do? Unlike all the diligent urban students who pass him by, why should he even bother to try to do his home-work?

One of the more amusing bits in the otherwise exhausting *Arcades Project* is Benjamin's claim that for a short period in the nineteenth century it was considered elegant to walk around Paris with a tortoise attached to a string, as if it were a dog on a leash. This was designed to be an effective method of immersion in the city streets. A tortoise either cannot or need not walk fast because, regardless, it carries its home on its back. Homeless persons do not have a home where they can leave their minimal possessions for safekeeping, so they carry everything with them in plastic bags or shopping carts, which is one of the reasons that mobility (literally and metaphorically) is very difficult in their case. So everything slows to a glacial pace.

🕊

EDGAR ALLAN POE wrote "The Man of the Crowd" in 1840 while living in New York. Yet he set his story in London, probably because its urban landscape was more developed at the time. It is a strange tale of a decrepit and filthy old man, feverishly walking through the metropole's crowded streets from evening until morning without ever taking a break. The big question that looms throughout is what keeps the man going. He seems to be driven by a sense of terror: that if he stops, even for a moment, he will have to confront his own nothingness. "To Poe," Benjamin writes, "the flâneur was, above all, someone who does not feel comfortable in his own company. This is why he seeks out the crowd."

But there may be an even deeper motive, one that Edwin Burrows and Mike Wallace clarify in their definitive history of New York City up to 1898: "The flâneur's confidence in civic legibility, Poe suggests, is shallow and misplaced. Crowds and cities are indecipherable." It is as if Poe already knew in the mid-nineteenth century that the flâneur would eventually become the homeless person, someone who could not care less about his peripatetic impressions of the urban scene. For the homeless, the city is not a book; or if it is a book, then it is illegible; or if it is legible, then it is locked inside a safe. This explains why Benjamin comments that the compliment that someone "has the key to the street" is reserved for those to whom the door is forever closed.

If Benjamin is right that the flâneur is "a spy for the capitalists, on assignment in the realm of consumers," then the homeless person can be understood as an economic terrorist. For the homeless individual, the entire city with its buildings and people is an object of indifference, scorn, or despair. Everything is nothing to this urban hunter-gatherer. The only way he can fight the economic system from which he has been jettisoned is by being himself, by presenting his inhuman condition, by implanting his misery smack in the middle of luxury's face. The bomb is not strapped to his waist; it is his very form of life.

Whereas the flâneur busies himself in a phenomenology of the cityscape, the homeless person is engaged in its deconstruction. The flâneur is not a terrorist but a kind of local tourist. He never ceases to discover the world in which he already lives. Like a moth, he cannot help flying straight into the capitalist flame. The masses form the smokescreen that obfuscates the flâneur's ability to see how hellish the city is. He is intoxicated by the urban landscape, and he cannot wean himself off the streets. The homeless person, in contrast, is capital's hangover. His is a naked city.

"In the flâneur," Benjamin writes, "is reborn the sort of idler that Socrates picked out from the Athenian marketplace to be his interlocutor. Only, there is no longer a Socrates. And the slave labor that guaranteed him his leisure has likewise ceased to exist." One day, after reading a book about the lives of the ancient Cynic philosophers in the New York Public Library, Benjamin passed by a disheveled homeless person during the walk back to his apartment. Then it hit him. The homeless person is not Socrates's interlocutor but a reluctant Diogenes, the great

Cynic who concealed nothing from his fellow Athenians, living "like a dog" in the public eye. For example, Diogenes used to urinate and even masturbate in the marketplace; he slept inside a wooden barrel; and his only earthly possession was a bowl for food, which he then got rid of after noticing that little children cup their hands to drink from the fountain.

Without even intending to do so, homeless people present to the homeful city inhabitants the most radical example of "an other life," not in the sense of a life to which we need to aspire or from which we should take our distance, but in the sense of a life that is simply other than the one we otherwise thoughtlessly, conceitedly, take for granted. The fundamental point of the Cynic's provocations is not to show us that we are necessarily wrong about the way we live. It is, rather, to help us realize that we are not necessarily right, either. In Cynicism (and, Benjamin adds, in urbanism), culture and nature, lawfulness and lawlessness, humanism and barbarism, lose their sharp distinctions. And they do so in ways that do not seem to be dangerous but virtuous.

This is the reason that lowering the homeless population in the streets of New York—either by policing them away, as the last few mayors tried to do; or by putting them on a boat made of reinforced concrete, as Le Corbusier envisioned in the late 1920s; or by senselessly killing them, as Patrick Bateman does in *American Psycho*—is a sure way of reducing city life to an unexamined life, which, as you probably know, is not worth living. The homeless person is the sentry who watches over sheer life's radical depth. When he is caught off guard—when urban misery is just a billboard on a bus advertising the Broadway version of Hugo's *Les Misérables*—the shallow banality of evil begins to creep in: "There is an idea of a Patrick Bateman, some kind of abstraction, but there is no real me, only an entity, something illusory, and though I can hide my cold gaze and you can shake my hand and feel flesh gripping yours and maybe you can even sense our lifestyles are probably comparable: *I simply am not there*."

🕊

IN 1947, Heidegger declared that "homelessness is coming to be the destiny of the world." Being homeless, however, was not understood there as a material condition but as an existential one. It is not a matter of a housing shortage or of being out of luck. Heidegger's point is that instead of "dwelling in the truth of being," we have come to realize that this home is foreclosed.

Heidegger's work is dedicated to asking the question of the meaning of being. It is triggered by his realization that humanity has almost completely forgotten this question. This explains why instead of the word *existence* he sometimes writes "ek-sistence," which is meant to echo the word *ecstasy*, which originally meant to stand outside oneself. Our state of being—he is trying to tell us in his usual convoluted way—is being outside of being.

"Homelessness so understood consists in the abandonment of beings by being. Homelessness is the symptom of oblivion of being." Put differently, we are alienated from being; it is unfamiliar to us; we find it uncanny (*Unheimliche*, which literally means not homely, since everything at home is familiar and knowable). As a result we feel angst, which can be distinguished from the kind of anxiety directed toward this or that being (the plane, the tower). Angst is directed toward being as such. We just cannot bring ourselves to feel at home in the world. We are homeless in that we are worldless. This is like stepping into a cocktail party and feeling uncomfortable, as if we do not belong, estranged from everyone around. Only that in angst the entire world feels like one big cocktail party.

But why *should* we feel at home at a boring cocktail party? Are we required to just be comfortable about the shallow chatter and meaningless smiles? Normally, Heidegger argues, we go about our average everyday life with "tranquillized self-assurance." We are absorbed in the familiar social world and entangled in our habitus. The condition of not-being-at-home, of being homeless, is not to be understood merely as something negative, as a privation that must be avoided at any cost. Homelessness is, rather, a more primordial state of being, the kind of being that may save us from falling prey to thoughtless normative behavior.

This explains Heidegger's great fascination with Novalis's observation: "Philosophy is really homesickness, an urge to be at home everywhere." Heidegger thinks that this is a very strange definition, especially because he believes that today homesickness is on the wane: "Has not contemporary city man, the ape of civilization, long since eradicated homesickness?" But even if homesickness still exists, it is hard to imagine that the urge to be at home (somewhere or everywhere) can ever be fulfilled. The task of the homeless philosopher is therefore to remind us what it felt like before we took the first sip from that glass of wine and began to get comfortable, perhaps a little too comfortable, in the world. This is the light in which we should read the following line from Oswald Spengler, which Benjamin copied in his *Arcades Project*: "Man as civilized being, as *intellectual nomad*, is again wholly microcosmic, wholly homeless, as free intellectually as hunter and herdsman were free sensually."

To be homeless is to live in unconcealment. Practically, you need to do almost everything in public. Others cannot not mind your own business. It is very difficult to hide anything from anyone, even from yourself, without having at least minimal privacy. Even repression becomes a luxury. But when one leads a life that is bare, almost naked, then truth, which is always a kind of scandal, also seems to be closer than ever before. Truth in Greek is *alethea*, which, Heidegger tells us, means "not hidden." In a landscape built of sheer life, the homeless are that truth.

THIRTY-EIGHTH CHAPTER # THE HOMELESS PHILOSOPHER

WORKING FOR HOURS ON END at the long communal reading tables at the New York Public Library, one is tempted to scrutinize at moments of distraction the other patrons and muse about their lives. It is an easy enough task to single out the occasional homeless persons from the rest. They usually doze off, or stare blankly at the ceiling, or amble about at random. The difficulty begins when one starts to notice a special type of patron who cannot be confused with either the seemingly dejected homeless persons or the seemingly dignified users. Benjamin refers to those threshold characters as "homeless philosophers." With their slightly unkempt attire, jumbles of papers and other personal belongings, obsessive daily research, and questionable reading material (often a heavily used copy of the Bible), these outsider scholars are a recurrent object of curiosity in his *Manhattan Project*.

At one point in the manuscript Benjamin questions his ability to scan the assorted library patrons sitting around the reading tables and positively identify who might be a professional philosopher and who a homeless one. Keenly aware of his own marginal and anonymous existence, he knew that other patrons might mistake him for just one more of those dubious characters. The librarian Beatrice Wald perceived him in this way for many years, before the two came to know each other on a more personal level. In other words, Benjamin's interest in homeless philosophers shows that he did not consider their condition completely extraneous to his own. One fragment from *The Manhattan Project*, titled "Lives of Unpublished Authors," is an unrealized plan for a book of short intellectual biographies dedicated to a few of these shabby thinkers, whom Benjamin came to know so intimately from his years of daily visits to the library—though only by sight.

One homeless philosopher did make it into the pages of the surviving manuscript. He was one of the first that Benjamin noticed when he had begun to frequent the library's main branch in the 1950s, though he never saw him again in the decades to follow. This man used to sit all the way in the back of the Genealogy Division room on the first floor. He was short and bald, with a jaunty disposition and a bushy beard. He always wore the same hand-me-down, three-piece suit that was two sizes too big for him. He rarely bothered to read any of the library materials, and when he did, he could be heard mumbling curses at the books' authors. Most of the time he was scribbling with a fountain pen in a battered grammar school composition book, writing something and crossing it out, writing and crossing out, as if possessed. His name, Benjamin learned only years later, was Joseph Ferdinand Gould.

Gould was a legendary character in Greenwich Village even before Joseph Mitchell wrote a piece on this self-proclaimed "last of the bohemians" for the *New Yorker* magazine in 1942. (All other bohemians, Gould is quoted in the opening paragraph, "fell by the wayside. Some are in the grave, some are in the loony bin, and some are in the advertising business.") Another way to describe Gould is to simply say that he was an alcoholic bum, constantly afflicted by what he called "the three H's"—Homelessness, Hunger, and Hangovers. When friends wondered how he got by, he informed them that he lived on "air, self-esteem, cigarette butts, cowboy coffee, fried-egg sandwiches, and ketchup," which he mixed in a mug with boiling water to make tomato soup. To keep himself warm during the punishing New York winters, he stuffed newspapers between his shirt and undershirt. "I'm snobbish," he once told Mitchell. "I only use the *Times*."

Although he was raised in a distinguished New England family and graduated from Harvard in 1911, Gould was treated by teachers, parents, and neighbors alike as a natural-born failure. "In my home town," he wrote in one of his composition books, "I never felt at home. I stuck out. Even in my own home, I never felt at home. In New York City, especially in Greenwich Village, down among the cranks and the misfits and the one-lungers and the has-beens and the might've-beens and the would-bes and the never-wills and the God-know-whats, I have always felt at home."

Yet even in the streets and barrooms of the bohemian capital of American culture, Gould was perceived as an amusing curiosity at best; at worst, an intolerable nuisance. The former can be gleaned from a picture taken at his fifty-fourth birthday party, during which he performed his famous stomp while holding a beer growler in each hand. The latter became the consensus on the day he stood outside the Brevoort Café on lower Fifth Avenue, a favorite hangout for radical Leftists, and recited his latest poem with much bravado: "Behind these barricades, the Comrades die! The Comrades die! The Comrades die! And behind these bar-ricades, the Comrades die—of overeating."

BUT THERE WAS ANOTHER WAY Gould wished to be perceived by his contemporaries and remembered for posterity. This was also the way a few of his friends and admirers viewed him, among them the writer William Saroyan, the painter Alice Neel, and the poets Ezra Pound and E. E. Cummings. For all of them, Joe Gould was the author of *The Oral History of Our Time*, a monumental work-in-progress, eleven times as long as the Bible, destined to enter the literary pantheon of the West.

"What we used to think was history," Gould says, "is only formal history and largely false." His task, to which he dedicated forty years of his life, was therefore to record whatever he saw or heard in order to "put down the informal history of the shirt-sleeved multitude—what they had to say about their jobs, love affairs, vittles, sprees, scrapes, and sorrows." His sprawling chronicle of life in New York City was bound to become an even greater intellectual achievement than Gibbon's *History of the Decline and Fall of the Roman Empire*, if only because of the latter's unfortunate remoteness from his subject matter. *The Oral History* was written before, not after the flood. Gould believed that his work "might have great hidden historical significance. It might have portents in it . . . portents of cataclysms, a kind of writing on the wall long before the kingdom falls."

But a lingering uncertainty surrounded Gould's magnum opus. The problem was that no one had ever read an actual chapter from *The Oral History*. There were a few autobiographical sketches and a few essays full of digressions (and digressions of digressions) circulating among his acquaintances. But the real thing was said to be stored away in the cellar of a retired librarian's farmhouse, located in an isolated tract of rural land out on Long Island. Some of the most important publishers in the city tried to convince Gould to let them take a look at the manuscript, but nothing came of it. Mitchell heard Gould reciting a few chapters from memory over seven long nights and over innumerable drinks in a bar on Sixth Avenue, but all his attempts to gain access to the archive of the actual notebooks were rebuffed with various excuses. Gould did publish a few short essays during his lifetime (two of them in the *Dial*, the journal of record of modernist literature), but these were not exactly transcriptions of what other people said. They were mostly concerned with the single subject that never failed to fascinate Gould: himself. Mitchell singles out one sentence from one of these essays: "I have a delusion of grandeur. I believe myself to be Joe Gould."

GOULD DIED IN 1957. Seven years later Mitchell wrote a second article, recounting his many years of intricate relationship with the man who continued to be a part of his life long after the original piece went to print. The crux of this masterpiece of long-form journalism is a plain revelation: *The Oral History* does not exist. Perhaps Gould intended to one day put in writing whatever he had heard and seen and did not forget. But the only thing he really wrote over those long years, Mitchell claims, were endless revisions of the handful of texts already in circulation about his own life story and his own circuitous ideas. There were no notebooks hidden in the librarian's farmhouse because there was no farmhouse and no librarian. It was all just one big hoax. When Mitchell mustered the courage to confront Gould, accusing him of being too lazy to write down his book, which, at best, existed only in his mind, Gould replied that it "wasn't a question of laziness." Neither of them addressed the subject ever again.

In the end Mitchell came to realize that Gould was more than just a pathological liar. All things considered, not writing *The Oral History* was probably much wiser than actually trying to write it. Gould's true masterpiece was not written in ink on paper; it was his very life. His major work was himself: "He had come to Greenwich Village and had found a mask for himself, and he had put it on and kept in on. The Eccentric Author of a Great, Mysterious, Unpublished

Book—that was his mask. And, hiding behind it, he had created a character a good deal more complicated," Mitchell concludes, "than most of the characters created by the novelists and playwrights of his time."

Joe Mitchell sympathized with Joe Gould's predicament mainly because, from an early age, he also had a dream of writing a monumental monograph. It was supposed to be a novel about New York. Inspired by Joyce's *Ulysses*, he wanted it to revolve around a day in the life of a young reporter walking through the streets of a city that he perceived as "a kind of Hell, a Gehenna." Needless to say, this semi-autobiographical book was never written. "Talking to Joe Gould all those years," Mitchell confessed in 1992, "he became me in a way, if you see what I mean."

For more than thirty years after "Joe Gould's Secret" was published, in 1964, Mitchell went to his *New Yorker* office every workday, closed the door behind himself, and sat at his desk with paper and pencils from morning till evening. He told his colleagues that he was writing a new piece, but he never submitted a single word to the editors, who nevertheless kept him around until the day he died, in 1996.

By now it probably doesn't really matter anymore, but it seems like a good place to mention that the existence of Benjamin's *Manhattan Project* may also be contested.

FIFTH THRESHOLD   A TALE OF TWO CITIES

ONE OF THE FINEST and most frequently recited accounts of life in twentieth-century New York was actually written with late eighteenth-century Paris and London in mind: "It was the best of times, it was the worst of times, it was the age of wisdom, it was the age of foolishness, it was the epoch of belief, it was the epoch of incredulity, it was the season of Light, it was the season of Darkness, it was the spring of hope, it was the winter of despair, we had everything before us, we had nothing before us, we were all going direct to Heaven, we were all going direct the other way."

A knee-jerk reaction is to say that Dickens is only making a blanket statement. But a second thought may lead one to realize that there are only certain times when certain places warrant such contradictory descriptions. These stark polarities cannot be explained away by saying that some people are optimistic in nature while others are more pessimistic, that some see heavenly puffy clouds where others see hellishly scorching fires, some are rich and others poor, some are lions and others lambs, some live uptown and others downtown, or some have caffeine in their blood while others have alcohol. It seems more likely that these groups are living in two different cities. One need only watch Martin Scorsese's *Mean Streets* or *Taxi Driver* back to back with Woody Allen's *Annie Hall* or *Manhattan* to understand this strange cognitive dissonance at the heart of New York's collective consciousness.

It is, however, more interesting to think of situations in which the same person sees the darkness quite clearly but still insists on searching in it for the light, or vice versa. Marx once said that the desperate situation filled him with hope. Benjamin, too, was inclined to find miniature redemptions even in the most colossal images of desolation. Scorsese's films also tend to adhere to this school of thought, finding the best of times in the worst of times. Think, for example, of the epilogue to *Taxi Driver*, when Robert De Niro's character, hallucinating or not, metamorphoses from psychopath to hero.

At the same time and in the same place, and because of the same difficulty in distinguishing between reality and fantasy, Allen tends to follow the opposite path, finding the worst of times in the best of times. For example, whenever someone addresses his character in *Annie Hall* with the word *you*, he hears *Jew*. In this respect, Scorsese's and Allen's parallel depictions of late 1970s New York develop the complementary perspectives on early 1960s Rome that can be gleaned from Pier Paolo Pasolini's *Accattone* and Federico Fellini's *La Dolce Vita*. These four filmmakers come together in their adherence to the basic urban rule in Calvino's *Invisible Cities*: "Seek and learn to recognize who and what, in the midst of the inferno, are not inferno, then make them endure, give them space."

SINCE THE DAYS OF AUGUSTINE, the Western tradition has been held captive by the dualistic split of the city into its earthly and heavenly manifestations: one of man, one of God. It is anachronistic to imagine that, before Augustine disseminated this idea (with some theoretical assistance from Plato), people had any reason to believe that atop the Acropolis in Athens or the Temple Mount in Jerusalem stood nothing more than embassies representing ephemeral cities of an otherworldly character. Rather than a simulacrum of heaven, the ancient city was the center of pre-Christian imagination, a sacred place in and of itself, surrounded by profane rural land.

Nor is it surprising that, around the time Nietzsche had his scuffle with God, the modern metropolis returned to its original position as the focal point of an immanent world, a point that represents all our human hopes and despairs simultaneously, with no transcendence in sight. If all the city's a stage, then it must be comedy and tragedy wrapped into one. In comparison to both the classical and modern worlds, the urban centers in the medieval world were pretty weak. The truly magnetic capital city that stirred the people's hearts was the heavenly one. So maybe the dark ages can be defined as the time, or any time, in which humanity treats the city of man as distinct from the city of God.

The nearly half century that Benjamin spent in New York eventually forced him to acknowledge something he had not been ready to admit: the modern city begins to make sense only once it is understood as a space that exists beyond good and evil. Any other approach obfuscates the actual urban constellation through the paradisal overtones or infernal undertones we readily attach to it. The city should neither be renounced nor lauded but reckoned with. This led Benjamin to be critical of any description of New York that made it look like either Sin City or Zion, either a paradise lost or found—and virtually every urban account, including my own, tends to tip in one of these directions.

These considerations led Benjamin to align his *Manhattan Project* with Arendt's opening statement in *The Origin of Totalitarianism*: "This book has been written against a background of both reckless optimism and reckless despair. It holds that Progress and Doom are two sides of the same medal; that both are articles of superstition, not of faith." Only after he stopped thinking about his work as a modernistic theology of heaven and hell was Benjamin able to approach his intellectual project in the same way he left it for posterity: as the detailed cartography of a vital urban scape, compiled by someone who was "within and without, simultaneously enchanted and repelled by the inexhaustible variety of life" that New York had to offer.

✦

MANY NEW YORKERS BELIEVE that Gehenna is the underworld into which they descend whenever they need to commute from one part of town to another. They also believe that Eden is wherever the rent is the highest. Lame jokes aside, there is still a serious philosophical point that needs to be made before we move on to the last part of this book. This argument does not appear in this exact form in Benjamin's *Manhattan Project*. I should also note that it borrows heavily from Wittgenstein's "Lecture on Ethics."

Imagine an omniscient person who knows all the movements of all the bodies, dead or alive, throughout twentieth-century New York. He also knows all the states of mind of all the human beings who lived in this city during those years. Now suppose this person were to write down all he knows in a big fat book. Such a book would contain the complete description of the city over the same period that stands at the center of Benjamin's own book project. The point of this thought experiment is that the omniscient person's book would contain no moral judgment about what is good and what evil, or anything that could logically imply such a judgment. All the facts within its endless pages would stand, as it were, on the same level. No proposition would be sublime or loathsome, important or trivial. There would be no meta-statements about other statements.

This brings to mind the words of Hamlet: "Nothing is either good or bad, but thinking makes it so," though this quotation can lead to a misunderstanding. It seems to imply that good and bad, while not qualities of the city around us, may still stem from our states of mind. But the point is that no single idea that anyone ever entertained in his or her mind in twentieth-century New York, considered as a fact, can in itself be good or bad, or right or wrong, which is precisely why all these ideas can be included in our thick city-book.

By way of example, imagine that we read therein the description of a murder, such as the 1965 assassination of Malcolm X at the Audubon Ballroom in upper Manhattan, in all its details, physical and psychological. The mere description of these facts will contain nothing that we can call a moral proposition or a moral judgment. The gunshot will be treated on exactly the same level as any other event, for instance, the dropping of a penny. The description of this assassination might well provoke in us pain or rage or any other emotion, but we are external to the book. We might read in the book about the pain or rage that many New Yorkers felt at the time, but these would simply be facts, facts, and more facts. There would be no morality, no theology, no good, no evil, no redemption, no damnation, no heaven, no hell.

SIXTH PART

New York, and then desolation.

—LOUIS ZUKOFSKY

THIRTY-NINTH CHAPTER HARD-KNOCK LIFE

THE OLDEST SURVIVING SENTENCE written in any alphabet—the first recording, in effect, of a human being's speech—also happens to be "the most basic and touching form of communication" imaginable. Four millennia ago, in the Sinai desert, someone wrote on the wall of a turquoise mine: "I was here." We do not know who that person was, but there are very good reasons to believe that this could not have been the work of a member of some cultural or social elite. The community that invented the first alphabet (it was invented only once and from there spread all over) did not belong to the ruling class. These people were neither learned scribes nor government officials, as was once assumed. They were most likely the mine's lowly Canaanite laborers.

Since the workers did not have the education necessary for mastering the thousands of pictograms that made up the Egyptian hieroglyph system, they figured that they could still use a tiny fraction of these intuitive symbols to stand for the most elementary sounds in their vernacular. Initially, every letter was a schematic picture of an object that began with the same sound (like a drawing of an apple for *A*, of a boy for *B*). This made it easy for everyone to decipher the code with a bit of work and imagination.

Over the centuries the symbols lost their graphic sense, though the names of quite a few letters in various Semitic alphabets still bear witness to the original hieroglyphs. (For example, *bet*, the second letter in Hebrew, also means house, which was rendered in the first alphabet as a simple square.) This later development, which coincides with the appropriation of the alphabetical system by the ruling class, was much more difficult for uneducated communities to master. But in opposition to our modern association of illiteracy with low social class, the birth of our alphabet, probably the most profound media revolution in human history, suggests otherwise.

IN THE SUMMER OF AD 1970 a high school senior in upper Manhattan carried with him a thick black Magic Marker wherever he went around town. He used it to write on any smooth surface he came across: ice-cream trucks, subway cars, building windows, and bathroom stalls. He always wrote the same thing, *Taki 183*, which stood for his street name and the street number where he lived. It wasn't long before many teenagers began to use this simple method of anonymous (but free) self-advertisement, and many more law-abiding New Yorkers began to notice their tags. It also wasn't too long before the *New York Times* ran an article about Taki, directing the public's attention to the mushrooming of graffiti across the city.

The *Times* piece does not dwell on the motives behind this phenomenon beyond indirectly quoting Demetrius (Taki's given name) and claiming that "it is something he just has to do." There was, after all, no financial gain to be made in those early days from writing on public surfaces. The possibility of getting caught, or getting hurt, was always on the horizon. Most graffiti was erased within weeks. And because the writers had to hide their true identities, they could not even enjoy their temporary fame. What, then, brought so many people to engage in such a seemingly thankless activity, only a sliver of which was documented? Would it be too far-fetched to claim that the New York pioneers of modern graffiti wished to convey the same message their Canaanite brothers and sisters were trying to convey four millennia ago? "I was here."

It is no coincidence that the signature of one of the most celebrated graffiti writers of the 1970s was *Seen*. It also explains why the slogan for the city's anti-graffiti campaign in the 1980s was, "Make your mark in society, not on society." Rene Ricard introduces the same general idea in the essay that helped transform Jean-Michel Basquiat from an obscure graffiti writer who slept on park benches to a rich and famous legitimate artist: "Any tag by any teenager on any train on any line is fairly heartbreaking. In these autographs is the inherent pathos of the archaeological site, the cry down the vast endless track of time that 'I am somebody,' on a wall in Pompeii, on a rock at Piraeus, in the subway graveyard at some future archaeological dig, we ask, 'Who was Taki?'"

As the movement of graffiti writers exploded in the 1970s and early 1980s, it became clear, given the crowded competition, that marking one's presence with an "I was here" gesture was not going to cut it. It was also less relevant what one chose to write as long as it was consistent. Even the question of how many surfaces one managed to bomb turned out to be secondary. The most important issue became *how* one was executing one's tags, throw-ups, or pieces. Graffiti was above all about style. The leading practitioners distinguished themselves through their fresh layouts and color schemes. At a certain point "wild style" was the term used to describe graffiti that became intricate to the point of near illegibility, while "style wars" were said to be raging on every conceivable city surface, with writers going over each other's names in order to get even a shred of noticeability.

This style was not limited to wall writing alone, although it is notable that graffiti was the vanguard of what is arguably the most influential and original cultural movement to emerge from twentieth-century New York. The term "hip-hop" encompassed not only new strands of music, art, dance, and poetry. It was also the synthesizer of a distinct fashion, dialect, body language, and sprawling web of references into a complete lifestyle. Most notably, this movement gave rise to rap, an art form that, unlike graffiti, is truly indigenous to New York. Rap songs are usually self-referential and autobiographical because one of the rapper's main aims is to poeticize the entire spectrum of this form of life: from articulating its radical politics to pumping up its mad parties, from criticizing socioeconomic conditions to bragging about pimps and hoes, from chronicling the drugs hustled on street corners to boasting about the multimillion-dollar record deals signed in corporate boardrooms.

MARSHALL BERMAN, who grew up in the Bronx during the 1940s and 1950s, offers an insightful meditation on how hip-hop emerged from his childhood borough in the 1970s and 1980s, decades when the Bronx was stricken by unprecedented levels of poverty and crime. Things were so bad back then that frustrated land-lords set fire to their own buildings in devious attempts to collect insurance money, avoid paying the property taxes, and get the hell out of neighborhoods that seemed to have no future whatsoever. Yet for the young people who grew up in the midst of this devastation, hell was also a playground. As Grace Paley, another Bronx native, puts it in one of her stories: "The block is burning on one side of the street, and the kids are trying to build something on the other." More philosophically, we could say, after Hegel (who had never been to the Bronx), that "spirit is a power only by looking the negative in the eye and living with it." Living in this urban negativity was the magic power that brought the spirit of hip-hop into being.

"It makes me wonder how I keep from going under," Grandmaster Flash rapped in 1982. The answer seems to lie in the question, that is, in the praxis of hip-hop itself. A similar sentiment, three years earlier, may have led James Baldwin to write: "Music is our witness, and our ally. The 'beat' is the confession, which recognizes, changes and conquers time. Then, history becomes a garment we can wear, and share, and not a cloak in which to hide; and time becomes a friend." By introducing a split and a stop into the temporal progression, rhythm offers a new structure that resists the already established, prevailing schemes. By jumping on the beat or chopping it up, the rapper's flow plays with the given chronology in-stead of capitulating to it. By extracting from the archives of our musical tradition a certain phrase and then repeating it again and again, the linearity of the old song, the immutability of what was, faces the new song's merciless and contagious return of the same.

When Benjamin was twenty-four, he declared it a "metaphysical truth that all nature would begin to lament if it were endowed with language." Seventy years later he added that if the city were able to speak, it would probably rap. Hip-hop music, blasting from passing cars and open windows, is "sonorial graffiti"; it is New York's sound system, an ephemeral strategy to occupy the city's streets. Gradually, however, this sound of the city crossed over, breaking along the way many geographic and social boundaries (sometimes erected especially to forestall its advance) to become a global phenomenon that even overtook sleepy suburbia. In the twenty-first century graffiti and rap can still irritate those who would prefer to see them erased and censored. Others are fed up with the endless and senseless output of the commercial hip-hop industry. Either way, the voice that is being silenced or ignored through rage or indifference is the very voice of the city that emerged from the specific experience of late twentieth-century New York.

ϟ

BENJAMIN, who, despite his old age, observed the rise of hip-hop with great fascination, developed an interesting theory that, as far as I can tell, offers a yet-to-be-explored connection between modern New York and ancient Athens. In Greek culture, the song's melody (*melos*) was originally supposed to correspond very closely to the rhythm of speech (*logos*). When this traditional link was first broken (during a recitation of the Homeric poems), a new word, *parodia*, was introduced to designate this new technique of singing, or speaking, alongside the song (*para ten oiden*). This insertion of parody into rhapsody, this brash attempt by a few Greek performers to disjoin music and language, song and word, felt so strange to Athenian ears that it "provoked irrepressible fits of laughter."

Parody is inseparable from rap (Benjamin even talks at one point about *rapody*, though it might just be a typo). This is true not only in the etymological sense of rapping alongside the song, instead of singing by following a melody, but also in the contemporary sense of parody. Rap songs are often a pastiche, appropriation, or citation of recorded materials scavenged from different sources (first by DJs spinning vinyl records and then by producers using digital samplers), which is one common way to define parody. Rappers are the proudest ragpickers. Moreover, certain rappers can proclaim or perform their lifestyle with such self-awareness that they are responsible for some of the most elaborate examples of self-parody in recent memory. "Double-consciousness," which W. E. B. Du Bois defines as the ability to look "at one's self through the eyes of others," plays a pivotal role in the rap game.

The perplexed approach rap with such seriousness that they judge the genre according to traditional categories of authenticity while treating the rapper's intricate persona, or act, as a show of earnestness. Nevertheless, we must still distinguish between parody and fiction. Fiction calls into question the reality of its object. In parody the object is too real, "intolerably real," so it has to be kept at the parodic distance. To keep it real, reality must be kept at arm's length.

FORTIETH CHAPTER   SEX AND PHILOSOPHY

"OF ALL THE FAMOUS MEN WHO EVER LIVED," Woody Allen confessed, "the one I would most like to have been was Socrates. Not just because he was a great thinker, but also because I have been known to have some reasonably profound insights myself, although mine invariably revolve around a Swedish airline stewardess and some handcuffs." Allen's universe is ruled by two forces whose paths rarely cross in Western culture. Metaphysics and flesh, meaning and moaning, philosophizing and philandering: Allen's incessant engagement with both suggests that neither fulfillment nor relinquishment is a viable option. He cannot let go of his two obsessions despite (or because of) his inability to really get what he is looking for. Sometimes they even get dangerously mixed up, as in "The Whore of Mensa," a story about a married man who pays young women, fresh out of Vassar College, to secretly engage with him in an exchange of abstract ideas instead of bodily fluids.

This improbable quest for an ultimate answer and supreme pleasure is infinitely demanding. It is also morally questionable and comically infantile. It is difficult to keep a straight face while thinking about Allen (the man) or Woody (his character) as an object of (intellectual) reverence or an object of (sexual) desire. Why does that photo in which he is seen crossing a New York street together with a tall black woman with a big Afro and a short skirt seem so incredible? Are they together or did they just happen to walk side by side? Though Allen's sexuality is often unsettling, his philosophy is rather baffling. His love life in a nutshell: "I was involved in an extremely good example of oral contraception. Two weeks ago I asked a girl to go to bed with me, and she said no." His theory in another nutshell: "There is no question that there is an unseen world. The problem is, how far is it from midtown and how late is it open?" Ultimately the joke is on the inevitable senselessness of philosophy and the senseless inevitability of sexuality.

ONE OF ALLEN'S FANS, intrigued by the possibility of developing this line of thought into a book chapter, met the filmmaker for coffee in an Upper West Side cafeteria. We publish here a transcript of this interview with Allan Stewart Konigsberg (aka Woody Allen), conducted by Walter Bendix Schönflies Benjamin (aka Carl Roseman), which took place in 1985. Sandor Needleman, a retired Columbia University professor who arranged the meeting and took these notes, stipulated that they should be "published posthumously or after his death, whichever comes first."

> WALTER: Most people think about *Manhattan* the film as your love letter to Manhattan the place. I disagree. For me it is a declaration of war. What was on your mind when you made it?

WOODY: You're right. I said before that I wrote the script while thinking about what is happening to American culture, where relationships between human beings are becoming harder and harder to have, and it is becoming harder and harder to be honest and not to sell out. New York has to fight every day for its survival against the encroachment of all this terrible ugliness that is gradually overcoming all the big cities in America. This ugliness comes from a culture that has no spiritual center, a culture that has money and education but no sense of being at peace with the world, no sense of purpose in life.

WALTER: Do you consider your art in redemptive terms? Is this your way of fighting this empty entertainment machine, this culture industry, which distracts us from facing a philosophical problem like the meaning of life?

WOODY: Not really. I hate when art becomes a religion. I feel the opposite. When you start putting a higher value on works of art than on people, you're forfeiting your humanity. To answer your second question, art to me has always been no more than entertainment for intellectuals, or pseudointellectuals. Mozart or Rembrandt or Shakespeare are entertainers on a very, very high level. But at bottom it is still meant to distract us from life, which is either miserable or horrible.

WALTER: In *Stardust Memories* the choice is between the train that you are trapped in, which is full of sickly, grim-looking individuals, and a second train, where beautiful, well-dressed people are having a party. As you are fighting to escape your gloomy train and join the celebration on the other one, both reach their final destination: a garbage dump, a landfill site.

WOODY: Yes, life is a lose-lose situation.

WALTER: And then you die alone.

WOODY: Well, there are worse things than death. Many of them playing at a theater near you.

WALTER: But even if there is no afterlife, you can still achieve immortality through your work. Imagine people watching a film you made or reading a book I wrote long after we are both dead.

WOODY: Rather than live on in the hearts and minds of my fellow man, I'd prefer to live on in my apartment.

WALTER: So this is the best of all possible worlds.

WOODY: It's certainly the most expensive.

WALTER: Then explain to me how being a comedian fits into this despairing condition of living without feathers, which is your rejoinder to Emily Dickinson's "hope is the thing with feathers"?

WOODY: The way I see it, there is nothing really redeeming about tragedy. Tragedy is tragic, and it's so painful that people try to twist it and say "it's terribly hard, but look, we've learned something." This is a weak attempt to find some kind of meaning in tragedy. But there is no meaning. There is no upside. Suffering does not redeem anything; there is no positive message to learn from it. The argument can therefore be made that the comic filmmaker or playwright is doing a better service to humanity than the tragic one. In the end the comic is helping you more, you're okay for a little while longer.

WALTER: In this sense you seem very much like an inverted Kafka. I'm also reminded here of Nietzsche's claim that the only enemies who can harm the ascetic ideal are its comedians.

WOODY: Every event first appears as tragedy and then as farce. I'm interested in the latter, in this comedy of errors.

WALTER: I once read a humorous piece in the *New Yorker*, not by you—it was actually published a decade before you were even born—about a visit by Plato to twentieth-century Manhattan. He is dismayed by the complete chaos, so he asks a passerby where one can still find hope and happiness, and the answer is: go to the movies.

WOODY: Like many Americans of my generation, watching so many films while growing up in Brooklyn led me to escape to fantasy and resent reality. Even today I see many people around me who are unable to shake off this attitude. They are still trying to write scenes into their own lives.

WALTER: But you escaped into a life in the cinema on the *other* side of the camera rather than the audience side of it. It's not the audience that escapes—it's you!

WOODY: That's because I never felt truth was beauty. Never. I've always felt that people can't take too much reality. I like being in Ingmar Bergman's world. Or in Louis Armstrong's world. Or in the world of the New York Knicks. Because it's not this world. You don't spend your whole life looking for the truth. You spend your whole life searching for a way out. Otherwise you just get an overdose of reality.

WALTER: We all know the same truth, and our lives consist of how we choose to distort it.

WOODY: The point for me is that, unfortunately, we must choose reality, but in the end it crushes us and disappoints. I hate reality, but it's the only place where you can get a good steak dinner.

WALTER: But don't you think that your films owe something to the *real* New York?

WOODY: In some sense they do, but in another sense they don't. I'm always known as a New York filmmaker who eschews Hollywood and in fact denigrates it. No one sees that the New York I show is the New York I know only from Hollywood films that I grew up on. The New York that Hollywood showed the world, which never really existed, is the New York that I show the world because that's the New York I fell in love with. In this sense, I feel I owe very little to reality.

WALTER: You create a phantasmagoria of New York that only a fool will confuse with the real thing. Still, as you show in *The Purple Rose of Cairo*, the living want their lives to be fiction, and the fictive characters want their lives to be real.

WOODY: Let me put it this way. Almost all my work is autobiographical and yet so exaggerated and distorted it reads to me like fiction.

WALTER: In *Annie Hall*, for example, your character suffers from anhedonia, which was the film's original title. Annie explains that you're "incapable of enjoying life. . . . Your life is New York City. . . . You're like this island unto yourself."

WOODY: By the way, my anhedonia is even worse in real life. I almost always work. Having what most people would call fun is something I don't really care for. If I have fun doing anything it's working. Constantly. Leaving the city on the weekend is something I more dread than look for. I'm strictly pavement.

WALTER: Another, related idea in *Annie Hall* is that you always try to get things perfect in art, because it is so difficult to do in life. But I still wonder whether life can imitate art.

WOODY: Usually, life imitates bad television.

WALTER: But how's anyone going to come up with a movie or a book or a painting or a symphony that's going to compete with a great city?

WOODY: I agree. So much so that I might use this in one of my movies. (*Woody is smiling. Walter is nodding.*) But don't you think that the life of a city is still very different from an individual's life, or the life of an artwork?

WALTER: Of course it is. City life is sheer life.

WOODY: I see, I guess. (*looking puzzled, pausing for a moment*) Look, I'm sorry but I have to run. (*picking up the check*) I got it. No problem. The prices in this place, as Hannah Arendt told me once, are "reasonable without being historically inevitable."

IT IS THE SAME ARENDT who once described those moments when "the comedy breaks into the horror itself, and results in stories, presumably true enough, whose macabre humor easily surpasses that of any Surrealist invention." What in Benjamin's philosophy is called sheer life is transformed in Allen's into "mere anarchy." No rational explanation or logical plan can ever organize the absurdity of it all. The absence of the eye of God means that we would "rather be lucky than good." Enlightened reason is a dark fantasy, or a setup for a joke.

The word *gag* has two seemingly unrelated meanings in modern English. A gag is either a joke or an object put in a person's mouth to prevent speech or an outcry. The discrepancy between the two senses is dispelled when we take into account a third use. In nineteenth-century theater, actors who began to improvise because they had forgotten their lines were said to be gagging. "Whereof one cannot speak, thereof one must gag." The one-sentence seventh chapter in Wittgenstein's *Tractatus Logico-Philosophicus* should consequently be read not as a mystical pronouncement but as the book's bona fide punch line. "Laughter," Benjamin agrees, "is shattered articulation."

Allen explains the anatomy of his jokes by saying that every punch line should be preceded by a "straight line"—a character, a life, that feels real and true: "You can only go where the straight line honestly enables you to go." Otherwise, you arrive at what both Karl and Groucho Marx call the alienation of humor. As outlandish as Allen's comedy can get, it never feels estranged from life.

Annie Hall concludes with an old joke: This guy goes to a psychiatrist and says, "Doc, my brother's crazy. He thinks he's a chicken." And the doctor says, "Well, why don't you turn him in?" And the guy says, "I would, but I need the eggs." New York life, all life, really, is totally irrational. But we stay with it because most of us need the eggs, from which new, absurd lives will hatch. Or as Ralph Ellison writes in *Invisible Man*, it is "better to live out one's own absurdity than to die for that of others."

FORTY-FIRST CHAPTER   **AN IMAGE OF EXISTENCE**

A THING, Socrates teaches us, "is not seen because it is visible but on the contrary it is visible because it is seen." Helen Levitt should be credited, maybe more
than any other photographer, for making the New York street visible, for seeing, through her camera's lens, the city's sheer life like never before and, most
likely, like never since. Unfortunately, she rebuffed almost all requests to explain
in words what it was, exactly, that she saw. To begin to understand the significance
of her body of work, which spans the last seventy years of the twentieth century,
we turn to her friend James Agee for some guidance: "The streets of the poor
quarters of great cities," he writes, "are, above all, a theater and a battleground.
There, unaware and unnoticed, every human being is a poet, a masker, a warrior,
a dancer: and in his innocent artistry he projects, against the turmoil of the street,
an image of human existence."

These lines are from the opening statement of *In the Street*. Released in 1948,
the film is a fourteen-minute montage of everyday scenes of street life: kids playing in the middle of the road with water coming out of an open fire hydrant; an
old, heavyset woman passing by with a small dog on a leash; a young boy riding
his bicycle behind a carriage; a couple flirting on a stoop; neighbors checking
out the scene; a toddler pressing his face to the windowpane; a young woman
on a sidewalk chatting with someone upstairs. Though *In the Street* has neither
sound nor color, neither plot nor discernible logic, Benjamin considered it one
of the most important documentaries ever made about New York. It is the city in
miniature.

Made by Levitt in collaboration with Agee and Janice Loeb, the film also
remains a rare example of a seamless translation of a photographer's sensibility
between still and moving pictures. In both media, Levitt was looking for that "decisive moment": the point in time and space at which all the elements in the street
align to form an aesthetic composition, or a philosophic constellation, framed
from just the right angle. "There is a delicate empiricism," Benjamin writes of
Levitt, "which so intimately involves itself with the object that it becomes true
theory." It is not difficult to imagine that the continuous motion of *In the Street* is
precisely what Levitt saw through her Leica's viewfinder as she hawkishly awaited
for the right instant to press the shutter-release button.

What Levitt's film and her photography also have in common is the clandestine method in which they were made. The poor image quality of *In the Street* is
the result of filming with a hidden camera that allowed her to capture life as it

is rather than life when it puts on a show for the ethnographer-photographer. Although her portable still camera could be easily spotted by any suspicious passersby, it was equipped with a right-angle viewfinder (called a *winkelsucher*) that enabled her to appear as if she were shooting the scene in front of her, when in fact she was shooting sideways. In 1938, a couple of years after she discovered this device, she also began to accompany Walker Evans on his long subway trips during which he photographed unsuspecting riders with a lens peeping out of his winter coat. During one of those rides he photographed Levitt herself as she was gazing deadpan at his camera.

ONCE LIFE IS AWARE that it may become art, once we know that someone is taking our picture, we act like the subatomic particles that change their course after they have been detected by the scientist's measuring device. In a Diane Arbus portrait, as in Evans's picture of Levitt, there is a sense of full disclosure. We can almost read the subjects' minds as they look at Arbus's camera with an odd mixture of pride and sadness, thinking to themselves, "She is taking my picture." Levitt's work eschews this sense of self-awareness, as well as photographer-awareness. She might not go so far as Warhol, who used to complain that whereas other people feel self-conscious when they are being filmed, he feels self-conscious whenever he films others. But unlike Arbus, Levitt does not assert her own presence in her pictures, and her subjects rarely seem to be saying to themselves, "I am a subject." The reason so many of Levitt's pictures feature children is not that they are cute but that they are unselfconscious. The people in her photographs are simply "going about the business of living in a city."

One difference between Benjamin's two favorite New York photographers is that whereas the background in Arbus's frontal portraits remains decidedly in the back, keeping the individual in full focus, in Levitt's stolen glances street life and city life reach their full significance. For example, it is hard to look at the black-and-white photo, which she took early in her career, of a group of children playing by the curb and think of street and life, or city and life, independently of one another. The center of gravity is not Levitt, or the persons she photographed, or even the street in which they are all standing, but somewhere in the middle of this serendipitous triangle.

Nevertheless, viewers looking at her photographs are compelled to recognize that they are *not* a part of the picture, that they are definitely not *in the street*. The sort of communion that viewers can have with an Arbus photo is intentionally withheld. If the existential comportment of a Levitt photo is *being-there* (in the street, that is), then the observer is relegated to the position of *no-longer-being-there*. This, at least, is what the cross-eyed child in this photograph seems to be signaling to us with his arms.

IN THE STREET is more than an odd extension of Levitt's more substantial and sustained work as a still photographer. The film's position within the history of cinema hearkens back to its earliest origins, to actualities, as some turn-of-the-century movies were called. Many of these shorts depict unscripted and unedited street scenes with no discernible plot. A famous example of an actuality is *What Happened on Twenty-Third Street, New York City* (1901), an unremarkable one-minute depiction of people walking up and down the sidewalk, peering from time to time at the odd contraption that is registering their movements (with or without their knowledge). Near the end of the clip, we see an elegant woman passing over a grating that is blowing some air. For a second, her dress billows out, revealing her shins, more than half a century before Marilyn Monroe pulled a very similar trick, some thirty blocks to the north.

Many of Warhol's films from the 1960s can also be comfortably classified within this neglected genre of actualities. Like Levitt before him and the pioneers of cinema before her, Warhol was not trying to mold reality into a narrative. It would also be inaccurate to claim that any of these movies have a director, in the sense of an auteur, because the persons responsible for their creation understand that the more they allow what is to simply be, the better the film becomes. Warhol's aim, like Levitt's, is to silk-screen reality. Because Levitt and Warhol resist the temptation to manipulate the footage and to construct a larger argument or a more coherent story line, the power of their intentionally raw films only grows. Siegfried Kracauer, another German-Jewish intellectual who lived in New York until his death in 1966, fully understood this achievement when he spoke of the photographer's ability "to represent significant aspects of physical reality without trying to overwhelm that reality—so that the raw material focused upon is both left intact and made transparent."

What Happened on Twenty-Third Street already encapsulates the other direction that cinema took in the twentieth century: an unwritten contract between filmmaker and viewer stipulating that by the movie's end something has to *happen*. Though many things occur in rapid succession in Levitt's *In the Street*, to the person habituated to the language of modern cinema it may still seem as if nothing is happening at all. Questioning this type of reaction, Warhol observes that people can "sit by a window or on a porch all day and look out and never be bored, but then if they went to a movie or a play, they suddenly objected to being bored."

🐦

LEVITT'S ACHIEVEMENT has something to do with her ability to use the spectacular mediums of photography and film to depict what one critic called "the society of the unspectacle." Arbus's work is also an attempt to grapple with the glossy world of commercial photography, which she knew personally through her family's business. The fringes of spectacle are a central theme of her work, and her favorite topics include freak-show performers, abandoned theme parks, unused movie sets, and nearly empty theaters. By seizing the means of reproduction, Arbus posits a kind of anti-spectacle, or at least an alternative one. One of the most evocative displays of her underlying aim can be seen in the portraits she took in the last years of her life during repeated visits to residences for people with mental disabilities.

Levitt had a different strategy. The people she photographed give the impression of being untouched by the spectacle in which we otherwise all live. Her street is not exactly a theater, as Agee claims. It is instead a zone where, against all odds, unmediated or unalienated human interactions remain possible. At times it even becomes a slightly romanticized place where people make their children a Halloween costume with what little they have, where people are not at home glued to a screen but are hanging out together—sometimes in an abandoned lot or by the gutter—but still together. As the century progressed, Levitt discovered that those instances of unspectacled existence were increasingly difficult to find in the growing unreality of her city's streets. But she kept on trying because, well, otherwise what would be the point?

The unreal is not the same as the surreal. One of Levitt's only statements about her own work—that "the poetry of photography is surreal"—was sharpened by Agee when he wrote that in her photos "the surrealism is that of the ordinary metropolitan soil which breeds these remarkable juxtapositions and moments, and that what we call 'fantasy' is, instead, reality in its unmasked vigor and grace." Arbus's visual world is meticulously constructed and sometimes even a bit belabored; Levitt's seems to arise from a mixture of patience and instinct, skill and luck. If the stasis in Arbus's photos captures the city's melancholy, the movement in Levitt's proves its porosity. Arbus's images are like a collection of rare fish in an aquarium; Levitt's look as if they have just been plucked out of the ordinary urban sea.

"Truth, for all its multiplicity, is not two-faced." From this Baudelairean lesson, Benjamin concluded that "the truth will not run away from us" is as false as a notion can get. Like both men, Levitt knew perfectly well that "the true image of the past flits by," that "the past can be seized only as an image that flashes up at the moment of its recognizability, and is never seen again." Truth is that woman who passed Baudelaire by in the Parisian street, that beauty dressed in black whose fleeting glance he perceived as his sudden "rebirth," as a strobe of light in an everlasting night. Click.

FORTY-SECOND CHAPTER **NO IDEAS BUT IN THINGS**

"A MAN IN HIMSELF IS A CITY, beginning, seeking, achieving and concluding his life in ways which the various aspects of a city may embody." William Carlos Williams treats the mind as a mirror, though he no longer sees it as a mirror of nature. The modern mind must be a reflection of the modern city in all its miseries and glories and twists and turns. A true modern city cannot be the embodiment of one person's thought (as in L'Enfant's Washington, or Oscar Niemeyer's Brasilia). But a truly modern person can be the ensoulment of a single good city. New York is just such a city, and Benjamin is just such a man. He seems to be the only one who can step into Baudelaire's shoes.

Williams predates Warhol in his insistence that the most mundane subject matter stand at the center of his creative imagination. He was interested in the profane, not the profound. Nevertheless, he deemed New York too formidable an object for his poetry, too elevated, too insular. So he decided instead to dedicate his greatest masterpiece to Paterson, New Jersey, a congenial city of a hundred-and-some thousand residents whose main draw is a waterfall. The Manhattan cynics who smirk at the mere mention of the state on the other side of the Hudson (Question: Why are New Yorkers so depressed? Answer: Because the light at the end of the tunnel is New Jersey) will surely try to claim that *Paterson* the poem transcends Paterson the place. Yet it is hard to imagine how this single poetic composition—even if it took its brilliant author twelve years to write its five epic parts—could really do justice to such an intricate and delicate urban constellation. As intimately as Williams knew his subject matter, the signified necessarily exceeds the signifier. *Paterson* is not Paterson.

Benjamin's attitude falls somewhere in between these two extremes. He considers *Paterson* an experiment with controllable variables, conducted in an urban laboratory small enough to be well monitored and large enough to have general validity. Williams's work offers an excellent confirmation of the viability of Benjamin's own literary experiment, which draws on the colossal setting of New York City and a considerably larger set of sources. The epic quality of *Paterson*—a courageous attempt to poeticize the prosaic—is confronted with the philosophical diligence of Benjamin's *Manhattan Project*, written in what he once called "liberated prose." The result is a text as complex and as overwhelming as the city it is about.

One of the most striking pages in Benjamin's manuscript consists of a single sentence, written again and again in his barely decipherable small script, like the chalkboard handiwork of an unruly student forced to stay after school. The sentence, "For the philosopher there are no ideas but in things," is a riff on Williams's identical claim about the task of the poet. In other words, a thought that tries to transcend the actual city—this most complicated constellation of things ever created by humankind—is irrelevant and provincial. Theories cannot be imposed on the urban landscape from above. They must somehow emanate from it. To appropriate another of Williams's formulations, we could say that the philosopher "does not permit himself to go beyond the thought to be discovered in the context of that with which he is dealing." Ideas are not about things but in them. Ideas cannot be abstracted from things, in the same way that we cannot extract the soul from the body and still keep the two alive. "The order and connection of ideas," Spinoza confirms, "is the same as the order and connection of things."

These things, however, are not only objects like buildings and bridges. A poem is a thing. A photograph is also a thing. These are not just the mimesis of things. Whatever Benjamin found in the library's archives was a particular thing that was an inseparable part of New York City, and within every one of these things he located a singular idea. Once all these ideas crystallized into his *Manhattan Project*, they were like a thousand little mirrors glued on a single wall. In front of this wall stood a life. Though this life was the city's and not Benjamin's own, the latter had truly become nothing other than a refracted and fragmented reflection of the former.

Half a century before Williams wrote *Paterson*, Edmund Husserl had already cast his philosophical work as an attempt to go "back to the things themselves." He dedicated his thought to a scrupulous analysis of his most minute impressions of the world in which he lived, or the lifeworld, as he eventually came to call it. But whereas Husserl, like Proust, attuned himself to his inner experiences, to his stream of consciousness, Williams and Benjamin attuned themselves to existence as such, to being, to things. They gave themselves without reservation, almost resigning themselves to the staggering multiplicity and particularity of the external world of which, since Descartes, philosophers cautioned us to be extremely wary. "What profoundly fascinated Benjamin," Arendt agrees, "was never an idea, always a phenomenon."

There are no ideas but in things, or at least in the way those things appear to us. The metaphysical assumption that the highest ideas are about the most abstract things is reversed in Benjamin, whose earliest philosophical texts suggest that the relationship between ideas and things is like that between constellations and stars. Things surround us wherever we go, though their multiplicity, variety, and utter artificiality in a modern urban setting surpass by a quantum leap all that human beings had ever previously known. Inspired by Williams, Benjamin shows us how to open ourselves to these things without owning them, how to welcome them into our selves without fetishizing them, and how to turn the ideas embedded in them into the topography of a thoroughly urban and modern mind. The ultimate goal is therefore not to be *in* a city but, as strange as it may sound, to *be* a city, to let it affect us—with no fear and no remorse—to such an extent that we become it rather than expect it to become more like us.

🐦

ARCHEOLOGISTS can take just a fraction of a thing, like a piece of clay or thread, and use it to reconstruct the complete artifact, be it a jug or a necklace. But they can also reconstruct from these objects a culture or a form of life. Even ideas can be deduced from the remnants of what people leave behind, covered by centuries of welcomed oblivion. Yet contemporary objects also clamor for our attention. It is from this perspective that Benjamin's work as an urban archeologist makes sense.

We misunderstand the word *ruin* when we think only about the physical object now defunct. What is ruined in a ruin is not just the thing itself but the life that had to do with that thing. We never care about a ruin unless we at least try to imagine the persons who built it, or dwelt in it, or used it, or even just looked at it. The ruins of a way of being are infinitely more fascinating than the ruins of an inanimate being. The physical structure or infrastructure of a city is not unlike a tortoise's shell; it is the organic extension of the living, acting bodies that occupy it. In this way, even the house in which we grew up, even if it is still occupied by our aging parents, may be contemplated with detachment as a ruin, especially if we feel that we are no longer the children we used to be. At the moment we acknowledge that our recently purchased, secondhand shirt was once worn by someone else (we often prefer to repress this thought), that shirt turns into a ruin.

New York is also a city of ruins as far as the eye can see, even though its only structure that faintly resembles a classic ruin is Castle Clinton in Battery Park, which, before its current use as an oversized ticket booth, housed an aquarium, a theater, an immigration hall, and a beer garden, but was never used in battle. It took Gibbon six volumes to describe the decline and fall of the Eternal City of Rome. A comparable account of New York—where the gap between the opening ceremony and the wrecking ball is almost negligible—could be as long as a report of a man falling off a building. "Everything is torn down before you have had time to care for it," James Merrill writes in "An Urban Convalescence." What makes the work of the New York archeologist most difficult is not lack of findings but that once one life is ruined, another one quickly takes its place. In this city, Henry James laments, "one story is good only till another is told." And nothing is left fallow long enough to be covered with a nice layer of dust. Things are over before they even start.

Where impermanence is the only permanent thing, the solid becomes air while the air becomes solid. If a factory vacates a cast-iron building, an art gallery takes its place. If a Jewish family moves out of a tenement, a Puerto Rican family moves in. If a subway line deserts a tunnel, the mole people take over. But the fact that no structure is allowed to disintegrate for long before a new form of life reclaims its quarters, or before it is obliterated to make place for a newer structure, does not change the fact that, in New York, there are layers and layers of ruins everywhere we look. Monuments are ruins long before they begin to crumble. And Benjamin made it his task to attend to all these ruins, to excavate the ideas in the things, the lives from the walls. Because if a city is a text, it must be a palimpsest.

The human mind is a hoarder of its own memories. According to Freud, even the psyche of an infant continues to live in that of the adult. But a city, he claims in *Civilization and Its Discontents*, functions very differently than a brain. As old parts of a city like Rome are destroyed and new ones rise up, the urban landscape cannot help betraying its past. Does colonial New York, or New Amsterdam, or the Lenapehoking of the Native Americans live on in today's New York? If a city were indeed like a mind, Freud reasons, then all the different structures that ever occupied this or that block would appear superimposed one on top of the other. So if one were to sit on a bench in Columbus Park, one would see not only today's Chinatown and civic center but also, with a slight shift of perspective, the infamous Five Points neighborhood that used to surround it, just as I can recall my eighth birthday and then, without even blinking, my twenty-eighth.

Benjamin's reasoning, however, is the exact opposite of Freud's. His basic question is not whether an urban experience can replicate psychic experience. He is much more interested in whether our mental life can function like city life.

FORTY-THIRD CHAPTER   **THE MARRIAGE OF REASON AND SQUALOR**

NO MATTER HOW SATISFIED the reader might be with Benjamin's depiction of twentieth-century New York, the city's simultaneity and muchness are such that people will always wonder why he didn't say something, or say more, about this figure or that phenomenon, this idea or that sensibility. For instance, this is the perfect spot to insert a chapter about the minimalist movement in the arts, especially in sculpture and music, but also in fashion and design. Although Benjamin viewed minimalism (as he did hip-hop) as a comprehensive form of life endemic to New York, he did not make more than a few offhand remarks about this subject. Speculating on his hidden intentions would be a violation of one of the basic laws of hermeneutics. There are, though, some things that can be deduced with a modicum of certainty.

Conflicting messages prevent us from situating the movement's precise position in Benjamin's philosophy of New York. In some ways, the minimalists assume the role played by the surrealists in his early thought. In this regard, reality is no longer something to quarrel with. Reality is now stripped bare, like the exposed floorboards of Donald Judd's SoHo loft. Drapery is crime. Art transposes the viewer to its own setting. The question of Being is answered by the *as is*. A fluorescent light bulb glaring from a vapid office's ceiling might very well become one of the most iconic sculptures of the twentieth century. The encounter with the real is neither traumatic nor wishful but studious. The pedestrian is not to be surmounted; it calls instead for repetition. In a city where aesthetics becomes a kind of anesthesia, where the poverty of experience is cultural capital, being plain—as a person, an artist, or an artwork—marks the highest of achievements.

Another way to consider the spirit of minimalism in 1960s and 1970s New York is to contrast the movement's impact with the way Benjamin understood the effect of art nouveau (*Jugendstil*) on Parisian culture during the 1890s and 1900s. We might then say that the artifact's attempt to imitate the truth of nature (the ornate entrances to the metro in Paris) gives way to the artistic search for the true or elemental nature of the artifact (the sans serif typeface on a New York subway sign). Inspiration is more likely to be found in the hardware store than in the flower shop. The result is that interior design of the minimalist kind can lead one "to feel homesick, even though one is at home." Instead of inserting nature into the design of the city, minimalist art puts the city back into the city. This may be why Richard Serra felt the need to plant a steel ring, twenty-six feet in diameter, in the middle of a desolate, dead-end street in the Bronx. This clinical piece functions as a clear manifestation of what Carl Andre once called "the marriage of reason and squalor." In a letter to Benjamin, Gretel Adorno also described New York's surreal "contrast between the most modern and the most shabby."

If we compare a canvas completely covered with layers of seemingly random, abstract expressionist paint drops to an empty white room with nothing but a few strings of yarn meticulously stretched from floor to ceiling, it becomes possible to think of minimalist aesthetics as the opposite of hoarder aesthetics. Less versus mess. Yet Herb and Dorothy Vogel—a postman and a librarian who spent every penny they pinched to amass one of the most impressive collections of minimalist art in their cluttered one-bedroom apartment on the Upper East Side—might well be seen as art hoarders. Once again, New York proves that reason and squalor are closer than previously imagined.

EVERY PHILOSOPHY requires a sound track to put the reader in the right mind-set. Musical tastes diverge, of course, but for my money, the ideal accompaniment to *The Manhattan Project* would be a few pieces by the New York minimalist composer Steve Reich. Yet we should not assume that minimalist art can show us what Benjamin's philosophy is trying but failing to say. Sol LeWitt's formulation leaves little room for doubt: "The philosophy of the work is implicit in the work and it is not an illustration of any system of philosophy." This is true about every artwork but especially true regarding minimalism, in which the surface is fetishized even more than in Warhol. Frank Stella clarifies: "Only what can be seen there *is* there. . . . You can see the whole idea without any confusion. . . . What you see is what you see." And what you hear is what you hear.

You visit MoMA to experience its art. You visit New York to experience its life. There can be something very disorienting about these encounters, especially the first time. In both cases, the best bet is to follow E. E. Cummings's advice: "Don't try to despise it, let it try to despise you. Don't try to enjoy it, let it try to enjoy you. *Don't try to understand it, let it try to understand you.*" This is not to imply that, in matters pertaining to either aesthetics or ethics, the pregnant silence of the inexplicable became Benjamin's choice of last resort. Because every letter of his *Manhattan Project* is meant to operate in the small gap between art and life.

FORTY-FOURTH CHAPTER   # CRITIQUE OF PURE MOVEMENT

THE ANCIENT GREEKS did not have one term to express what we mean by the word *place*. They had two: *topos* and *chora*. It was only after Aristotle claimed that both words mean more or less the same thing, and after they both got translated into Latin as *locus*, that the distinction began to lose its clear contours.

A simple example suffices to illustrate the original difference between the two concepts. I am writing this paragraph while sitting in a coffee shop around the corner from Avenue C and East Ninth Street. Understood as *topos*, this place is simply a location, a spot that can be easily found on any map of Manhattan. We can begin to understand the same place as a *chora* once we take into account the other people in the room, its layout and design, even the garden across the street and the social makeup of the surrounding neighborhood. *Chora* is always the place of specific bodies. It is, as Heidegger explains, "what is taken up and occupied by what stands there." It often gets its meaning from the embodied human engagements that take place within it. There is always something, or someone, in a *chora*. Things happen. Otherwise it is not a *chora* but a *kenon*: an empty space, a void.

Another example should clarify the relevance of this linguistic distinction to Benjamin's urban thought. It can be said that Robert Moses treats New York City as a *topos*, whereas Jane Jacobs treats it as a *chora*. Superficially, it can be argued that they hold divergent views of the same place. But on a deeper level we need to recognize that their very definition of place is not the same. Moses's approach resembles that of an army general in conquest of a city. Jacobs's resembles that of a Greek philosopher trying to make sense of it. The site where Moses ordered the construction of a new public pool is a *topos*. The site of Jacobs's intricate ballet of the street is a *chora*. Whereas Moses sees geometric shapes, like points and lines, or bureaucratic variables, like budget allocations and masses of people, Jacobs sees forms of life, interactions between persons, relations between built and lived elements, a plurality of uses and unexpected events, none of which are easily localized.

Chora, Plato writes in a classic yet still elusive passage, is "apprehended by a kind of bastard reasoning that does not involve sense perception, and it is hardly even an object of conviction. We look at it as in a dream when we say that everything that exists must of necessity be somewhere, in some place and occupying some space, and that that which doesn't exist somewhere, whether on earth or in heaven, doesn't exist at all." These observations lead Plato to an impasse. He admits that *chora* is neither rationally intelligible nor empirically sensible, neither an immutable being nor a fleeting becoming, neither a transcendent idea nor a lowly phenomenon. It therefore remains an in-between, strange entity that he finds difficult to explicate beyond calling it, metaphorically, either the receptacle or the mother of everything that comes into being.

How, then, are we to make sense of the word *place* if we want to understand it as *chora*? Circumventing Plato's mystifying text, as well as the readings of it by contemporary thinkers such as Julia Kristeva and Jacques Derrida, Benjamin's strategy even bypasses the direct use of language. His reasoning seems straightforward enough: if topography is the practice dedicated to *topos*, then the practice best suited to give us access to *chora* is choreography. *Choreia* was a type of circle dance in ancient Greece; and *choreo*, a verb that meant "to make room." The usual etymology of choreography is dance-writing. Benjamin, however, approaches choreography as an ethereal text whose ultimate subject matter is always the *chora*. Choreographers inscribe the *chora* in ways that architects never even imagine possible: by using transient, usually silent lives and little else. Dancers do not mimic onstage the everyday place in which they already live. They enact something that was never written: not a utopia but a *uchoria*.

It is no coincidence that when Jacobs speaks of the *chora* of her city, she describes it as a dance; and when Merce Cunningham speaks about dance, he describes it as the obliteration of the linear, measurable, agreed-upon space and time of the performance (not only its *topos* but also its *chronos*, as indicated on ticket stubs). The task of a Cunningham dancer is to constitute a new *chora*: "A prevalent feeling among many painters that lets them make a space in which anything can happen is a feeling dancers may have too. Imitating the way nature makes a space and puts lots of things in it, heavy and light, little and big, all unrelated, yet each affecting all the others."

TO CREATE THIS *CHORA*, this new yet unapproachable "place of suspended possibilities," as Trisha Brown later called it, twentieth-century choreographers and dancers—a majority of the most groundbreaking among them were New Yorkers—had to embody, and hence exemplify, consciously or not, a premise Spinoza developed at the dawn of modernity: *We still do not know what the body can do.* We know that, along with Descartes, Spinoza rejected the prevalent medieval view of the body as the prison of the soul. If a human body cannot determine the mind to think, then our thoughts can be autonomous and free. But this argument often ignores Spinoza's corollary critique of a Cartesian assumption that became deeply ingrained in our modern culture: the belief that my body parts simply do the bidding of my various thoughts; that the mind can "determine the body to motion or rest, or to anything else (if there is anything else)," that the soul is, in other words, the prison of the body.

Spinoza argues that those who hold this opinion are those who do not yet know what the body can do. Pressed to offer a counterexample, he mentions sleepwalkers, who seem to act contrary to their mind's will. But if Spinoza had spent his days in twentieth-century New York instead of seventeenth-century Amsterdam, he would have been drawn to modern, postmodern, and contemporary dance as a paradigm case, the one best tailored to prove his point.

The liberation of the body from the sovereignty of the mind does not necessarily mean that one can dodge bullets or bend spoons with a piercing gaze. Spinoza wants us to figure out what our body can do *according to the laws of its own nature*. This figuring out requires scrupulous attention. It takes time and effort to develop the body's proprioception, study its motions and rests, listen to its proclivities and limits, test its gestures and postures through repeated experiments and daily practice, see how it influences and is influenced by other bodies through improvised and choreographed interactions, and map the intricate economy of the emotions that sway it in every which way.

Yvonne Rainer best summed this attitude up when she called her seminal choreographic work *The Mind Is a Muscle*, though the reverse is just as true. Dancers often speak in this vein of body memory, or about the intelligence of different body parts. The mind's aim is therefore not to dictate to the body what it ought to be doing according to some cold, rational plan but to understand this body in a clear manner. It is not a question of top-down obedience but of self-restraint. There is nothing less free than an undisciplined body that moves impulsively. A passive individual can become active and hence free, just as a child who takes ballet classes from an early age, after years of hard work and some luck, can dance on a New York stage. "All things excellent," writes Spinoza at the end of his *Ethics*, "are as difficult as they are rare."

The *Ethics* can thus be read as a training manual for modern dancers. "Kinetics," it has recently been proclaimed, "is the ethics of modernity." Whereas the sacrifice of the dancer's body through the grueling training that forces it to do things contrary to its own nature still informs classical ballet, modern choreographers tend to side with Spinoza, who finds it absurd to pursue an idea that negates, destroys, or deforms one's body, even though pain is inevitable. More than any modern philosopher, the modern dancer may best manifest the full power of Spinoza's ethical thought. Watching a troupe of gifted dancers is one of the best opportunities we have to witness the realization of Spinoza's idea of blessedness in everyday life.

But what, precisely, do we witness? The answer to the perennial question of what this or that dance piece means is that, more often than not, the question is wrong to begin with. Ever since Cunningham stopped treating dance as mimesis, distilling it to "movement in itself, without external references," and ever since Brown took things a step further by focusing on what she called pure movement, it makes less sense to keep searching for the choreography's semantic or even semiotic content. Only metaphorically speaking does a dance have a language. What the choreographer writes and the audience reads is essentially glossolalic. Hence the realization, extending from Heinrich von Kleist to Giorgio Agamben, that dance operates in a "zone of nonknowledge."

Only when we stop hunting for a literal or symbolic meaning can we cease to be blind to the choreography's emotive and somatic affects. We may then notice that these kinesthetic experiences and motor possibilities pass between the dancers' bodies, seep into the bodies of the spectators, spill from theater to street, or from street to theater (unless, as in many of Brown's early works, the street *is* the theater). We may then know a little better what the body can do and what the *chora* can become. This may not be the most direct way to imagine a form of life, but it is probably the most beautiful.

❧

IT SHOULD COME AS NO SURPRISE that the previous considerations are not intended as universal claims, applicable to any body, any place, or any dance. To give Benjamin's dance theory the right proportions, we need to think less about Plato and more about Cunningham, less about Spinoza and more about Brown, to whom I dedicate the remainder of this longish chapter. Benjamin treats Brown's body of work as a crystallization of twentieth-century New York dance and considers *Locus*, a piece she made in the mid-1970s, the axis around which her evolving artistic production turns. *Locus* is also the piece that articulates some of the main concerns of Benjamin's overarching approach to both dance and place.

Like Spinoza's *Ethics*, Brown's *Locus* was composed in a geometric fashion. She began by drawing in her notebook a diagram of twenty-seven equidistant points on a three-dimensional cube (nine on each side, plus one at the center). Then she assigned to each point a number and a letter of the English alphabet, leaving the twenty-seventh point at the center to represent the space between each word. Standing inside this imaginary cube, she could then relate with different parts of her body to the different points of the cube. Sentences written on paper become movements that are structured, clustered, and ordered according to their corresponding points in space. The main text that Brown wrote and then spelled onstage began with a short autobiography and evolved into a concise manifesto:

> Pure movement is a movement that has no other connotations. It is not functional or pantomimic. Mechanical body actions like bending, straightening or rotating would qualify as pure movement providing the context was neutral. I

use pure movement, a kind of breakdown of the body's capabilities. . . . I may perform an everyday gesture so that the audience does not know whether I have stopped dancing or not. . . . I make radical changes in a mundane way. . . . I do not promote the next movement with a preceding transition and, therefore, I do not build up to something. . . . If I am beginning to sound like a bricklayer with a sense of humor, you are beginning to understand my work.

Pure movement, Benjamin adds, exists "within the sphere of means themselves, without regard to the ends they serve." The problem is that these means without end, these pure movements, can easily be obfuscated by a slew of other elements: a stage or a set, costumes or lights, a story line or a verbal script, the assumption of roles or the display of emotions, the accompanying music or the general sense of a spectacle. Equally distracting are elements codified by previous modern choreographers (Martha Graham is the all-powerful example here), in which the evocation of certain moves, gestures, and expressions carry very specific, undeniable connotations.

Influenced by Cunningham and the peers with whom she performed at the Judson Memorial Church on Washington Square Park during the 1960s, Brown eliminated some or all of the previously mentioned variables in an attempt to investigate and present movement as such. For example, dancing in silence ensured that the choreography would not be constricted by a tempo, by the tyranny of the musical score. It then became possible to instruct the performers, as Brown often did, to "allow a movement to take the time that it takes." Another example is the cultivation of a virtuosity that remains potential. Balletic splits and spins draw the occasional "ooh" and "aah" from an enchanted audience. Yet Brown preferred not to do many of the things that her body was evidently capable of doing. What a dancer like Brown can *not* do (not to be confused with what she *cannot* do) is as important as what she can do.

Brown was also allergic to the expression of clichéd emotions and lyrical posturing. In her work, affects may emerge only from movements, not the other way around. The dancer's face may convey a sense of calm, concentration, maybe joy, but nothing more. In the words of one observer, the result of this stripping down of the performance is that "Brown appears to simply *be* there, over and over, intentionally empty of anything—except the profoundly existential." Her pure movement is therefore a good expression of what Heidegger calls *Dasein* (being there) and what Benjamin calls sheer life.

FOR ABOUT TWO DECADES Brown created minimalist pieces, many of which can be approached as kinesthetic lab experiments, during which her dancers were dressed in all white, as in *Group Primary Accumulation*, seen here performed in Central Park. The choreographies usually amounted to nothing more than a task she gave the performers in advance. She called these pieces "dance machines." Then, around 1980, she began to implement her body of kinetic knowledge into the composition of more traditional choreographies for the proscenium stage. These pieces had a beginning, a middle, and an end, as well as music, costumes, and lights. The transition seemed like a sharp departure, conveniently dividing Brown's oeuvre to an early and a later period. Yet the persistent force of the early, more elementary pieces is what lends her mature, elaborate productions their quiet air of mastery. Once one becomes attuned to pure movement, not much can get in the way. Unlike many contemporary choreographers who are primarily driven by theatrical and conceptual agendas, for Brown, pure movement was always what was at stake.

Here is one example of how the early pieces laid the groundwork for Brown's kinetic fingerprint. When neuroscientists are asked to point to where thinking takes place, they usually talk about synapses. When dancers talk about movement, especially if they are influenced by Brown, they sooner or later begin to talk about joints. The real question is not what the body can do but, more accurately, what the joints can do: how they get articulated by bending, straightening, and rotating. The body, after all, is not a single, solid mass. It can hold on to certain static shapes by flexing the muscles, but only through the release of these tensions is movement, pure or not, born.

If we now ask ourselves what the human body *cannot* do, a common first reaction is that it cannot fly. Gravity is the force that, for our lack of feathers, keeps us close to the ground. In classical ballet one can detect a near defiance of this simple law of nature. To this day the words most often heard in ballet classes are *lift* and *hold*. The ballerina's joints rarely give in. This explains how the unique quality of Brownian motion can be traced back to the way "gravity was enlisted as a collaborator, a machine for making dances." Extension gives way to release. Limbs and spine repeatedly drop and swing. The enemy of the body becomes its closest ally.

None of this made much sense before April 18, 1970, when one of Brown's dancers, secured to a rope, walked on the side of a building in SoHo, face down, from roof to street. On the same day, Brown presented a second piece that was in appearance much simpler but is actually quite difficult to execute. Do try this at home (I mean, in the street): Replicate the posture documented in this photograph of *Leaning Duets*. Stand next to a partner with your feet touching his or hers. Hold hands and lean sideways to form a triangle. During this balancing act, begin to walk, making sure that your feet are still touching each other whenever they touch the ground.

ALL OF BROWN'S WORK, in her own words, "is about change—of direction, shape, velocity, mood, state. There are total, instantaneous shifts from one physical state to another. This is tumultuous to perform, but if the momentum is just right, there is an ease." Most of the time we think of movement and change (the Greek *kinesis* encapsulates both) only in view of the ends they serve. We think of our body as an instrument that performs certain tasks. It is to stop a passing taxi that we lift our arm, to see who called our name that we turn our head, to protect our eyes from the sun that we squint.

Dancers see and do things differently. They can display pure movement and pure change as such rather than in view of some end. They do not erase their potentiality by actualizing it but exhibit it as potentiality, as power. Brown likes to tell the story of an early improvisation session she conducted with a broom, during which she used the momentum generated from the mundane, end-oriented gesture of sweeping to lift her body in the air until she levitated parallel to the floor.

In 1971 Brown instructed a dozen dancers, all dressed in red, to stand on different rooftops throughout downtown Manhattan. The first dancer generated slow, improvised movements that a second dancer was able to see and copy. A third dancer who had a clear line of sight to the second mimicked those same movements, and so on, in what looked like a kinetic version of Chinese whispers. In the middle of the performance the order was reversed, as the first dancer (Brown) who originated the movement became the last to receive it.

LET ME NOW POSE THE QUESTION I previously advised against: What does *Roof Piece* mean? What is this choreography about? What information was relayed from dancer to dancer and from dancer to viewer? Notice that at least part of the reason these questions are particularly impossible to answer is that no one ever saw this piece in its entirety. As Babette Mangolte's iconic photo of this performance makes clear, no matter where the spectators or dancers were positioned, they had to miss most of the action. This evokes one reason why it is so difficult to say what New York City is about. One can write very eloquent short stories or long novels about the life of one or several New Yorkers, but the multitude and magnitude of this *chora* leave all but the most arrogant quite speechless.

It is similarly a mark of vanity to pile up all unanswerable questions into a single, indistinguishable heap. Sometimes it is useful to simply sort them out to find certain similarities. The method will not supply definitive solutions, but it will help to better cope with some unsolvable puzzles. Compare, for instance, the search for the meaning of the choreography called *Roof Piece* with the search for the meaning of the *chora* called New York. What is to be gained from the realization that in both cases we are basically searching for the same thing?

Benjamin had just such a question in mind when he formulated a simple set of rules for his choreography as a pedestrian:

1. Walk down a random Manhattan sidewalk until you reach the corner.

2. Always cross in the direction indicated by the walk sign.

3. Keep on walking until you reach another light; then repeat the last step for a few hours.

4. Never jaywalk, rush, or slow down to catch the light of your choice.

Benjamin's *Walk Piece* draws on Cunningham's chance operations and Brown's simple movement tasks, as well as on Vito Acconci's *Following Piece*, in which the artist was led by random strangers that he shadowed around town. Another clear influence on Benjamin's dance is Guy Debord's "Theory of the Dérive," which outlines a similar technique for drifting through the streets of Paris. But unlike Debord, who relied on random psychological cues to move from street to street, Benjamin relinquished his inevitably biased urban intuition, as well as the illusion of self-control, which enabled him to experience New York as never before.

FORTY-FIFTH CHAPTER **LIFE SENTENCE**

IN THE SUMMER OF 1974, Tehching Hsieh (pronounced dur-ching shay), a twenty-four-year-old Taiwanese sailor, jumped ship when his oil tanker docked in the Delaware River. From there he took a bus to Manhattan, where he lived as an illegal alien for the next fourteen years. Speaking broken English and working odd jobs, he remained a perpetual outsider. Back then there was little reason to take seriously Benjamin's prediction that one day Hsieh would be considered one of the greatest New York artists of the twentieth century. This epithet still raises many contemporary eyebrows in the art world. But after decades of near-complete obscurity—during which Hsieh developed an underground art economy and an alternative aesthetic sensibility to reflect his marginalized position in the city—he is now beginning to gain recognition for his unsettling achievement.

For his first artwork, or lifework, Hsieh locked himself in a cage for an entire year. Built inside his loft on Hudson Street (one mile from where Bartleby the Scrivener "preferred not to"), Hsieh's cell was equipped with a bed, a sink, a bucket, and nothing else. Outside he posted a printed statement in which he declared, "I shall *not* converse, read, write, listen to the radio or watch television, until I unseal myself on September 29, 1979." He paid a friend to come once a day to give him food, clean his refuse, and take his picture. He carved a line on the wall for each day spent in his self-inflicted prison. Once a month the studio was opened to the public during usual gallery hours, but Hsieh did not even make eye contact with the few curious visitors. After the show closed, a lawyer certified that no deception was involved.

Despite these minimal living conditions, or because of them, Hsieh maintained the ability to concentrate on his art and contemplate his life during the seemingly endless, uninterrupted hours spent in his cage. So for his second *One Year Performance* he decided to deprive himself of precisely this privilege. He chose to punch a time clock every hour, on the hour, twenty-four hours a day, seven days a week, for a total of 8,760 stamps. He also recorded with a camera a single frame, showing himself standing next to the clock every time he punched the card, which eventually turned into a six-minute stop-motion movie clip. He wore the same generic work uniform every day, though his growing hair, which was shaved at the beginning of the year, marked the passing of time. In the end he produced a report detailing the 133 punch-ins (or punch-outs) he had missed, tabulated by month and by reason (because he was asleep, or because he mistakenly stamped the card a minute too early or a minute too late). The piece illustrates Hsieh's basic idea that wasting time is the true meaning of life, that "whatever you do, living is nothing but consuming time until you die."

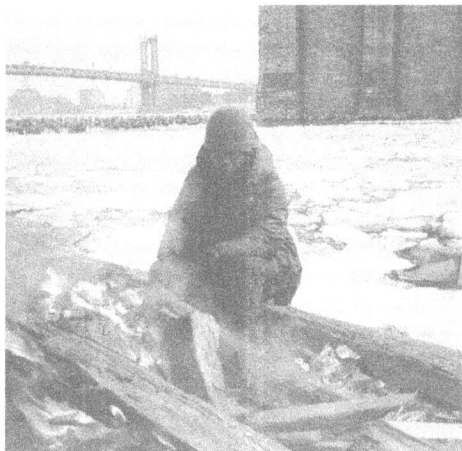

IF HIS FIRST ARTWORK prevented Hsieh from experiencing the surrounding city in which he lived and the second required him to stay within a few blocks' radius of his studio, his third year-long performance deprived him of what the previous two grueling years had not dared to call into question: the fact that he still had shelter. "I shall stay *outdoors* for one year, never go inside," his statement from 1981 reads. "I shall not go into a building, subway, train, car, airplane, ship, cave, tent." Carrying only a backpack with a sleeping bag and a few other necessities, he performed homelessness among thousands of others who did not perceive their condition as art, just as he once performed imprisonment in solitary confinement and then performed factory work on a never-ending shift. Instead of observing him in his studio, the growing number of spectators were instructed to meet this living artwork under the Brooklyn Bridge on certain dates, including the dead of winter, when the East River nearly froze. (The reproduced photograph, like other documentations of his performances, is not considered part of the piece but only its trace.) Once, he was arrested for a few hours. He was dragged into the First Precinct police station despite his anguished protest. It was the only time that the show did not go on. When his case was discussed in court, the judge addressed the question of habeas corpus: "I don't see any reason to bring him indoors [for the hearing]. These days anything is art. Staying outside may be art. I'm getting old and nothing surprises me."

The fourth *One Year Performance* again addressed something Hsieh had not relinquished in any of his previous pieces: his solitude. In collaboration with the performance artist Linda Montano, he agreed to never be alone for an entire year. The couple (they did not know each other before the work began, and they did not get along that well during it) were able to go about their normal lives. They went to the movies, did some work, renovated a studio, and met with friends. But they remained tethered to each other by a rope eight feet in length, tied at waist level at all times. The ties were secured by two seals and signed by two witnesses. Montano and Hsieh also vowed to never touch each other during this period. As can be seen from the poster advertising the performance, which was called *Art/Life*, this time around there were only four formal presentations, probably because the spectacle of a man and a woman walking down the street connected by a rope was unavoidable for ordinary downtown residents.

HSIEH'S LAST TWO PERFORMANCES form together the natural conclusion to his six-part masterpiece. But they also problematize his position within the history of art. The penultimate piece, which was the last to span an entire year, began on July 1, 1985. (Between each piece he took a few months off, which he considered "life time" rather than "art time.") On the face of it, it was the least arduous of the performances he had ever undertaken, yet it may well have been the most radical of them all. The statement he issued announces that he will "not do *art*, not talk *art*, not see *art*, not read *art*, not go to *art* gallery and *art* museum for one year." Instead, he will "*just go in life*." He managed to succeed in this endeavor only by leaving New York for most of the year. In opposition to the previous works, there could be no documentation, no witnesses, and no traces whatsoever that could attest that the performance really took place, because those would have constituted a breach of contract. Given Hsieh's history of complete dedication to his work, there is little reason to doubt his word.

There is something ironic about no art as art, about a performer performing a nonperformance. This conundrum led to Hsieh's announcement of his ultimate lifework, a thirteen-year performance that was to end on the last day of the twentieth century. According to the plan, he was allowed to make art but only in secret. No one but he was supposed to know what he was up to until the very end. None of his past or present art could be displayed publicly during those years. Once again, Hsieh relinquished something that all the previous one-year performances had retained: the desire to be recognized by others, without which it is nearly impossible to even be considered a person.

On January 1, 2000, Hsieh revealed the work that had taken him thirteen years to complete. In a ceremony at Judson Church on Washington Square, he released a pithy statement: "I kept myself alive." In a sense, all of his pieces are remarkable in that he survived them. But this was not his original intention. His plan was to disappear. Disappearance, not perseverance, was meant to be his supreme performance. It is not hard to guess why Benjamin was so drawn to this disappearing act, which he himself had first entertained upon reading Brecht's *Reader for City Dwellers*: "The man who hasn't signed anything, who left no picture, who was not there, who said nothing . . . Erase the traces."

Today Hsieh admits that he failed to realize his final work. He was on his way to Alaska when he began to question his willingness to do such a thing for the sake of art. Of all the hellish conditions to which he subjected himself, disappearance was too much to bear. He retired after this sixth, incomplete performance, believing that he has nothing else to say. "I don't do art anymore since 2000," he said in a recent interview. "Now I'm just doing life." Nevertheless, Hsieh is an artist whose medium of expression has always been his own life. Reading about his lifeworks remains a conceptual exercise until one realizes that these are not just ideas whose execution is a "perfunctory affair," but that a person actually subjected himself to them for quite extended periods. The banality of everyday life is completely radicalized once it comes into contact with this everyday art, and vice versa. The performative event is stretched until it can no longer be recognized as such. There is probably no better example of a person who transformed so much of his life into a work of art. This is so true that it is not easy to speak about the artist behind the work. In this case, even the word *art* becomes almost superfluous. It might even be interpreted as an insult.

In such a context, it is helpful to think about Yves Klein's "Leap into the Void," a 1960 photo showing the artist diving from the roof of a small house located in a side street of a Parisian suburb. His friends, who stretched a tarpaulin to catch his fall, were erased from the published image. In an early piece Hsieh performed in 1973, when he was still living in Taiwan, he jumped from the second floor of a building to the sidewalk and broke both of his ankles. A frame-by-frame photographic record of the leap and its aftermath is the only physical trace left of the performance, in addition to the chronic pain Hsieh endured for years thereafter. But he claims that he did not *mean* to hurt himself. He also insists that none of his mature works were designed to inflict pain or to jeopardize his mental or physical well-being. Suffering, like error or failure, is not the point of Hsieh's art, but, as in life, it is virtually inescapable because, as he realized, art and life are both largely beyond our control.

IN THE LAST PAGES of *The Manhattan Project* one can find a predominantly descriptive account of Hsieh's work. Little effort is made to theorize it. In the margins Benjamin adds, "I needn't *say* anything. Merely show." I cannot explain exactly how Hsieh's life and art affected Benjamin's thought and work, or even my own. The most I can say is that now I realize how much of *The Manhattan Project* was written as a response to this affect.

SIXTH THRESHOLD   # SPINOZA IN NEW AMSTERDAM

MANY OF THE THEORIES, stories, dreams, and dramas that revolve around the modern city fail to see it as a natural phenomenon. It is not uncommon to approach a place like New York as a "kingdom within a kingdom" that disturbs rather than follows the order of its surrounding environment.

Economy is often perceived as the great enemy of ecology. The economic system is seen as an unstoppable force behind the constant destruction of our planet. It is therefore somewhat surprising that in the late nineteenth century, when botanists began to analyze communities of plants rather than individual specimens, they referred to the intricate relationships they came to discover as an economy. When these botanists-turned-ecologists started to investigate how different animals, plants, and their shared environment depend on one another, they found it helpful to describe this ecological system as the "economy of nature."

As the twentieth century was nearing its end, Jacobs composed a Platonic dialogue between several imaginary New York friends. She called it *The Nature of Economies*, a work that might be read as a peculiar contribution to systems theory. It is her attempt to think of ecology and economy as sister sciences. She thus insists on using expressions like *the economy of nature* and *the nature of economy* in their literal sense. In her mind, they point to a single field of interconnected networks composed of different organisms and natural elements. This means, on the one hand, that "economic life is ruled by processes and principles we didn't invent and can't transcend, whether we like it or not." On the other hand, it means that only the most "misanthropic ecologists" can continue to renounce or denounce the place of human beings within the overall ecosystem, recently renamed the Anthropocene.

What we currently think of as economics could be reconceived as an integral field within an ecology that specializes in human interactions. And ecology might properly be understood as natural economy. But this is easier said than done, so Jacobs offers some hypothetical examples that enable us to let go of the seemingly unbridgeable gap that separates the economic system from the ecological system, human from animal, city from nature. She thereby demonstrates how expansion, survival, and collapse are processes that follow the very same logic in both realms. Is a savanna with snakes and birds necessarily different from a downtown with traders and artists? "What are the perils of jungle and prairie," Baudelaire asks, "compared to the daily shocks and conflicts of civilization?"

A belief that man's mastery over nature was the ultimate goal of technology eventually "betrayed man and turned the bridal bed into a bloodbath." With this graphic image in mind, Benjamin goes on to argue that the purpose of education is not the mastery of children by adults but, above all, the "ordering of the relationship between generations and therefore mastery (if we are to use this term) of that relationship and not of children." This, he concludes, enables us to rethink technology not as the mastery of nature but of the *relationship* between nature and man. The same logic applies to the mastery of the relationship between city and country, which is the basis for Jacobs's provocative suggestion that economy and ecology come together as a single, unified field.

🐦

IN 1958 JACOBS PARTICIPATED in a protest against Moses's plan to allow car traffic to run through Washington Square Park, which was a crucial part of his grander plan to build an expressway right through the middle of downtown Manhattan. She probably noticed then the inscription, attributed to George Washington, on the attic story of the monumental arch located at the park's northern edge. "The event is in the hand of God" are the words of the man who almost single-handedly rewrote the city's history. Think of New York as a protracted event. If this event is not in the hand of this land's proto-sovereign, then it is surely in no one's at all.

Gotham needs a hero from time to time, but even Batman eventually hangs up his suit and returns to his cave. Washington's words are not a declaration of blind trust in the machinations of the Almighty or an expression of nihilistic resignation in the face of an ungovernable chaos. They are an articulation of disenchanted distrust or pragmatic humility. What Washington meant to say was that even if we were to "raise a standard to which the wise and honest can repair," instead of merely aiming to "please the people," the rest would remain pretty much out of our hands. Doing the right thing is no guarantee that things will not fall apart.

THE WASHINGTON ARCH IN NEW YORK, like the Arc de Triomphe in Paris and Brandenburg Gate in Berlin, is a modern replica of a Roman structure under which the victorious army passed when it returned to the city from yet another conquest. Such a rite of passage at the metropolitan threshold carried religious undertones: the troops can be seen as having escaped hostile elements, as clearing themselves of "some stain, separating off contagion or the spirits of the dead, who cannot follow through the narrow opening." It was also a juridical ceremony necessary for transforming soldier into citizen, war into peace, and an exceptional state of nature into a civilized urban order.

The line that marked this neat separation, without which Rome's bloody imperial project would have probably been unbearable, has all but disappeared in modernity. "We have grown very poor in threshold experiences," Benjamin realized one afternoon while observing the lively crowd in Washington Square Park, as people were passing under the arch, completely unfazed. Today, everything interpenetrates everything else. Nothing is left behind: neither war nor work, neither private pain nor public shame, neither the sacred nor the profane, neither our nature nor our culture. Modern life's porosity precludes the introduction of clear boundaries. The thresholds that do exist are as much exits as they are entrances. Once we do encounter what seems like an opening to the other side, we are overcome by a Kafkaesque paralysis that stops us in our tracks. Then again, maybe every moment or place in a modern city like New York is a small gateway or a secret entrance of sorts.

THERE IS SOMEONE who understood all this long before and much better than Washington, Jacobs, or even Benjamin. This individual had never been to New York, for it did not even exist when he was alive, at least not under its present name. Nevertheless, growing up in Amsterdam, the undisputed capital of the seventeenth century, Spinoza was keenly aware of New Amsterdam on the other side of the Atlantic, which had been founded only six years before his birth. When he was twenty-two (the year his father died and two years before his excommunication), a few Dutch Jews landed in Manhattan and established their first congregation in North America. Peter Stuyvesant, the governor of the colony at the time, was adamant that they should be expelled from his territory, but the executives of the West India Company back in Amsterdam thought otherwise.

Spinoza's name is rarely mentioned in Benjamin's European writings. In America, however, the relation of his *Manhattan Project* to Spinoza's *Ethics* is like that of a blotting pad to ink. The former is saturated with the latter, even though this ink is of the invisible kind. Whereas the protagonist in Spinoza's metaphysics is God, or nature, it is New York, or sheer life, that stands at the center of Benjamin's thought. Like Spinoza's substance, Benjamin perceives the city as a pure immanence. But when he is pressed to either elaborate this claim or face its problematic nature, he only wraps the riddle in a mystery by saying that the *aura* of New York is "*a life*, and nothing else."

It is common to make sense of Spinoza's *Ethics* by linking it to Maimonides's religious thought, Hobbes's political thought, Descartes's philosophical thought, or Newton's scientific thought. It is less common to approach this work by linking it to Rembrandt's art: as a vivid reflection, almost a representation, of the urban life that emerged in the rapidly expanding cosmopolitan hub of Amsterdam during that city's golden age. Following this lead, the city is no longer just the soil on which Spinoza's philosophy thrives. It is, rather, what his strange theory of modes, attributes, and affects is ultimately about. His goals: to see the city *sub specie aeternitatis*, to promote an intellectual love of the city.

FORTUNATELY, only the place can prove the theory, not the other way around. For "while facts never become obsolete or stale," as Isaac Bashevis Singer argues, "commentaries always do." And in any event, philosophy, like the city, can never be finished; at most, it can be abandoned.

So we will abandon this textual ship in the same way we boarded it. Imagine Benjamin wandering into the Catalog Room of the New York Public Library. While browsing through various titles, he comes across a manuscript dating back to the seventeenth century. It turns out to be a commentary on the book of Genesis. Benjamin's initial hunch only intensifies as his close examination of the manuscript progresses. The author of this unknown and unsigned treatise can be none other than Spinoza. It remains uncertain whether, in the face of his persecution, Spinoza sent this wildly heretical book to America for safekeeping. Maybe he even wrote it in New Amsterdam, where he, like so many others since, found refuge from a life unlivable elsewhere.

Philosophy is actually never abandoned; it is only shelved until another hand reaches out for its spine. In the meantime, Benjamin should get the last word:

These pages, devoted to life in twentieth-century New York, were begun under an open sky of cloudless blue that arched above the foliage; and yet—owing to the thousands of leaves that were visited by the fresh breeze of diligence, the stertorous breath of the researcher, the storm of youthful zeal, and the idle wind of curiosity—they have been covered with that century's dust. For the painted sky of summer that looks down on the writer who sits in the Public Library's main reading room has spread out over his words a dreamlike ceiling.

ACKNOWLEDGMENTS

THIS BOOK was made possible by generous support from the Institute for Cultural Inquiry in Berlin and Emerson College in Boston. It is only in Berlin that I got suspicious of those "we" who "take" in Leonard Cohen's "First We Take Manhattan" the two cities where I have spent my adult life. It is only in Boston that I got the meaning of Kafka's claim in *Amerika* that this city is connected to New York by a bridge that "hangs delicately over the Hudson and trembles if one narrows one's eyes." Reciting this line every time I board the train to go teach there turns the long commute into a relative joyride.

I wish to thank these good people for their guidance and friendship: Yael Almog, Daniel Barber, Bobby Benedicto, Roy Ben-Shai, Emily-Jane Cohen, Alice Gavin, Graeme Gilloch, Pavel Godfrey, Antonia Grousdanidou, Kit Heintzman, Cynthia Lindlof, Stefan Pedatella, Yehuda Safran, and Sandrine Sanos. And Netta Yerushalmy, who is so real that losing her fictional representation for argument's sake was one of the easiest moves in this entire book.

It is dedicated to the eight million.

NOTES

QUOTATIONS placed within quotation marks, along with epigraphs, block quotations, and parts of the conversation in the fortieth chapter, are all genuine unless otherwise noted. They are cited here in order of appearance, with their first few words highlighted in bold. Two abbreviations are used:

AP   Walter Benjamin, The Arcades Project, trans. H. Eiland and K. McLaughlin (Cambridge, MA: Harvard University Press, 1999).

SW I–IV   Walter Benjamin, Selected Writings, 4 vols., ed. M. Bullock and M. W. Jennings (Cambridge, MA: Harvard University Press, 1996–2003).

PREFACE: I CAN'T AFFORD TO ♥ NY

Never use: *SW* II, 603. **a confession**: Friedrich Nietzsche, *Beyond Good and Evil*, ed. R. P. Wilhelm and J. Norman (Cambridge: Cambridge University Press, 2001), 8. **read an *H***: *AP*, 776. **They're so intimate**: F. Scott Fitzgerald, *The Great Gatsby*, ed. M. J. Bruccoli (Cambridge: Cambridge University Press, 1995), 41. **the only home**: Edward W. Said, *Reflections on Exile* (Cambridge, MA: Harvard University Press, 2000), 184.

INTRODUCTION: THE ROSEMAN HYPOTHESIS

the theater: Walter Benjamin, *The Correspondence of Walter Benjamin 1910–1940*, ed. G. Scholem and T. Adorno (Chicago: University of Chicago Press, 1994), 359 (amended). **The historical method**: *SW* IV, 405. **What does it matter**: Samuel Beckett, quoted in Michel Foucault, "What Is an Author?," in *The Essential Foucault*, ed. P. Rabinow and N. Rose (New York: New Press, 2003), 239. **city-as-text**: Graeme Gilloch, *Myth and Metropolis: Walter Benjamin and the City* (Cambridge, UK: Polity Press, 1996), 182. **ghostwriter**: Rem Koolhaas, *Delirious New York* (New York: Monacelli Press, 1994), 11. **that which is placed**: Giorgio Agamben, "The Thing Itself," *SubStance* 53 (1987), 23. **One can read**: *AP*, 464. **commentary on a reality**: ibid., 460.

FIRST PART

Benjamin merges: Susan Sontag, "Introduction," in *One-Way Street*, by Walter Benjamin (London: Verso, 1979), 13.

FIRST CHAPTER: BENJAMIN IN NEW YORK

There is not enough time: quoted in *AP*, 946 (presumably written on a postcard handed to Henny Gurland, his companion in Portbou, who destroyed the original not before committing its contents to memory). **Speech conquers**: *SW* I, 458. **Action can**: *SW* III, 7. **Sad is Eros**: W. H. Auden, "In Memory of Sigmund Freud," in *Selected Poems*, ed. E. Mendelson (New York: Vintage, 2007), 103 (amended). **where, he used to say**: Hannah Arendt, "Reflections: Walter Benjamin," *New Yorker* (October 19, 1968), 96. **the last New Yorker**: A. J. Liebling, "That Was New York," *New Yorker* (October 12, 1963), 143–68. **star devoid**: Friedrich Nietzsche, quoted in *AP*, 369. **mass**: Theodor W. Adorno, "On Jazz," in *Essays on Music*, ed. R. Leppert (Berkeley: University of California Press, 2002), 470–95; Max Horkheimer and Theodor W. Adorno, *Dialectic of Enlightenment* (Stanford, CA: Stanford University Press, 2002), 112 (on laughter). **who so thoroughly studied**: Marx talking about Balzac, quoted in *AP*, 776. **Philosophy is about**: cf. Carl Andre, "Art is what we do, culture is what is done to us," in *Cuts*, ed. J. Meyer (Cambridge, MA: MIT Press, 2005), 31. **abandonment**: Theodor W. Adorno and Walter Benjamin, *The Complete Correspondence 1928–1940*, ed. H. Lonitz (Cambridge, MA: Harvard University Press, 2000), 106. **eddy in the stream**: Walter Benjamin, *The Origin of German Tragic Drama*, trans. J. Osborne (London: Verso, 2003), 45. **Few things**: *AP*, 82–83 (interpolated). **organic totality**: Gilles Deleuze, "Whitman," in *Essays Critical and Clinical*, trans. D. W. Smith and M. A. Greco (London: Verso, 1998), 56. **the description of confusion**: *AP*, 331.

SECOND CHAPTER: NOT TO LOOK UPON

terrible affair and **all those women**: James Joyce, *Ulysses* (New York: Vintage, 1990), 239, 182. Richard Ellmann stands behind the seemingly settled explanation that Joyce chose this date to mark an event of a personal kind: the first time he went out with Nora Barnacle, his future wife (*James Joyce* [Oxford: Oxford University Press, 1983], 155–56). **Shot Heard Round**: Don DeLillo, *Underworld* (New York: Scribner, 1997), 95. **Isn't it possible**: ibid., 59–60. **doesn't change**: ibid., 32. **In one respect**: Ambrose Serle, quoted in *New York Diaries*, ed. T. Carpenter (New York: Modern Library, 2012), 407; cf. Acts 17:21. **It used to be**: E. B. White, "Here Is New York," in *Empire City: New York through the Centuries*, ed. K. T. Jackson and D. D. Dunbar (New York: Columbia University Press, 2005), 710. **gloomy awareness**: *AP*, 97 (amended). **lofty target**: White, "Here Is New York," 711. **if it were to go**: ibid. **What makes the general**: Henry James, *The American Scene*, in *Collected Travel Writings: Great Britain and America* (New York: Library of America, 1993), 445–46 (amended). **Central Park**: *SW* IV, 161–99. **The right reason**: Joseph Mitchell, "Old Mr. Flood," in *Up in the Old Hotel* (New York: Vintage, 2008), 408. This quotation and the slightly abbreviated version of the story that follows are originally presented as a way to explain the attraction of Manhattan's Fulton Fish Market.

THIRD CHAPTER: BACK TO THE FUTURE

In a dream: *SW* I, 477. **Before we have learned**: Anne Robert Turgot, quoted in *AP*, 477–78 (interpolated). **Tomorrow was the party**: Alice Gavin, "Tensed," unpublished paper, 2013. **repeat the past**: Fitzgerald, *The Great Gatsby*, 86. **the gaze**: *AP*, 10. **erected on the idea**: *SW* III, 305. **Philosophy will have conscience**: Ernst Bloch, *The Principle of Hope*, vol. 1, trans. N. Plaice, S. Plaice, and P. Knight (Cambridge, MA: MIT Press, 1986), 7. **that people do not**: Frank O'Hara, *Meditations in an Emergency* (New York: Grove Press, 1996), 38. **20th century's**: Koolhaas, *Delirious New York*, 9. **we live in the description**: Wallace Stevens, *Letters of Wallace Stevens*, ed. H. Stevens (Berkeley: University of California Press, 1996), 494. **A further word**: G. W. F. Hegel, *Elements of the Philosophy of Right*, ed. A. W. Wood (Cambridge: Cambridge University Press, 1991), 23 (amended). **love at last sight**: *SW* IV, 25. **It is one and the same**: *AP*, 347 (amended). **It is very vulgar**: A. J. Liebling, *Back Where I Came From* (New York: Sheridan House, 1938), 270. **Nothing at all**: *AP*, 833.

FOURTH CHAPTER: THINK LOCALLY

Can we actually: Woody Allen, "My Philosophy," in *The Complete Prose* (New York: Picador, 1998), 170. **Where are we**: Hannah Arendt, *The Life of the Mind* (New York: Harcourt, 1981), 197. **You have to understand**: Roger Berkowitz, "Remembering Hannah Arendt: An Interview with Jack Blum," in *Thinking in Dark Times*, ed. R. Berkowitz, T. Keenan, and J. Katz (New York: Fordham University Press, 2009), 265. *amor mundi*: Elisabeth Young-Bruehl, *Hannah Arendt: For Love of the World* (New Haven, CT: Yale University Press, 2004), 318–24. **arguing the world**: Joseph Dorman, *Arguing the World: The New York Intellectuals in Their Own Words* (Chicago: University of Chicago Press, 2001). **presence of mind**: *SW* II, 147. **arrest** and **monad**: *SW* IV, 396. **perpetual living mirror**: Nicholas Rescher, *G. W. Leibniz's Monadology* (London: Routledge, 2002), 24. **Give me a place to stand**: quoted in Gregory Crane, *Thucydides and the Ancient Simplicity* (Berkeley: University of California Press, 1988), 44. **If I can make it**: Frank Sinatra, Fred Ebb, John Kander, "Theme from *New York, New York*," Capitol Records, 1977. **In this large town**: René Descartes, *The Philosophical Writings of Descartes*, vol. 3, ed. J. Cottingham, R. Stoothoff, and D. Murdoch (Cambridge: Cambridge University Press, 1984), 31.

FIFTH CHAPTER: IMPLOSION

honor, loyalty: Karl Marx, "The German Ideology," in *The Marx-Engels Reader*, ed. R. C. Tucker (New York: Norton, 1978), 173. **urban implosion**: Lewis Mumford, *The City in History* (New York: Harcourt, 1968), 34–35. **During the last**: Lewis Mumford, *Sidewalk Critic*, ed. R. Wojtowicz (Princeton, NJ: Princeton Architectural Press, 1998), 230. **human beings** and **because they are**: Jane Jacobs, *The Death and Life of Great American Cities* (New York: Vintage, 1992), 220–21. **If as one people**: Genesis 11:6. *tsimtsum*: Gershom Scholem, *Major Trends in Jewish Mysticism* (New York: Schocken Books, 1995), 260. **God is the place**: quoted in Karen Armstrong, *A History of God* (New York: Random House, 1993), 74. **My home**: Agnes Heller, "Where Are We at

Home?," in *Aesthetics and Modernity*, ed. J. Rundell (Lanham, MD: Lexington Books, 2011), 203. **the place where:** Jorge Luis Borges, "The Aleph," in *Collected Fictions*, trans. A. Hurley (New York: Penguin, 1998), 281.

SIXTH CHAPTER: SHEER LIFE

landscape built: quoted in *AP*, 83 (amended), 417, 880 ("countless lives" is another way to render *lauter Leben*). **bare life:** *SW* I, 250 (amended); cf. Giorgio Agamben, *Homo Sacer: Sovereign Power and Bare Life*, trans. D. Heller-Roazen (Stanford, CA: Stanford University Press, 1998). **each city:** Italo Calvino, *Invisible Cities* (New York: Harcourt, 1978), 18. **the bare needs:** Aristotle, *The Politics and the Constitution of Athens*, ed. S. Everson (Cambridge: Cambridge University Press, 1996), 13. **share in happiness:** ibid., 73.

SEVENTH CHAPTER: A SECRET ABOUT A SECRET

Men can see: quoted in Guy Debord, "Theory of the Dérive," in *Situationist International Anthology*, ed. K. Knabb (Berkeley: Bureau of Public Secrets, 2007), 63. **a secret about a secret:** Diane Arbus, *Revelations* (New York: Random House, 2003), 278. **mirror that remembers:** Robert de Montesquiou, quoted in *AP*, 688. **propose that we collect:** Susan Sontag, *On Photography* (New York: Picador, 1990), 82. Unfortunately, Benjamin could not have read Sontag's reevaluation of her own position in *Regarding the Pain of Others* (New York: Farrar, Straus and Giroux, 2003). **chronological specifiability:** *AP*, 691. **was as important:** William R. Taylor, quoted in Ann Douglas, *Terrible Honesty: Mongrel Manhattan in the 1920s* (New York: Farrar, Straus and Giroux, 1996), 59–60. **When one knows:** *SW* IV, 53. **New York Elderhood:** apocryphal; cf. "Berlin Childhood around 1900," in *SW* III, 344–413. **the proof that something:** Arbus, *Revelations*, 226. **stillness:** ibid.

FIRST THRESHOLD: INTERPENETRATION

What can I know: Immanuel Kant, *Philosophical Correspondence, 1759–1799*, ed. A. Zweig (Chicago: University of Chicago Press, 1986), 205. **theology of hell:** *AP*, 854. **dream city:** ibid., 410. **no outside:** ibid., 406. **world in miniature:** ibid., 3. **capital of perpetual:** Koolhaas, *Delirious New York*, 11. **jealous custodian:** Manfredo Tafuri, *Venice and the Renaissance* (Cambridge, MA: MIT Press, 1995), xi. **seems pregnant:** Karl Marx, "Speech at the Anniversary of the *People's Paper*," in *The Marx-Engels Reader*, 577. **forest of symbols:** Marshall Berman, *All That Is Solid Melts into Air* (London: Verso, 1983), 289. **Do not insist:** quoted in Esther Leslie, *Walter Benjamin: Overpowering Conformism* (London: Pluto, 2000), 235 (amended). **The finest thing:** Liebling, *Back Where I Came From*, 13. **dialectical fairyland:** *AP*, 937. **for a boy:** Henry Miller, *Tropic of Capricorn* (New York: Grove Press, 1987), 215.

SECOND PART
things are real: Jane Jacobs, interview with Roberta Grotz, Jane Jacobs Papers, Boston College, Box 22.

EIGHTH CHAPTER: LIVINGRY
Some people: Andy Warhol, *The Philosophy of Andy Warhol (From A to B and Back Again)* (New York: Harcourt, 1977), 111. **What is the city**: William Shakespeare, *Coriolanus* (Oxford: Oxford University Press, 1998), 257. **inside-out**: In 1924 Benjamin translated "La photographie à l'envers," Tristan Tzara's essay on Man Ray (see Leslie, *Walter Benjamin*, 57). **The great goal**: Victor Fournel, quoted in *AP*, 401. **whose eyes**: Allen Ginsberg, *Howl and Other Poems* (San Francisco: City Lights, 1985), 21 (amended). **The architectural profession**: Buckminster Fuller, *Critical Paths* (New York: St. Martin's, 1981), xxv. **city indoors**: *AP*, 532. **one umbrella**: Edward Bellamy, quoted in *AP*, 136. **glorious canopy**: Isaiah 4:5–6. **crystal canopy**: Léo Claretie, quoted in *AP*, 109.

NINTH CHAPTER: THINGIFICATION
thing theory: Jane Jacobs, *The Nature of Economies* (New York: Vintage, 2000), 32. **For all reification**: Adorno and Benjamin, *The Complete Correspondence*, 321. **the most poignant**: Alfred Dalvau, quoted in *AP*, 435.

TENTH CHAPTER: REALITY OVERDOSE
wishful frivolity: Jacobs, *Death and Life*, 345. **since the world**: quoted in Koolhaas, *Delirious New York*, 9. **Why do we have**: quoted in ibid. *theoretical* **Manhattan**: ibid., 11. **exist in a world**: ibid., 10. **factory of man-made**: ibid. (amended). **two-dimensional discipline**: ibid., 20. **indefinitely postponed**: ibid., 110. *retroactive manifesto*: ibid., 9. **Reality Shortage**: ibid., 241. **So many a day**: Edwin Denby, "Mid-Day Crowd," in *Dance Writings and Poetry*, ed. R. Cornfield (New Haven, CT: Yale University Press, 1998), 15 (amended). **fetal Manhattan**: Koolhaas, *Delirious New York*, 30. **Luna parks**: *SW* I, 487 (amended). **experiment in moral**: Koolhaas, *Delirious New York*, 39. **Delirious No More**: *Wired*, June 2003, http://goo.gl/W1eXbs. **surrealism is invisible**: Koolhaas, *Delirious New York*, 261. **surrealism was born**: *AP*, 82. **no face**: *SW* II, 211. **in each minute**: ibid., 218. **During the war**: Denby, "The Thirties: An Essay," in *Dance Writings and Poetry*, 3. **There's something**: Simone de Beauvoir, *America Day by Day* (Berkeley: University of California Press, 2000), 18.

ELEVENTH CHAPTER: THE DISENCHANTED ISLAND
pouring water: Edwin G. Burrows and Michael L. Wallace, *Gotham: A History of New York City to 1898* (New York: Oxford University Press, 1999), xiv. **More fools**: ibid. **the Idiotic Building**: Ric Burns and James Sanders, *New York: An Illustrated*

History (New York: Knopf, 2003), 232. **Great Lobotomy**: Koolhaas, *Delirious New York*, 177. **architectural ideology**: Manfredo Tafuri, *Architecture and Utopia: Design and Capitalist Development* (Cambridge, MA: MIT Press, 1985), 135. **It is not by mere chance**: ibid., 33–34. **to dispel myths**: Horkheimer and Adorno, *Dialectic of Enlightenment*, 1. **elevation of urban life**: Roger Caillois, quoted in *AP*, 555. **that takes itself**: E. B. White, "Why I Like New York," *New Yorker* (August 22, 1925), 10. **added value**: Manfredo Tafuri, "The Disenchanted Mountain," in *The American City: From the Civil War to the New Deal*, trans. B. L. La Penta (Cambridge, MA: MIT Press, 1979), 451–57. **were stripped**: ibid., 461. **represented the final**: ibid., 483. **the disenchanted mountain**: ibid., 493. **The realism**: ibid., 484. **intent on communicating**: ibid., 500. **technological civilization**: ibid. **a city under**: Raymond Hood, quoted in Koolhaas, *Delirious New York*, 176.

TWELFTH CHAPTER: DEMOCRACITY
those who search: Tafuri, *Architecture and Utopia*, 24. **existence is elsewhere**: André Breton, *Manifestoes of Surrealism* (Ann Arbor: University of Michigan Press, 1972), 47. **factories of dreams**: Jacques de Lacretelle, quoted in *AP*, 405. **one entered**: quoted in Burns and Sanders, *New York*, 514. **From the conservative**: W. H. Auden, "September 1, 1939," in *Selected Poems*, 96–97 (amended). **city of tomorrow**: Le Corbusier, *The City of To-morrow and Its Planning*, trans. F. Etchells (New York: Dover, 1987). **I could make promises**: Joan Didion, "Goodbye to All That," in *Writing New York: A Literary Anthology*, ed. P. Lopate (New York: Washington Square Press, 1998), 889.

THIRTEENTH CHAPTER: (AD)DRESS
The Skyline of New York: see Koolhaas, *Delirious New York*, 126–27. **Houses of the best taste**: James, *The American Scene*, 449. **Every fashion**: *AP*, 79. **the beauty of the body**: Odon of Cluny, quoted in *AP*, 402. **Madam Death**: quoted in ibid., 62. **inhere in the darkness**: ibid., 393. **To dwell means**: ibid., 9. **dwelling is diminished**: ibid., 221. **Poor people**: Eugène Montrue, quoted in ibid., 71 (amended). **camouflage**: ibid. **always new**: ibid., 544. **the barrier**: ibid., 74. **tolerant**: a slogan for Manhattan Mini Storage, 2012. **The eternal**: *AP*, 463. **new currents**: ibid., 64. Adorno scribbled in the margin of the manuscript: "I would think: counterrevolutions." **The New Yorker**: *New Yorker* (February 6, 1926), 6.

FOURTEENTH CHAPTER: NONARCHITECTURE
the integrity: Herbert Muschamp, "Public Spirit, Private Money and a New New Deal," *New York Times* (March 24, 2002), A36. **an offense**: Don DeLillo, *Cosmopolis* (New York: Scribner, 2004), 65. **built canals**: Edwin Denby, "Elegy—The Streets," in *The Complete Poems*, ed. R. Padgett (New York: Random House, 1986), 13. **absence of monuments**: *AP*, 385. **against any (further)**: Koolhaas, *Delirious New York*, 20.

windowless house: *AP*, 532 (interpolated). **conditions**: Giorgio Agamben, *Stanzas*, trans. R. L. Martinez (Minneapolis: University of Minnesota Press, 1993), *xvi*.

FIFTEENTH CHAPTER: TRUTH IS CONCRETE

In the street: Henry Miller, "Black Spring," in *Writing New York*, 614. **the dwelling place**: *AP*, 423. **is precisely that**: Jacobs, *Death and Life*, 55. **By its nature**: quoted in ibid., 238. **stranger feels at home**: Arendt, "Reflections," 102. **Soon**: quoted in *AP*, 224. **a place to sleep**: *New Yorker* (February 21, 1925), 30. **the place where you dressed**: Lloyd R. Morris, *Incredible New York: High Life and Low Life from 1850 to 1950* (New York: Syracuse University Press, 1996), 316. **the second most consumed**: Mark Kingwell, *Concrete Reveries: Consciousness and the City* (New York: Viking, 2008), 238. **approximately one Hoover Dam**: David Owen, "Concrete Jungle," *New Yorker* (November 10, 2003), 81. **objectify vacuity**: Koolhaas, *Delirious New York*, 249. **The truth**: quoted in Howard Eiland and Michael W. Jennings, *Walter Benjamin: A Critical Life* (Cambridge, MA: Harvard University Press, 2014), 252. **act or process**: *New Oxford American Dictionary*, 3rd ed., 2010.

SECOND THRESHOLD: INFRASTRUCTURE

micrological: Theodor W. Adorno, *Prisms* (Cambridge, MA: MIT Press, 1983), 238. **world of secret**: *AP*, 540. **language of this lamp**: *SW* I, 63. **precisely as**: *AP*, 392.

THIRD PART

There are certain sections: Rick Blaine to Major Heinrich Strasser, *Casablanca*, dir. Michael Curtiz, 1942.

SIXTEENTH CHAPTER: EMPIRE

endow any soup can: *SW* II, 526. **When Queen Elizabeth**: Warhol, *The Philosophy of Andy Warhol*, 101. **there was more awake**: Andy Warhol and Pat Hackett, *POPism: The Warhol Sixties* (New York: Harcourt, 1980), 33. **stillies**: quotes by Klaus Biesenbach, "Image Body Machine," in *Andy Warhol: Motion Pictures* (Berlin: Kunst-Werke, 2005), 14. **Isn't life a series**: quoted in Jane Dillenberger, *The Religious Art of Andy Warhol* (New York: Continuum, 2001), 116. **in the beginning**: John Locke, *Two Treatises of Government*, ed. P. Laslett (Cambridge: Cambridge University Press, 1988), 301.

SEVENTEENTH CHAPTER: THE URBAN REVOLUTION

painter of modern life: Charles Baudelaire, *Painter of Modern Life and Other Essays*, ed. J. Mayne (London: Phaidon, 1964). **trademark**: *AP*, 372. **global cities**: Saskia Sassen, *The Global City: New York, London, Tokyo* (Princeton, NJ: Princeton University Press, 2001). **Other Spaces**: Michel Foucault, "Of Other Spaces," *Diacritics* 16:1 (Spring 1986), 22–27. **mongrel**: Douglas, *Terrible Honesty*, 5. **class consciousness**:

Georg Lukács, *History and Class Consciousness*, trans. R. Livingstone (London: Merlin Press, 1971).

EIGHTEENTH CHAPTER: HYPOTHESES ON MODERN CITIES

the first *communio*: *AP*, 793. **cities are battlefields**: *SW* IV, 233. **The revolution**: David Harvey, *Rebel Cities: From the Right to the City to the Urban Revolution* (London: Verso, 2012), 25. **symbolic economy**: Sharon Zukin, *The Culture of Cities* (Cambridge, MA: Blackwell, 1995), 3. **to chart the path**: David Harvey, *Social Justice and the City* (Baltimore: Johns Hopkins University Press, 1973), 314. **Truth and Politics**: Hannah Arendt, *The Portable Hannah Arendt*, ed. P. Baehr (New York: Penguin, 2000), 545. **dual city**: Manuel Castells, *The Informational City: Economic Restrictions and Urban Development* (Oxford: Blackwell, 1989), 172–228. **right to the city**: Henri Lefebvre, *Writings on Cities*, ed. E. Kofman and E. Lebas (Oxford: Blackwell, 1996), 63–177. **tripartite**: Henri Lefebvre, *The Urban Revolution* (Minneapolis: University of Minnesota Press, 2003), 32. **More than ever**: Rem Koolhaas, *S,M,L,XL* (New York: Monacelli Press, 1995), 971.

NINETEENTH CHAPTER: URBAN PHILOSOPHY

The manner of living: Jean-Jacques Rousseau, *The Confessions* (London: Reeves and Turner, 1861), 327. **It is in the country**: ibid., 387. **only the wicked**: quoted in Leo Damrosch, *Jean-Jacques Rousseau: Restless Genius* (Boston: Houghton Mifflin, 2007), 292. **Is not a man**: Ralph Waldo Emerson, *Political Writings*, ed. K. Sacks (Cambridge: Cambridge University Press, 2008), 73. **The town is the seat**: Hegel, *Elements of the Philosophy of Right*, 273. **political society**: Alexis de Tocqueville, *Democracy in America*, trans. A. Goldhammer (New York: Library of America, 2004), 111. **Tocqueville's central idea**: Jean Baudrillard, *America* (London: Verso, 1995), 91. **space for politics**: Hannah Arendt, "What Remains? The Language Remains," in *The Portable Hannah Arendt*, 17. **Landscapes and trees**: Plato, *Phaedrus*, in *Complete Works*, ed. J. M. Cooper (Indianapolis: Hackett, 1997), 510. **chief sin**: Mumford, *The City in History*, 152.

TWENTIETH CHAPTER: HOME RULE

So we have two: quoted in Jane Kramer, "Paterfamilias II," *New Yorker* (August 24, 1968), 42. **life in all its variety**: *SW* IV, 19. **Compared to cities**: Jane Jacobs, interviewed by Claire Parin, 1999, Jane Jacobs Papers. **The Burrow**: Franz Kafka, *The Complete Stories*, ed. N. Glatzer (New York: Schocken, 1946), 325. **Liberty**: Burrows and Wallace, *Gotham*, 211. **New Yorker**: see "Washington, George" in *The Encyclopedia of New York City*, ed. K. T. Jackson (New Haven, CT: Yale University Press, 2010), 1380. **culprit**: letter from George Washington to Henry Knox, April 1, 1789, http://goo.gl/iJg6u. **two centers**: Burrows and Wallace, *Gotham*, 306. **concord**: Thomas Bender, "New York as a Center of Difference: How America's Metropolis Counters

American Myth," *Dissent* (Fall 1987), 429–35. **seeing like**: James C. Scott, *Seeing Like a State* (New Haven, CT: Yale University Press, 1998).

TWENTY-FIRST CHAPTER: CITY OF REFUGE

insular city: Herman Melville, *Moby-Dick, or, The Whale* (New York: Penguin, 2001), 3. **For by art**: Thomas Hobbes, *Leviathan* (New York: Touchstone, 1997), 19. **Call me Ishmael**: Melville, *Moby-Dick*, 3. **The drama's done**: ibid., 625. **it is not down**: ibid., 61. **petrified unrest**: *AP*, 329. **real state**: *SW* IV, 392 (amended). **To recover confidence**: James, *The American Scene*, 427. **alienism**: ibid. **one belongs to New York**: Thomas Wolfe, *The Web and the Rock* (New York: Harper, 1958), 315.

TWENTY-SECOND CHAPTER: ARENDT'S CITY

Ford to City: Burns and Sanders, *New York*, 543. **was interpreted by Christians**: Hannah Arendt, *Between Past and Future* (New York: Viking, 1961), 66. **the most absolute**: Agamben, *Homo Sacer*, 166. **the laws, like the wall**: Hannah Arendt, *The Human Condition* (Chicago: University of Chicago Press, 1998), 194. **lies between people**: ibid., 198. **we insert ourselves**: ibid., 176–77. **the space where I appear**: ibid., 198. **One, if not the chief**: ibid., 197 (interpolated). **the common good**: Fran Lebowitz, *The Fran Lebowitz Reader* (New York: Knopf, 1994), 35. **quality of temptation**: Hannah Arendt, *Eichmann in Jerusalem* (New York: Penguin, 2006), 150. **in the very nature**: ibid., 273. **holes of oblivion**: ibid., 232. **even in Antiquity**: Max Weber, *The City* (New York: Collier Books, 1962), 99. **lost treasure**: Hannah Arendt, *On Revolution* (New York: Penguin, 1990), 215–81. **emphasize how the spirit**: *AP*, 777. **Private faces**: W. H. Auden, "Shorts," in *Collected Poems*, ed. E. Mendelson (New York: Vintage, 1991), 54 (amended).

TWENTY-THIRD CHAPTER: HERE COMES EVERYBODY

husks of people: Rainer Maria Rilke, *The Notebooks of Malte Laurids Brigge*, trans. B. Pike (Champaign, IL: Dalkey Archive, 2008), 28. **contacts**: Samuel R. Delany, *Times Square Red, Times Square Blue* (New York: NYU Press, 1999), 111. **whatever singularity**: Giorgio Agamben, *The Coming Community*, trans. M. Hardt (Minneapolis: University of Minnesota Press, 1993), 1. **everything is possible**: Arendt, "Total Domination," in *The Portable Hannah Arendt*, 122. **in New York everything**: quoted in Douglas, *Terrible Honesty*, 118. **Today, I should say**: Walt Whitman, *Complete Poetry and Collected Prose* (New York: Library of America, 1982), 824. **Just as you feel**: ibid., 309–11 (amended). **avail not**: ibid., 308. **pours my meaning**: ibid., 312.

THIRD THRESHOLD: ECOPOLIS

took the inside: Warhol and Hackett, *POPism*, 3. **the street becomes room**: *AP*, 406. **economic and political**: Thomas Piketty, *Capital in the Twenty-First Century* (Cambridge, MA: Harvard University Press, 2014), 577. **hold two**: F. Scott Fitzgerald, *The Crack-Up*, ed. E. Wilson (New York: New Directions, 1993), 69. **contradictory and mobile**: Walter Benjamin and Gershom Scholem, *The Correspondence of Walter Benjamin and Gershom Scholem, 1932–1940* (Cambridge, MA: Harvard University Press, 1992), 108–9 (amended).

FOURTH PART
It is more important: O'Hara, *Meditations in an Emergency*, 38.

TWENTY-FOURTH CHAPTER: THE LIBRARY
the whole city: quoted in Carpenter, *New York Diaries*, 169. **more full of reflections**: quoted in Douglas, *Terrible Honesty*, 59. **No one knows**: *New Yorker* (August 28, 1926), 11.

TWENTY-FIFTH CHAPTER: THE ECONOMY OF PHILOSOPHY
even in the kitchen: quoted in Aristotle, "Parts of Animals," in *The Complete Works*, vol. 1, ed. J. Barnes (Princeton, NJ: Princeton University Press, 1984), 1004. **whose movement controls**: Jean-Pierre Vernant, "Hestia-Hermes: The Religious Expression of Space and Movement in Ancient Greece," in *Antiquities*, ed. N. Loraux, G. Nagy, and L. Slatkin (New York: New Press, 2001), 128. **immutable and permanent**: ibid. **economic shit**: quoted in Werner Blumenberg, *Karl Marx: An Illustrated History* (London: Verso, 2000), 93. **the tidying up of a room**: quoted in Gordon C. F. Bearn, *Waking to Wonder: Wittgenstein's Existential Investigations* (New York: State University of New York Press, 1997), 84. **Happiness has its recipes**: *AP*, 638. **My father**: quoted in Ben-Ami Scharfstein, *The Philosophers: Their Lives and the Nature of Their Thought* (Oxford: Oxford University Press, 1989), 332. **Act only according**: Immanuel Kant, *Grounding for the Metaphysics of Morals*, trans. J. W. Ellington (Indianapolis: Hackett, 1993), 30. **always do** and **get paid**: *Do the Right Thing*, dir. Spike Lee, 1989. **we've got to fight**: Public Enemy, "Fight the Power," Motown Records, 1989. **If you want to know**: "Dorothy Parker: The Art of Fiction No. 13," interviewed by Marion Capron, *Paris Review* 13 (Fall 1956), http://goo.gl/jj5CO. **God is a luxury**: *Crimes and Misdemeanors*, dir. Woody Allen, 1989.

TWENTY-SIXTH CHAPTER: BUSINESS ART
If someone asked: Warhol, *The Philosophy of Andy Warhol*, 8. **The thing is to think**: ibid., 9. **I don't really use makeup**: ibid., 10. **I think buying**: ibid., 229. *real* **phony**: Truman Capote, *Breakfast at Tiffany's* (New York: Modern Library, 1994), 29. *exactly* **wrong**: Warhol and Hackett, *POPism*, 287. **money is a kind**: Wallace Stevens, *Opus Posthumous* (New York: Vintage, 1990), 191. **pretends to demand nothing**: Clement Greenberg, "Avant-Garde and Kitsch," in *Art and Culture: Critical Essays* (Boston:

Beacon Press, 1984), 10. **Business art**: Warhol, *The Philosophy of Andy Warhol*, 92. **aestheticization**: J. M. Bernstein, "Introduction," in *The Culture Industry*, by Theodor W. Adorno (London: Routledge, 2001), 24 (Bernstein flips Benjamin's logic [cf. *SW* IV, 270] in order to fit Adorno's). **department stores**: Andy Warhol, *America* (New York: Harper and Row, 1985), 22. **the notion that some part**: *AP*, 415. **got a glimpse**: ibid., 898 (originally pertains to surrealism). **Our movies**: Warhol and Hackett, *POPism*, 251. **the economic origins**: *AP*, 460. **Success Is a Job**: *Glamour Magazine* (September 1949). **Bianca was driving**: Andy Warhol, *The Andy Warhol Diaries*, ed. P. Hackett (New York: Warner Books, 1989), 647. **Jesus is the Messiah**: Giorgio Agamben, *The Time That Remains: A Commentary on the Letter to the Romans*, trans. P. Dailey (Stanford, CA: Stanford University Press, 2005), 129. **Andy Warhol Enterprises**: Warhol, *The Philosophy of Andy Warhol*, 91.

TWENTY-SEVENTH CHAPTER: MODES OF ASSOCIATED LIFE

aggravated assault: Louis Menand, *The Metaphysical Club: A Story of Ideas in America* (New York: Farrar, Straus and Giroux, 2001), 349. **modes of associated life**: quoted in Ryan Alan, *John Dewey and the High Tide of American Liberalism* (New York: W. W. Norton, 1995), 211. **marketplace of ideas**: Menand, *The Metaphysical Club*, 430–32. **cash-value**: William James, *Pragmatism and Other Writings*, ed. G. Gunn (New York: Penguin, 2000), 28. **credit system**: William James, "Pragmatism's Conception of Truth," in *Pragmatism: A Reader*, ed. L. Menand (New York: Vintage, 1997), 117. **We are free**: John Dewey, "Philosophies of Freedom," in *The Political Writings*, ed. D. Morris and I. Shapiro (Indianapolis: Hackett, 1993), 136. **are really rules**: quoted in Menand, *The Metaphysical Club*, 354. **Each thought**: *SW* II, 28 (the city in question is Moscow). **Consider what effects**: quoted in Menand, *The Metaphysical Club*, 227 (interpolated). **unstiffen**: James, "What Pragmatism Means," in *Pragmatism: A Reader*, 110. **Concepts are so clear**: Dewey, "The Need for a Recovery of Philosophy," in *Pragmatism: A Reader*, 228. **completely genial**: James, "What Pragmatism Means," 110. **pluriverse**: quoted in Menand, *The Metaphysical Club*, 88. **Nowhere more than here**: Jean-Paul Sartre, "Manhattan: The Great American Desert," in *The Empire City: A Treasury of New York*, ed. A. Klein (New York: Rinehart, 1955), 456. **the basis of the new**: *AP*, 394. **industry and its material**: Dewey, "Individuality in Our Day," in *The Political Writings*, 84. **The chief worth**: Oliver Wendell Holmes Jr., *Collected Legal Papers* (Clark: Lawbook Exchange, 2005), 248.

TWENTY-EIGHTH CHAPTER: JACOBS'S CITY

simple-minded: Jacobs, *Death and Life*, 50. **organized complexity**: ibid., 432. **is to make the mistake**: ibid., 373. **unselfconscious**: ibid., 228. **it is chance**: René Descartes, *Discourse on Method*, trans. D. A. Cress (Indianapolis: Hackett, 1998), 6. **render us unadaptable**: Jane Jacobs, "Responses to Remarks by Mr. Rose and Mr. Safdie,"

Jane Jacobs Papers. **What is responsible**: Lewis Mumford, "Mother Jacobs' Home Remedies," *New Yorker* (December 1, 1962), 163. **I had my doubts**: Jane Jacobs, interviewed by James Howard Kunstler, *Metropolis* (March 2001), http://goo.gl/wFIOS. **Just as nature heals**: *SW* II, 338. **When a place gets boring**: Quoted in Richard Florida, "Getting Jane Jacobs Right," *The Atlantic* (April 2, 2010), http://goo.gl/zOnyo.

TWENTY-NINTH CHAPTER: HOW NEW WORK BEGINS

is to mistake the results: Jane Jacobs, *The Economy of Cities* (London: Jonathan Cape, 1970), 48. **pristine economies**: Jane Jacobs, *Cities and the Wealth of Nations* (New York: Vintage, 1985), 129. **was probably risky**: Ian Hodder, *The Leopard's Tale: Revealing the Mysteries of Çatalhöyük* (London: Thames and Hudson, 2006), 88. *division of labor*: Jacobs, *The Economy of Cities*, 82. **further dividing**: ibid. **between people whose interests**: ibid., 249. **the separation of industrial**: *The Marx-Engels Reader*, 150.

THIRTIETH CHAPTER: TRANSACTIONS OF DECLINE

Poverty has no causes: Jacobs, *The Economy of Cities*, 121. **Never has a science**: Jacobs, *Cities and the Wealth of Nations*, 6–7. **from the sky**: Milton Friedman, *The Optimum Quantity of Money* (New Brunswick, NJ: Transaction, 2007), 4–5. **Choosing among the existing**: Jacobs, *Cities and the Wealth of Nations*, 28. **Nobody places more faith**: ibid., 31. **have been preoccupied**: ibid. **faulty feedback**: ibid., 156–81. **elephant hooked**: ibid., 172. **dog that realizes**: ibid., 214. **transactions of decline**: ibid., 182–203. **We are taught**: ibid., 214. **resist the temptation**: ibid.

THIRTY-FIRST CHAPTER: EMINENT DOMAIN

demolition artists: *AP*, 23. **Versailles**: Mumford, *Sidewalk Critic*, 258. **You will live**: quoted in *AP*, 129 (amended). **shock**: quoted in Robert E. Caro, *The Power Broker: Robert Moses and the Fall of New York* (New York: Vintage, 1975), 318. **snug luxury**: ibid., 33. **There was an exchange**: ibid., 807. **eminent domain**: ibid., 217. **impairing the obligation**: quoted in ibid., 615. **public authority**: ibid., 615–36. **is a thieves' game**: Shakespeare, quoted in ibid., 322. **This will destroy**: Victor Hugo, *Notre Dame de Paris* (New York: Collier, 1917), 181. **Encompassing**: *AP*, 459 (Breton and Le Corbusier are the names used in the original quotation).

FOURTH THRESHOLD: DEAD-END STREET

Hannah was part: e-mail exchange with the author, January 7, 2013. **that capitalism will not die**: *AP*, 667. **So you think capital**: Tom Wolfe, *The Bonfire of the Vanities* (New York: Picador, 2008), 154. **What are all the limestone**: ibid., 612. **Look at those people**: Niccolò Machiavelli, *The Discourses*, ed. B. Crick (New York: Penguin, 1984), 144. **Listen, I have rights**: Michel Foucault, *The Birth of Biopolitics*, trans. G. Burchell (New York: Palgrave, 2008), 283 (amended). **Behind each of those windows**: A. J.

Liebling, "Passage de crépuscule," *New Yorker* (January 11, 1964), 95. **Why live**: Sigmund Freud, *Letters of Sigmund Freud*, ed. E. L. Freud (New York: Dover, 1992), 436. **The less you eat**: *The Marx-Engels Reader*, 95–96. **"Life" is a "business"**: Martin Heidegger, *Being and Time*, trans. J. Stambaugh (Albany: State University of New York Press, 1996), 267. **Living? Our servants**: Auguste Villiers de L'Isle-Adam, *Axël*, trans. M. G. Rose (London: Soho Books, 1986), 170. **Just to keep itself going**: Jane Jacobs, *Dark Age Ahead* (New York: Random House, 2004), 159. **it is what people do**: Jane Jacobs, interviewed by Evan Solomon for CBC, *Hot Type* (April 14, 2000), http://goo.gl/208p8. **Economy is idealism**: *New Yorker* (March 13, 1925), 5 (it is a quote from Calvin Coolidge). **Making a living**: Elizabeth Hardwick, "Grub Street: New York," *New York Review of Books* 1:1 (February 1, 1963), http://goo.gl/X2jG22. **philosophes and philanthropists**: Burrows and Wallace, *Gotham*, 371–85. **Fex urbis**: Saint Jerome, quoted in Victor Hugo, *Les Misérables*, trans. N. Denny (New York: Penguin, 1982), 987. **Can you imagine**: overheard by the author.

FIFTH PART

Stand clear: recorded MTA message in twenty-first-century cars.

THIRTY-SECOND CHAPTER: AT NIGHT

At night: Miller, *Tropic of Capricorn*, 68. **At night**: Luc Sante, *Low Life: Lures and Snares of Old New York* (New York: Farrar, Straus and Giroux, 2003), 358. **naked city**: Weegee, *Naked City* (New York: Da Capo, 2002). **Money is their God**: Jacob A. Riis, *How the Other Half Lives: Studies among the Tenements of New York* (Ann Arbor: University of Michigan Libraries, 2011), 107. **the subject's voice**: Hakim Hasan, "Afterword," in *Sidewalk*, by Mitchell Duneier (New York: Farrar, Straus and Giroux, 1999), 327. **increasing fascination**: Sante, *Low Life*, 296. **the antithesis**: Theodore Dreiser, *The Color of a Great City* (Syracuse, NY: Syracuse University Press, 1996), 266. **innocence from sin**: Sante, *Low Life*, 278. **united under the single**: ibid., 214. **I do not know that I have**: quoted in Morris, *Incredible New York*, 229. **there is more law**: Sante, *Low Life*, 247 (amended). **honest graft**: ibid., 274. **Murder Inc.**: ibid., 232. **their mingled respect**: ibid., 235. **everybody remembers**: Colson Whitehead, *The Colossus of New York* (New York: Anchor, 2003), 80. **The already half-dead**: Richard Price, *Lush Life* (New York: Farrar, Straus and Giroux, 2008), 411. **Do I need to live**: apocryphal.

THIRTY-THIRD CHAPTER: GARBAGE STUDIES

Here we have a man: quoted in *AP*, 349. **The rags, the refuse**: *AP*, 860. **squinting minds**: Dante Alighieri, *The Inferno*, trans. R. Hollander and J. Hollander (New York: Anchor, 2000), 133. **progress**: see *SW* IV, 392. **Perhaps the most deeply**: *AP*, 211. **is that the object**: ibid., 204. **gone mad**: *The Marx-Engels Reader*, 334. **collector of nothing**: William Davies King, *Collections of Nothing* (Chicago: University of Chicago Press, 2008). **Between what a man**: William James, *Writings: 1878–1899*, ed. G. E. Myers (New York: Library of America, 1992), 174. **things into our space**: *AP*, 206. **time capsules**: Andy Warhol, *Time Capsules 1968–1973* (New York: Arena, 2003). **tribal sorcerer**: *AP*, 186. **catch up on the news**: Burns and Sanders, *New York*, 485. **How can you make**: E. L. Doctorow, *Homer and Langley* (New York: Random House, 2009), 80–81. **Each of us needs**: Dewey, *The Political Writings*, 88. **Give me your tired**: Emma Lazarus, "New Colossus," in *Selected Poems*, ed. J. Hollander (New York: Library of America, 2005), 58 (amended).

THIRTY-FOURTH CHAPTER: JUNK
Opium is the religion: quoted in Paul Kopasz, "Going Downtown (on an Uptown Train)," in *New York Calling: From Blackout to Bloomberg*, ed. M. Berman and B. Berger (London: Reaktion, 2007), 242. **profane illuminations**: *SW* II, 209. **character is so lost**: Henry James, *A Small Boy and Others: A Critical Edition*, ed. P. Collister (Richmond: University of Virginia Press, 2011), 166 (amended). **through almost any accident**: James, *The American Scene*, 445. **tremendous *muchness***: William James, "A Suggestion about Mysticism," in *Writings: 1902–1910*, ed. G. E. Myers (New York: Library of America, 1988), 1274. **indifference toward the distinctions**: Georg Simmel, "The Metropolis and Mental Life," in *The Blackwell City Reader*, ed. G. Bridge and S. Watson (Oxford: Blackwell, 2010), 106. **if God made anything better**: William S. Burroughs, *Junky*, in *Word Virus: The William S. Burroughs Reader*, ed. J. Grauerholz and I. Silverberg (New York: Grove Press, 1998), 175. **uptown** and **downtown**: Kopasz, "Going Downtown." **is not a kick**: Burroughs, *Junky*, 50. **when you give up junk**: ibid., 70. **Junk is the inoculation**: ibid., 68. **Many policemen**: William S. Burroughs, interviewed by Conrad Knickerbocker, *Paris Review* 35 (Fall 1965), http://goo.gl/eslLb. **most terrible drug**: *SW* II, 216. **I love those**: Friedrich Nietzsche, *Thus Spoke Zarathustra*, in *The Portable Nietzsche*, ed. Walter Kaufmann (New York: Penguin, 1976), 127.

THIRTY-FIFTH CHAPTER: LOST
If you're a Rockefeller: Warhol, *The Philosophy of Andy Warhol*, 127. **I was asking**: Whitman, *Complete Poetry*, 585 (amended). **my city**: Lewis Mumford, "From *Sketches from Life*," in *Writing New York*, 946. **Thus I take leave**: Fitzgerald, *The Crack-Up*, 33. **had all the iridescence**: ibid., 25. **archetype**: ibid., 26. **see New York whole**: ibid., 29. **the city was bloated**: ibid., 31. **From the ruins**: ibid., 32. **my lost city**: ibid. *the limits of my language*: Ludwig Wittgenstein, *Tractatus Logico-Philosophicus*, trans. D. F. Pears and B. F. McGuiness (London: Routledge, 2001), 68. **sprang from his Platonic**: Fitzgerald, *The Great Gatsby*, 77. **mark of spiritual** and **emotional bankruptcy**: quoted in Matthew J. Bruccoli, *Some Sort of Epic Grandeur: The Life of F. Scott Fitzgerald* (Columbia: University of Carolina Press, 2002), 126, 292. **But Sara**: ibid., 255. **whining**: quoted in Scott Donaldson, "The Crisis of Fitzgerald's 'Crack-Up,'"

Twentieth Century Literature 26 (Summer 1980), 174. **an indecent invasion**: ibid., 175. **Of course**: Fitzgerald, *The Crack-Up*, 69. **something you dominated**: ibid. **The blows**: ibid. **there was certainly**: ibid., 31. **lush and liquid**: ibid., 25.

THIRTY-SIXTH CHAPTER: PERFECT DAY

young boy: White, "Here Is New York," 699. **everything everybody**: J. D. Salinger, *Franny and Zooey* (Boston: Little, Brown, 1961), 26. **Hapworth**: *New Yorker* (June 19, 1965), 32–113. **A Perfect Day**: *New Yorker* (January 31, 1948), 21–25. **May Day**: F. Scott Fitzgerald, *May Day* (New York: Melville House, 2009). **not deprived of**: William Weigand, "J. D. Salinger: Seventy-Eight Bananas," in *J. D. Salinger: Modern Critical Views*, ed. H. Bloom (New York: Chelsea House, 1987), 6. **paranoiac in reverse**: J. D. Salinger, *Raise High the Roof Beam, Carpenters* (London: Penguin, 1964), 59. **who have been released**: Alfred Kazin, "J. D. Salinger: 'Everybody's Favorite,'" in Weigand, *J. D. Salinger*, 27.

THIRTY-SEVENTH CHAPTER: A THEORY OF THE HOMELESS

between one-third: Paul Ocobock, "Introduction," in *Cast Out: Vagrancy and Home-lessness in Global and Historical Perspective*, ed. A. L. Beier and P. Ocobock (Athens: Ohio University Press, 2008), 23. **in front of our noses**: *SW* I, 486. **signboards and street names**: *SW* II, 598. **New York was an inexhaustible**: Paul Auster, *The New York Trilogy* (New York: Penguin, 1990), 4. **The Man**: Edgar Allan Poe, *Selected Tales* (Oxford: Oxford University Press, 2008), 84–91. **To Poe**: *SW* IV, 27. **The flâneur's confidence**: Burrows and Wallace, *Gotham*, 701. **has the key**: G. K. Chesterton, quoted in *AP*, 437–38. **a spy for the capitalists**: ibid., 427. **In the flâneur**: ibid., 334. **like a dog**: Michel Foucault, *The Courage of Truth*, trans. G. Burchell (New York: Palgrave, 2011), 242–43. **an other life**: ibid., 244. **There is an idea**: Bret Easton Ellis, *American Psycho* (New York: Vintage, 1991), 376–77. **homelessness is coming to be**: Martin Heidegger, "Letter on Humanism," in *Pathmarks*, ed. W. McNeill (Cambridge: Cambridge University Press, 1998), 258. **dwelling in the truth**: ibid., 243. **ek-sistence**: ibid., 253. **Homelessness so understood**: ibid., 258. **tranquillized self-assurance**: Heidegger, *Being and Time*, 176. **Philosophy is really homesickness**: quoted in Martin Heidegger, *The Fundamental Concepts of Metaphysics*, trans. W. McNeill and N. Walker (Bloomington: Indiana University Press, 1995), 5. **Has not contemporary city man**: ibid. **Man as civilized being**: quoted in *AP*, 806. **not hidden**: Martin Heidegger, *The Essence of Truth*, trans. T. Sadler (London: Continuum, 2002), 103.

THIRTY-EIGHTH CHAPTER: THE HOMELESS PHILOSOPHER

homeless philosophers: apocryphal. **last of the bohemians**: Joseph Mitchell, *Joe Gould's Secret* (New York: Vintage, 1999), 3. **fell by the wayside**: ibid. **the three H's**: ibid. **air, self-esteem**: ibid., 4. **I'm snobbish**: ibid., 6. **In my home town**: ibid., 37–38.

Behind these barricades: ibid., 86 (amended). What we used to think: ibid., 12–13. put down the informal history: ibid., 13. might have great hidden: ibid., 40. I have a delusion: ibid., 96. wasn't a question of laziness: ibid., 152. He had come to Greenwich Village: ibid., 150. a kind of Hell: ibid., 145. Talking to Joe Gould: David Streitfeld, "The New Yorker's Joseph Mitchell, Past Pluperfect," *Washington Post* (August 6, 1992), D2.

FIFTH THRESHOLD: A TALE OF TWO CITIES

It was the best of times: Charles Dickens, *A Tale of Two Cities* (New York: Bantam, 1981), 1. Seek and learn: Calvino, *Invisible Cities*, 165. This book has been: Hannah Arendt, *The Origin of Totalitarianism* (New York: Harcourt 1985), vii. within and without: Fitzgerald, *The Great Gatsby*, 30. Lecture on Ethics: Ludwig Wittgenstein, *Philosophical Occasions: 1912–1951*, ed. J. Klagge and A. Nordmann (Indianapolis: Hackett, 1993), 36–44. Nothing is either good: ibid., 39.

SIXTH PART

New York, and then: Louis Zukofsky, *"A"* (New York: New Directions, 2011), 32.

THIRTY-NINTH CHAPTER: HARD-KNOCK LIFE

the most basic: Orly Goldwasser, "How the Alphabet Was Born from Hieroglyphs," *Biblical Archaeology Review* 36 (March/April, 2010), 48. I was here: Seth L. Sanders, "What Was the Alphabet For? The Rise of Written Vernaculars and the Making of Israelite National Literature," *Maarav* 11 (2004), 44. it is something he just: "'Taki 183' Spawns Pen Pals," *New York Times* (July 21, 1971), 37. Make your mark: *Style Wars*, dir. Tony Silver, 1983. Any tag: Rene Ricard, "The Radiant Child," *Artforum* (December 1981), 35–36. wild style: *Wild Style*, dir. Charlie Ahearn, 1983. The block is burning: quoted in Marshall Berman, "Introduction" to *New York Calling*, 9. spirit is a power: quoted in ibid. It makes me wonder: quoted in ibid., 28 (amended). Music is our witness: James Baldwin, "Of the Sorrow Songs: The Cross of Redemption," in *The Cross of Redemption: Uncollected Writings*, ed. R. Kenan (New York: Vintage, 2011), 153. metaphysical truth: *SW* I, 72. sonorial graffiti: Iain Chambers, quoted in Murray Forman, "Looking for the Perfect Beat," in *That's the Joint!*, ed. M. Forman and M. A. Neal (New York: Routledge, 2004), 449. provoked irrepressible fits: Giorgio Agamben, *Profanations*, trans. J. Fort (New York: Zone Books, 2007), 40. Double-consciousness: W. E. B. Du Bois, *The Souls of Black Folk* (Rockville, MD: Arc Manor, 2008), 12. intolerably real: Agamben, *Profanations*, 48.

FORTIETH CHAPTER: SEX AND PHILOSOPHY

Of all the famous: Allen, *The Complete Prose*, 335. The Whore: ibid., 51–57. I was involved: Woody Allen, *Standup Comic* (Rhino Records, 1999). There is no question:

Allen, *The Complete Prose*, 15. **published posthumously**: ibid., 7. **I wrote the script**: *Woody Allen, ou l'anhédoniste le plus drôle du monde* (Paris: Antenne 2, 1979). **I hate when art**: Woody Allen, interviewed by Michiko Kakutani, *Paris Review* 136 (Fall 1995), http://goo.gl/J3k9S. **entertainment for intellectuals**: Stig Björkman, *Woody Allen on Woody Allen* (New York: Grove Press, 2005), 103. **miserable or horrible**: ibid., 85. **lose-lose**: Eric Lax, *Conversations with Woody Allen* (New York: Knopf, 2009), 100. **worse things than death**: Woody Allen, "Hypochondria: An Inside Look," *New York Times* (January 13, 2013), SR8. **live on in the hearts**: Lax, *Conversations with Woody Allen*, 362. **the most expensive**: *Love and Death*, dir. Woody Allen, 1975. **hope is the thing**: quoted in Allen, *The Complete Prose*, 4. **Tragedy is tragic**: Woody Allen, interviewed by Helene Zuber, *Spiegel* (June 20, 2005), http://goo.gl/y1fAk. **ascetic ideal:** Friedrich Nietzsche, *On the Genealogy of Morals*, ed. W. Kaufmann (New York: Vintage, 1969), 160. **visit by Plato**: Yahoo, "Our Own Perfect State," *New Yorker* (May 16, 1925), 24. **I never felt truth**: John Lahr, "The Imperfectionist," *New Yorker* (December 9, 1996), 68–69. **We all know the same truth**: *Woody Allen: A Documentary*, dir. Robert B. Weide, 2012. **we must choose reality**: Lax, *Conversations with Woody Allen*, 19; cf. Björkman, *Woody Allen on Woody Allen*, 50. **I'm always known**: Lax, *Conversations with Woody Allen*, 266. **Almost all my work**: ibid., 7. **incapable of enjoying**: *Annie Hall*, dir. Woody Allen, 1977. **my anhedonia**: *Woody Allen, ou l'anhédoniste le plus drôle du monde*. **strictly pavement**: quoted in Lahr, "The Imperfectionist," 68. **life imitates bad television**: Björkman, *Woody Allen on Woody Allen*, 90. **how's anyone going to come up**: *Midnight in Paris*, dir. Woody Allen, 2011. **reasonable without being**: Allen, *The Complete Prose*, 443. **the comedy breaks**: Arendt, *Eichmann in Jerusalem*, 50. **mere anarchy**: Woody Allen, *Mere Anarchy* (New York: Random House, 2008). **rather be lucky**: Lefty Gomez, quoted in *Matchpoint*, dir. Woody Allen, 2005. **Whereof one cannot speak**: Wittgenstein, *Tractatus*, 89 (amended); cf. Giorgio Agamben, "Notes on Gesture," in *Means without End*, trans. V. Binetti and C. Casarino (Minneapolis: University of Minnesota Press, 2000), 59–60. **Laughter is shattered**: *AP*, 325. **straight line**: Lax, *Conversations with Woody Allen*, 101. **better to live**: Ralph Ellison, *Invisible Man* (New York: Vintage, 1995), 559.

is not seen: Plato, *Euthyphro*, in *Complete Works*, 9 (amended). **The streets of the poor**: *In the Street*, dir. Helen Levitt, Janice Loeb, and James Agee, 1948. **decisive moment**: Henri Cartier-Bresson, *The Mind's Eye* (New York: Aperture, 1999), 20. **There is a delicate**: Goethe, quoted by Benjamin apropos of August Sander in *SW* II, 520. **going about the business**: Adam Gopnik, "Improvised City," *New Yorker* (November 19, 2001), 88. **to represent significant aspects**: Siegfried Kracauer, *Theory of Film: The Redemption of Physical Reality* (Princeton, NJ: Princeton University Press, 1997), 23. **sit by a window**: Warhol and Hackett, *POPism*, 207. **the society of the unspectacle**:

David Levi Strauss, "Helen Levitt: International Center for Photography," *Artforum* (October 1997), 97. **the poetry of photography**: quoted in Thomas Dikant, "Helen Levitt: 10 Photographs," *PhiN* 25 (2003), 26. **the surrealism**: James Agee, "Foreword" to Helen Levitt, *A Way of Seeing* (Durham, NC: Duke University Press, 1989), xii. **Truth, for all its multiplicity**: Baudelaire, quoted in *AP*, 315. **the truth will not run, the true image**, and **the past can be seized**: *SW* IV, 390. **rebirth**: Charles Baudelaire, "To a Woman Passing By," in *Selected Poems of Charles Baudelaire*, trans. G. Wagner (New York: Grove Press, 1974), 79; cf. Gilloch, *Myth and Metropolis*, 179.

FORTY-SECOND CHAPTER: NO IDEAS BUT IN THINGS

A man in himself: William Carlos Williams, *Paterson* (New York: New Directions, 1992), xiv. **liberated prose**: *SW* IV, 406. **For the philosopher**: William Carlos Williams, *The Autobiography of William Carlos Williams* (New York: New Directions, 1967), 390. **does not permit himself**: ibid. **The order and connection**: Baruch Spinoza, *The Ethics*, in *Complete Works*, ed. S. Shirley and M. L. Morgan (Indianapolis: Hackett, 2002), 247. **back to the things**: Edmund Husserl, *Logical Investigations*, vol. 1, ed. D. Moran (New York: Routledge, 2001), 168. **What profoundly fascinated**: Arendt, "Reflections," 83. **Everything is torn down**: James Merrill, *Selected Poems* (New York: Knopf, 2008), 21. **one story is good**: Henry James, *The American Scene*, 420.

FORTY-THIRD CHAPTER: THE MARRIAGE OF REASON AND SQUALOR

to feel homesick: Søren Kierkegaard, quoted in *AP*, 218. **the marriage of reason**: Calvin Tomkins, "The Space around Real Things," *New Yorker* (September 10, 1984), 68. **contrast between**: quoted in Eiland and Jennings, *Walter Benjamin*, 587. **The philosophy of the work**: Sol LeWitt, "Paragraphs on Conceptual Art," in *Sol LeWitt: A Retrospective*, ed. G. Garrels (New Haven, CT: Yale University Press, 2000), 370. **Only what can be seen**: Bruce Glaser, "Questions to Stella and Judd," in *Minimal Art: A Critical Anthology*, ed. G. Battcock (Berkeley: University of California Press, 1968), 158. **Don't try to despise**: Quoted in Ross Wetzsteon, *Republic of Dreams: Greenwich Village, the American Bohemia, 1910–1960* (New York: Simon and Schuster, 2002), 463.

FORTY-FOURTH CHAPTER: CRITIQUE OF PURE MOVEMENT

what is taken up: Martin Heidegger, *Introduction to Metaphysics*, trans. G. Fried and R. Polt (New Haven, CT: Yale Nota Bene, 2000), 69. **apprehended by a kind of bastard**: Plato, *Timaeus*, in *Complete Works*, 1255. **A prevalent feeling**: Merce Cunningham, "Space Time and Dance," in *Merce Cunningham: Dancing in Space and Time*, ed. R. Kostelanetz (New York: Da Capo, 1998), 38. **place of suspended possibilities**: Trisha Brown, "All the Person's Person Arriving: An Interview by Marianne Goldberg," *Drama Review* 30 (Spring 1986), 169. **determine the body**: Spinoza, *The*

Ethics, 279. **All things excellent**: ibid., 382. **Kinetics is the ethics**: Peter Sloterdijk, "Mobilization of the Planet from the Spirit of Self-Intensification," *Drama Review* 50 (Winter 2006), 37. **movement in itself**: José Gil, "The Dancer's Body," in *A Shock to Thought: Expressions after Deleuze and Guattari*, ed. B. Massumi (London: Routledge, 2002), 117. **zone of nonknowledge**: Giorgio Agamben, *Nudities*, trans. D. Kishik and S. Pedatella (Stanford, CA: Stanford University Press, 2010), 114. **Pure movement**: Trisha Brown, "A Profile," in *Laurie Anderson, Trisha Brown, Gordon Matta-Clark: Pioneers of the Downtown Scene, New York 1970s*, ed. L. Yee (Munich: Prestel, 2011), 184. **within the sphere**: *SW* I, 236. **allow a movement**: Wendy Perron, "The Big Picture of Trisha Brown," *Dance Magazine* (January 2011), http://goo.gl/WjLT7. **Brown appears to simply *be***: Marianne Goldberg, "Trisha Brown, U.S. Dance, and Visual Art," in *Trisha Brown: Dance and Art in Dialogue, 1961–2001*, ed. H. Teicher (Andover, MA: Addison Gallery 2002), 35. **dance machines**: Brown, "All the Person's Person Arriving," 166. **gravity was enlisted**: Trisha Brown and Susan Rosenberg, "Forever Young: Some Thoughts on Selected Choreographies of the 1970s–1990s Today," program notes for a performance at Dia:Beacon (November 14, 2009), http://goo.gl/w47bk. **is about change**: Trisha Brown and Yvonne Rainer, "A Conversation about Glacial Decoy," *October* 10 (Fall 1979), 30. **Theory of the Dérive**: Debord, "Theory of the Dérive," 50–54.

FORTY-FIFTH CHAPTER: LIFE SENTENCE

preferred not to: Herman Melville, "Bartleby the Scrivener," in *Billy Budd Sailor and Other Stories*, ed. Harold Beaver (London: Penguin Books, 1985), 13. **I shall *not* converse**: Adrian Heathfield, *Out of Now: The Lifework of Tehching Hsieh* (Cambridge, MA: MIT Press, 2009), 66. **whatever you do**: ibid., 335. **I shall stay *outdoors***: ibid., 160. **I don't see any reason**: ibid., 328. **life time**: Karlyn De Jongh, "Art/Life: A Conversation with Tehching Hsieh," *Cmagazine* 105 (Spring 2010), http://goo.gl/ofz6d. **not do *art***: Heathfield, *Out of Now*, 296. **I kept myself alive**: ibid., 315. **The man who hasn't signed**: quoted in *AP*, 446 (amended). **I don't do art**: Tehching Hsieh, interviewed by Barry Schwabsky, "Live Work," *Frieze* 126 (October 2009), http://goo.gl/oYvS9. **perfunctory affair**: LeWitt, "Paragraphs on Conceptual Art," 369. **Leap into the Void**: cf. Heathfield, *Out of Now*, 322–23. **I needn't *say* anything**: *AP*, 460.

SIXTH THRESHOLD: SPINOZA IN NEW AMSTERDAM

kingdom within a kingdom: Spinoza, *The Ethics*, 277. **economy of nature**: Jane Jacobs, *Systems of Survival* (New York: Vintage, 1994), 124–25. **economic life**: Jacobs, *The Nature of Economies*, 11. **misanthropic ecologists**: ibid., 90. **What are the perils**: *AP*, 445. **betrayed man**: *SW* I, 487. **The event** and **raise a standard**: quoted in Walter Lippman, *The Essential Lippman*, ed. C. Rossiter and J. Lare (Cambridge, MA: Harvard University Press, 1963), 535. **some stain**: Ferdinand Noack, quoted in *AP*, 415.

We have grown: *AP*, 494. ***a life***: Gilles Deleuze, *Pure Immanence: Essays on a Life*, trans. A. Boyman (New York: Zone Books), 27. **while facts**: Isaac Bashevis Singer, interviewed by Harold Flender, *Paris Review* 44 (Fall 1968), http://goo.gl/WWmmL. **These pages**: *AP*, 457–58 (interpolated).

ACKNOWLEDGMENTS

we and **take**: Leonard Cohen, "First We Take Manhattan," I'm Your Man, Columbia Records, 1988. **hangs delicately**: Franz Kafka, *Amerika: The Missing Person*, trans. M. Harman (New York: Schocken, 2011), 96 (amended).

ILLUSTRATION CREDITS

The authorized representative in the EU for product safety and compliance is:
Mare Nostrum Group
B.V Doelen 72
4831 GR Breda
The Netherlands

www.ingramcontent.com/pod-product-compliance
Lightning Source LLC
Chambersburg PA
CBHW020843270326
41928CB00006B/519